LONGMAN STUDY GUIDES

GCSE
English

Elizabeth A. Cripps

LONGMAN

LONGMAN STUDY GUIDES

SERIES EDITORS **Geoff Black and Stuart Wall**

Titles available

Biology	Mathematics
Business Studies	Mathematics: Higher Level
Chemistry	Music
Design and Technology	Physics
Economics	Psychology
English	Religious Studies
English Literature	Science
French	Sociology
Geography	Spanish
German	World History
Information Technology	

Addison Wesley Longman Limited,
Edinburgh Gate, Harlow,
Essex CM20 2JE, England
and Associated Companies throughout the World.

© Addison Wesley Longman 1997

First published 1988
Third edition 1997

ISBN 0582-30484-9

British Library Cataloguing-in-Publication Data
A catalogue record for this book is available from the British Library.

Set by 8 in 9.75/12pt Sabon
Produced by Longman Singapore Publishers, Pte
Printed in Singapore

CONTENTS

► EDITORS' PREFACE

Longman Study Guides have been written by the people who set and mark the exams – the examiners. Examiners are aware that, due to lack of practice and poor preparation, some students achieve only the lowest grades: they are not able effectively to show the examiner what they know. These books give excellent advice about exam practice and preparation, and organizing a structured revision programme, all of which are essential for examination success. *Remember:* the examiners are looking for opportunities to *give* you marks, not take them away!

Longman Study Guides are designed to be used throughout the course. The self-contained chapters can be read in any order appropriate to the stage you have reached in your course. The examiner guides you through the essential parts of each topic, making helpful comments throughout.

We believe that this book, and the series as a whole, will help you establish and build your basic knowledge and examination technique skills. For additional help with exam practice and revision techniques, Addison Wesley Longman has published a series called **Longman Exam Kits**, which are available from all good bookshops, or direct from Addison Wesley Longman.

GEOFF BLACK AND STUART WALL

► ACKNOWLEDGEMENTS

All the Examination Boards referred to in this book are thanked for their prompt and helpful replies to enquiries. I am particularly grateful to the following for giving permission to reproduce questions from specimen papers: EDEXCEL (London); Midland Examining Group; Northern Examinations and Assessment Board; Northern Ireland Council for Curriculum, Examinations and Assessment; Southern Examining Group and Welsh Joint Education Committee. While permission has been granted to reproduce their questions, the answers or hints on answers are solely the responsibility of the author and have not been provided or approved by the Boards.

I should like to thank colleagues and pupils who have helped me in the preparation of this book and especially Miss Jean Hayes, Title Adviser and head teacher of Sir John Cass's Foundation and Red Coat Secondary School, Ms Anne Clarke and some of the pupils of Stockwell Park School, Mrs Zena Maddision of the Marcus Lipton Centre, Ms Caroline Footman and Mr Kenneth Uwah.

We are grateful to the following for permission to reproduce copyright material:

BBC Worldwide Ltd for an extract from *The Blue Peter Green Book*, by Lewis Bronze, Nick Heathcote & Peter Brown; the author's agents for an extract from *Native Ground* by Phillip Callow. © Phillip Callow (published by Heinemann, 1959); Belfast Telegraph Newspapers Ltd for a reader's letter reproduced in an examination paper by NICCEA; William Collins Sons & Co Ltd for an extract from *Intimate Relations* by Jacqui Durrell (pub. Collins, 1976); the author's agents for an extract from *If Only They Could Talk* by James Herriot (published by Michael Joseph, 1970); authors' agents on behalf the Estate of Frieda Lawrence Ravagli for part poems 'Peace' & 'Discord in Childhood' by D.H. Lawrence in *The Complete poems of D.H. Lawrence* & an extract from *Sons and Lovers* by D.H. Lawrence; the author's agents for an adapted extract from 'Through the Tunnel' in *The Habit of Loving* by Doris Lessing. © Doris Lessing 1954; the author's agents for the short story 'The Trout' by Sean O'Faolian; authors' agents on behalf Mark Hamilton as literary executor of the estate of the late Sonia Brownell Orwell & Martin Secker & Warburg Ltd. for an extract from *Animal Farm* by George Orwell. Copyright © Mark Hamilton.

We have been unable to trace the copyright holder of a short story by Enrique Serpa and would appreciate any information which would enable us to do so.

ELIZABETH CRIPPS

This book has been written as a course companion for use throughout your GCSE course in English. The first chapter focuses on skills required for examinations in English language, giving techniques for coursework (reading, writing and oral), written papers (rules, comprehension, creative and directed writing) and oral assessment. Chapter 2 examines the National Criteria, the marking schemes, attainment targets and assessment. Chapter 3 gives information about the different syllabus requirements for the main examination boards. You should read these first three chapters carefully as they give invaluable advice which will be useful throughout your English course.

Each of the following chapters, 4 to 18, deals with an important aspect of English language, including details about how to improve your language and writing style (see Chapters 4, 5, 9 and 12 in particular) and separate chapters on developing your oral, assignments, reading comprehension and written work (narrative, dialogue, persuasive, descriptive and personal writing) of poetry, drama or prose. We have also included a chapter presenting a typical student's coursework folder (Chapter 19), and some final tips on checking and correcting your work (Chapter 20). Remember that it is important always to re-read your work, even in the examination room, to ensure that it makes sense to the reader and is as accurate as possible.

Each chapter starts with a **Getting Started** section which is an introduction to the chapter. This includes a **Topic Chart**, a table which, at a glance, gives the main areas of the chapter. Where applicable, the Topic Chart also identifies which parts of the chapter are covered by your examination board (but some chapters are applicable to all Groups and so the examination boards are missing from the chart). The chart can also be used to check your study and revision progress over the two years. A Topic Chart looks like this:

LONDON	MEG	NEA	NICCEA	SEG	WJEC	IGCSE	TOPIC	STUDY	REVISION 1	REVISION 2
	✓					✓	Talk about personal experience			
	✓	✓	✓				Read and/or discuss a text			
✓		✓				✓	Give an individual talk			
✓	✓	✓	✓	✓	✓	✓	Describe or inform about something seen or read			
✓			✓				Informal roleplay			
✓			✓	✓	✓		Hypothesize and speculate			
				✓		✓	Talk about language use			

Key to the initials	
London	EDEXCEL Foundation (formerly ULEAC)
MEG	Midland Examining Group
NEAB	Northern Examining and Assessment Board
NICCEA	Northern Ireland Council for Curriculum, Examinations and Assessment
SEG	Southern Examining Group
WJEC	Welsh Joint Education Committee
IGCSE	International General Certificate of Secondary Education

Each topic listed is then explained in the **What you need to know** section – the core of the chapter. This section contains plenty of examples and tips to help you improve your style. To help you practise what you have just learnt, there are then a series of examination questions with suggested answers in one of the following two formats:

▶ An outline answer.
▶ A student's answer with examiner's comments.

Do not look at the answers until you have attempted to answer the questions yourself. Although there are no correct answers in English, the suggested answers may show you a more appropriate way of answering the question. The student's answers, some of which are excellent A grade answers and some of which may have faults or weaknesses, will help you to see what problems are identified by examiners and where you could improve your examination answers.

At the end of each chapter there is a **summary box** which briefly identifies the key points about topics covered in the chapter. You should check that you know, and understand more fully, each of the key points listed.

ADDRESSES OF THE EXAMINATION BOARDS

London EDEXCEL Foundation (previously ULEAC)
Stewart House, 32 Russell Square, London WC1B 5DN
Tel. 0171 331 4000

MEG Midland Examining Group
Robins Wood House, Robins Wood Road, Aspley, Nottingham NG8 3NR
Tel. 0115 929 6021

NEAB Northern Examinations and Assessment Board
12 Harter Street, Manchester, M1 6HL
Tel. 0161 953 1170

NICCEA Northern Ireland Council for Curriculum Examination and Assessment
Clarendon Dock, 29 Clarendon Road, Belfast, BT1 3BG
Tel. 01232 261200

SEG Southern Examining Group
Stag Hill House, Guildford, Surrey GU2 5XJ
Tel. 01483 503123

WJEC Welsh Joint Education Committee
245 Western Avenue, Cardiff CF5 2YX
Tel. 01222 265000

GLOSSARY

allegory	a story or poem in which characters and actions are simplified to represent good and bad qualities
alliteration	repeating same or similar consonants in a group of words
antithesis	putting together two opposite ideas or arguments in speech or writing
assonance	repeating same or similar vowels in a group of words
attainment targets	targets (ATs) laid down by the government for each subject in the National Curriculum AT1: Speaking and Listening, AT2: Reading, AT3: Writing, AT4–5: Presentation, Spelling and Handwriting
audience	the person or persons who receive a message, spoken or written
brainstorming	discussing something in a group; turning over ideas quickly and spontaneously
close reading	slow, careful reading for clear understanding and retention of what is read
dialogue	direct talk in a play or other dramatic text.
direct speech	the actual words of a speaker repeated exactly, as in a story or report
directed writing	writing, usually a report or summary, for a specified type of audience
drafting	first rough written version of a communication
elliptical sentence	leaving out words from a sentence, yet the meaning is clear
expressive writing	personal writing, with feeling of intimacy
extended metaphor	developing an image usually over several lines of text, sometimes throughout a text
fable	moral story with animals which have human attributes
figurative language	used in imagery; not the literal meaning
flow chart	a diagram showing how particular ideas or aspects of a topic interrelate
functional writing	to do with practical matters
idiom	a phrase which means something different from the literal meaning and is known through common usage
intensive reading	read carefully and re-read for total retention of meaning
key questions	questions that lead to the essential aspects of a topic
literal meaning	the exact meaning of words
metaphor	an implied comparison; not the literal meaning
onomatopoeia	a word which mimics a natural sound
open ending	leaving a conclusion undecided
outlining	planning a theme completely, but in broad terms
paradox	statement which appears false because it contains opposite ideas but which has some truth in it
personification	giving something inanimate human attributes
persuader word	adverb or adverbial phrase used in argument
prediction	working something out that will happen later
prefix	a group of letters added at the beginning of a word
proofreading	to read and correct before a final version of a text is arrived at
reflective reading	slow, thoughtful reading
rhetorical question	question asked for effect – not expecting an answer
roleplay	to take the part of a character in improvised drama
scanning	to read quickly but steadily, searching for the main lines of reasoning in a text
simile	imaginative comparison introduced by 'like' or 'as'
skimming	to read quickly to pick up the theme or key idea of text
suffix	a group of letters added at the end of a word
summarizing	to make a short general account of a longer, more detailed text
topic tree	diagram showing the main structure of an essay theme
verbal snapshot	short written sketch, collected in a notebook

Chapter

1

Revision, examinations and coursework

▷ **GETTING STARTED**

This chapter is concerned with general techniques which should help you to succeed in your English examination.

The first section considers techniques which will help you with coursework, the second section techniques for taking written papers, and the third section techniques for the oral examination.

TOPIC	STUDY	REVISION 1	REVISION 2
Coursework			
Written papers			
Oral assessment			

▷ **WHAT YOU NEED TO KNOW**

▷ **Coursework**

GCSE gives you opportunities to work in a variety of ways. You will have plenty of scope to try out ways of reading, writing, talking and listening, but may find yourself in areas that are unfamiliar to you. Many areas will be considered in detail in the following chapters of this book, but there are also certain **general ideas and techniques** to help with coursework.

'English as an integrated subject ...'

The stress on English as an integrated subject relates it closely to your experience. What you *write* may grow from what you discuss with friends, or in class, or from a story you have read. What you *read* may be stimulated by what you talk about, e.g. a discussion of the pollution of a river near where you live might raise such questions as: 'What really are the facts of the situation?'; 'Who might help in a campaign to protect the river?'; 'What was the river like twenty years ago?' and you might go on to research the subject in books, or listen to experts in the field or interview older people in the community. You might decide to write up what you had found out as a report, which could be part of your coursework.

Much of our listening and talking is stimulated by media other than books, and there is room for all kinds of stimuli in GCSE English. Students should develop the ability to 'understand and respond imaginatively to what they hear, read and experience in a variety of media'. So, it is hoped that English studies will become more closely related to life, and that some of your coursework will be based on experience of media such as television, films, computer programs, plays, music and art.

Reading techniques

Of course, a great deal of your reading will be suggested to you by your teacher or tutor, and for some groups (e.g. **NICCEA**) a list of literary works – as complete books, rather than extracts – for you to select from and study, will be part of the syllabus. This is a sample list from **NICCEA**, on the theme of *Family*:

Thornton Wilder   *Our Town**
P. King and F. Cary   *Sailor Beware!*
John van Druten   *I Remember Mama*
Keith Waterhouse   *Billy Liar**
Anne Frank   *Diary of Anne Frank**
Carson McCullers   *A Member of the Wedding**

Honore Morrow   *The Splendid Journey*
John Steinbeck   *East of Eden*
Florence McDowell   *Other Days Around Me*
Alexander Irvine   *My Lady of the Chimney Corner*
Barry Hines   *A Kestrel for a Knave*
Stan Barstow   *A Kind of Loving*

(*Available in drama and in prose form.)

As you can see, these works are very different, but each one has been chosen for its likely appeal to young people.

'Widen your reading!'

In a major survey of young people's reading interests, 15–16-year-old students said that they had comparatively little time for reading for pleasure. School work or homework took up so much time. One girl remarked: 'If they made the day longer, we'd all be reading'. Try, however full your timetable, to read widely, both fiction and non-fiction. Think about what you read, and take interesting ideas from it for your work.

Using reading in coursework

Here are some of the ways you can make use of your reading in coursework:

▶ **Continuing a story** – What might have happened to the characters during the next five years?
▶ **Alternative ending** – How else would I end the story?
▶ **Alternative version** – Tell the story from the point of view of a different character.
▶ **Dramatization** – Make part of the story into a play.
▶ **Diary** – Keep a diary, as one of the characters in the book.
▶ **Starting point** – Make the book the starting point for a piece of writing of your own, perhaps personal or imaginative.
▶ **Reader's response** – Write down your response to a story and get friends to tell you theirs.
▶ **Letters** – Write a letter to the author, explaining what you like and dislike about the book.
▶ **Review** – Write a 'taster' review to persuade others in your class to read the book.
▶ **Discussion** – Explore issues of plot, character and general significance.

'How to "interrogate the text"'.

As well as reading for ideas and creative response, remember also to do plenty of 'close' reading or 'interrogating the text', as it is sometimes called. Few readers bother to use a dictionary, but if you come across a word you don't really understand you should make the effort to find out precisely what it means.

Try reading the following extracts:

The day passed incredibly slowly. She never knew what to do ... and when, relying on some pert little girl for information, she had started a lesson, she did not know how to go on with it properly. The children were her masters. She deferred to them ... and before this inhuman number of children, she was always at bay. She could not get away from it. There it was, this class of fifty collective children, depending on her for command it hated and resented. It made her feel she could not breathe: she must suffocate, it was so inhuman.

In an atmosphere of which the most important constituent is oxygen, it follows that all ordinary examples of combustion are owing to the rapid oxidization of bodies at a high temperature. It would be wrong, though, to think that the word 'combustion' expressed no other actions. Many substances burn equally well in atmospheres from which oxygen is excluded altogether, and in some cases burn even more readily than they would under similar circumstances in pure oxygen.

Though both are difficult and need re-reading, I think you'll agree that many would find the second much more difficult. This is chiefly because of the unfamiliar words and ideas. Another reason why the second passage seems more difficult is because most people have read many more stories than they have books about science. With a story, we know pretty well what to expect: there will be a beginning, where characters are introduced and the scene set; some development or progress through the middle of the plot or action, perhaps to an exciting climax; and some sort of tying up of matters at the end, unless it is a sophisticated story where the reader is left guessing.

With non-fiction, we are less sure how the work is organized, and it may be worth while to look into this. Consider the following short passages:

(a) At the museum, we saw the first photograph taken of Queen Victoria. We enjoyed looking at the elegant china, and we also saw the display of court regalia. Finally, we looked at the royal portraits in the Queen's Room.

(b) At the museum, we saw the first photograph ever taken of Queen Victoria, and then looked at some old china, before moving to a display of court regalia. And finally we looked at the royal portraits in the Queen's Room.

(c) At the museum, I was most interested in the royal portraits and the first photograph ever taken of Queen Victoria, then in the displays of court regalia.

(d) At the museum, we looked carefully at the displays of old china and court regalia, and at the first photograph ever taken of Queen Victoria, so that we would be able to write a detailed report when we were back at school.

They are similar, but the first is merely a recital of seeing certain things at a museum, in no particular order. The second shows the order in which things were seen. The third concerns the visitor's reaction to seeing the things, and the fourth gives a motive for looking carefully at them. When you are studying a non-fiction passage, it may be useful to consider how it is organized. Is there a main idea and then a series of minor parts? Are there two contrasted main ideas? Thinking along these lines should help you to understand the passage better.

Ways of encouraging close reading

'Try reading in different ways'

Here are some suggestions for encouraging close reading of texts:

▶ **Finding the outline** – Discuss, with a friend, the structure of a passage.
▶ **Predicting what follows** – Cover up the latter part of a story. Read the first part, then, on the basis of the clues you have already, predict what is to come. Then read on, to see if you were right.
▶ **Gap filling** – Take a passage and delete every fifth word. Then discuss in a group what the missing words could be. You'll have to look very closely at the text to do this well.
▶ **Group comprehension** – Take a passage, and write a set of questions about it for another group in your class. Get them to write or record their answers, and to write a set of questions for you. Compare the responses.

More about close reading can be found in Chapter 10.

Writing techniques

Coursework gives opportunities for kinds of writing that could not be included in all traditional examinations because of the limited time available. In GCSE you can be examined on a much wider range of written work. Some of these types of writing are:

▶ topic work – handling information and ideas on a particular subject
▶ extended personal writing, e.g. autobiography
▶ writing stimulated by research carried out by the writer
▶ creative responses to literature, e.g. dramatization of a story
▶ writing preceded by a period of reflection, e.g. on an earlier visit to a historic house
▶ writing that goes through a series of drafts and revisions.

In the traditional written paper the choice of essay seemed wide: you could choose between descriptive, narrative, personal, discursive or dramatic writing, but would be required to write only one or at most two pieces. However, there are many more purposes, and styles to match them in writing. Coursework enables you to explore some of these:

'Eight different ways of writing'

▶ **Narrative/descriptive**, e.g. written response to a picture as a story or description.
▶ **Reflective/analytical**, e.g. discussion of motives of characters in a play you are studying.
▶ **Task controlled by examiner**, e.g. written comprehension paper.
▶ **Task controlled by writer**, e.g. piece of individual topic work.
▶ **Task based on first-hand experience**, e.g. personal writing.
▶ **Task related to knowledge from a second-hand source**, e.g. writing up an interview you had recorded.

> **Literary writing**, e.g. a story or poem.
> **Functional writing**, e.g. a report or an article.

Your coursework folder should also show that you can write for *different purposes and readers*, and in *different modes and styles*. The above list and scheme will help you to make sure that you will have a wide selection of pieces.

Talking and listening

These skills are discussed together because the National Criteria stress the importance of their 'interactive' nature. Some oral work that you do for the examination may not require a listener, or at least a listener who reacts to what you say. There is a place for including some speech of this kind:

> reading aloud
> a prepared talk
> a formal speech.

But mostly, though, you will speak *and* listen and will be assessed for both. You will be used to many kinds of talk in the classroom – directed discussion, paired talk, small group discussions, etc. – but most of it is not assessed. How can you become a better talker and listener? With any kind of speech it will be helpful to consider the following points:

> speaking to the purpose
> the nature of the audience
> the place where talk occurs.

Let us look at each in turn.

Speaking to the purpose

First of all, think positively about oral work. It is not a test of accent. Your main aim should be to *communicate something clearly*, so as to interest the listener.

Speaking can be an end in itself (known as **product**-type speaking) or can grow from some other activity (known as **process**-type speaking). Examples of the first kind are:

' "Product" and "process" type talking …'

> reading a poem aloud
> giving a prepared talk
> telling a story
> making a speech of thanks.

When you are doing any of these, even as an exercise, you will tend to be conscious of how well you are performing, but you will find it improves matters if you concentrate hard on what you are saying. It will often be helpful to practise beforehand with a tape recorder, or have a series of cards listing the points you wish to make, but finally you should remember you are trying to interest or persuade your listeners, and should attend to them and what you are saying, and forget yourself.

Examples of the second kind, where speaking grows from some other activity, are:

> 'brainstorming' in a group
> having a group discussion
> problem-solving in pairs
> interviewing someone
> discussing a poem.

All of these involve considerable skill as a listener; using talk to include shy or reluctant speakers and to quieten those who try to dominate; and knowing when to take charge and when to let another speaker put forward a point of view. Take turns in group work to be listener and speaker, and to take the lead in talk as well as to support other speakers. Playing back a tape recording of a group discussion with friends, assessing your own performances informally as a group, can teach you a great deal. Group orals are considered at length in Chapter 7.

The nature of the audience

Your talk will naturally be affected by *who* the listeners are. Try to forget that your talk is being assessed – most of the time it will not be. Try to talk with one other person, in a small group of friends and in a large group or the whole class. You will react very differently as a speaker each time. Notice how your speech becomes slower, more formal and careful as the size of the group increases.

Your audience will not usually be passive: even if they remain silent, there may be fidgeting, smiles of support, or interested or bored looks. You should take notice of all this and respond appropriately. If finally you must talk to an assessor, try not to be overawed!

The place where talk occurs

Physical conditions around us affect our responses as speakers and listeners. Imagine telling something to a friend, while hugging a radiator in the corner of a small room, during a chilly break, and then having to make an announcement about the same matter to an assembly of the whole school. If you have a choice, find a *place* you like and invite listeners to sit in a way that makes them and you comfortable. Ask your teacher or tutor, if you need help in such matters, too.

▷ Written papers

'Follow the rules!'

Rules to follow

In this section, we shall look at the general rules for taking any written paper, and then describe three types of GCSE papers. You should go through the rules carefully first, then think how they may be applied to each type.

1   Read the general instructions to the paper very carefully.
2   Read the questions very carefully.
3   Decide on the questions you wish to answer, if there is a choice.
4   Decide on the best order of answering questions.
5   Decide how much time you should allow for each question.
6   Plan your answers.
7   Make sure you answer relevantly.
8   Leave time for checking your work.

1   Read the general instructions to the paper very carefully

There are always some candidates who answer more than the number of questions required. Even though you will be assessed on your best answers, this is a dreadful waste of time. There are also candidates who ignore 'turn over' and do not read every page of a question. If you are asked to present your work in a particular way, do so. If you are given a word limit, do not exceed it.

2   Read the questions very carefully

Great care is taken by those setting questions to make the wording as clear as possible, so that you will not be confused or misled. But quite a few candidates give themselves problems by careless reading, because they are in a hurry to begin. It is worth spending a little extra time to make sure you have understood the question. For example, if you are asked to give the advantages and disadvantages of an issue, do not give only one side of the argument; if you are asked to write an account based on ideas in a set passage, do not depart from it and introduce ideas of your own.

3   Decide on the questions you wish to answer, if there is a choice

Most English papers of a 'Reading and Writing' type will not give you a choice of question. There are, however, still some examination boards setting essay-writing options, and here the title you choose may be very important. Know your own strengths and weaknesses and do not choose to write a play or a story that needs a great deal of conversation if you know your punctuation is weak! Choose to show your strong points.

4   Decide on the best order of answering questions

If you tend to have difficulty in timing your paper correctly, choose to do questions which carry most marks first.

5   Decide how much time you should allow for each question

Do not get carried away in an examination and write at very great length. You will probably make a lot of mistakes and will finally run short of time.

6   Plan your answers

A few minutes spent planning an answer is time well spent. Either think the answer through, or make a flow chart, a scheme or list of points, or a rough draft. Cross through all rough work when it is finished. It is worth knowing that if you fail to complete your final draft, examiners will look at your rough work to see if they can find the conclusion there. If they do, they will give you credit for it.

7   Make sure you answer relevantly

This is easier said than done. If you have read the question carefully and spent time thinking about it, you will have a better chance of seeing what is required and keeping to it. Avoid any temptation to be wildly original or over-subtle in examination answers.

8   Leave time for checking your work

You should leave five minutes or so for reading your answers and looking out for mistakes that you may have made. You may be surprised how many slips there are when you are working in examination conditions. See Chapter 20 for detailed advice on how to correct your work.

Understanding and response (comprehension) papers

This type of English paper will be set by all boards and is variously called 'Reading and Writing', 'Understanding and Response', 'Understanding and Appreciation', and so on. It consists of a general instruction, e.g. Part 1 of this examination consists of one or two extracts about which you will be asked to do some writing in Part 2. Fifteen minutes are allowed for reading the extract and for making any notes you wish, after which you will be given Part 2, with the questions based on the extract, and a passage or pair of passages for you to read (or listen to on a tape, while you follow the text).

A series of 'stepped' questions follows (see page 11 of this book), with the maximum marks to be awarded in brackets at the end.

All the general rules above apply (except 3) and before you begin you should, of course, read the passages themselves very carefully and think about what is required for each answer.

Examples of typical passages and questions can be found in Chapter 10.

Creative writing (composition) paper

These will variously be called 'Continuous Writing', 'Personal and Expressive Writing' (**MEG**), and so on.

You will be invited to write on one or two (from a set of seven or eight) essay titles, covering the whole range of narrative, descriptive, discursive, imaginative, personal and dramatic writing. A picture will often be included to which you will be expected to respond. The normal length of the essay is 450 words, but this will be specified in the instructions to candidates, as will any other requirements:

▶   Write on ONE of the following ... You should write between 350 and 600 words (**MEG**).

▶   Write approximately two sides on one of the following subjects. If, however, your handwriting is unusually large or unusually small, you should make some adjustments in the amount you write ... (**NEAB**).

All the general rules above apply, and (1), (2), (6) and (7) are particularly important.

Examples of typical essay topics for you to try can be found in Chapters 13–18.

Directed writing papers

These are set by **MEG**, **NICCEA** and **WJEC**. You will be given one or two passages about something factual – e.g. the Channel Tunnel – and asked to respond to a series of about four or five questions. You may be required to give a simple, factual answer, or your response may involve inference from evidence in the text or evaluation of opinion, summarizing, and so on.

All the general rules above (except 3) apply, and typical passages and questions of this kind are to be found in Chapters 12 and 15.

▷ Oral assessment

General rules

Most of your oral work will be assessed by your teacher or tutor, but there may be occasions when an external examiner is directly involved.

'Rules for the Oral ...'

1 Plan what you have to do beforehand.
2 Be polite and friendly to your audience.
3 Concentrate on what you have to say rather than the way you are saying it.
4 Try to speak as clearly as possible.
5 Speak a little more slowly than usual.
6 Try not to lose your audience's attention.

1 Plan what you have to do beforehand

This is, of course, essential, but the extent to which it is possible varies. If you are giving an unscripted talk or are taking part in a discussion, think out in advance points that you would like to make. Some cards with reminder headings on them help to make you feel more confident, but do not read the headings out. Do look at your audience as you are speaking, not down at your notes.

2 Be polite and friendly to your audience

However nervous you may be feeling, be pleasant, saying 'Good morning' or 'Good after-noon'. If your audience is enjoying the occasion it will help you to relax and do your best. If you are not sure about any instructions, ask politely for them to be repeated.

3 Concentrate on what you have to say rather than the way you are saying it

You will be assessed for effective and appropriate speech: this includes clarity of speech but also how you interact with others, and the content of what you say. The best advice is to try to enter into the experience as freely and naturally as you can.

4 Try to speak as clearly as possible

You must be audible and intelligible, so remember that you may be speaking to someone who is not used to your manner of speech. Take care to speak out fairly loudly and clearly.

5 Speak a little more slowly than usual

The normal tendency of a student in an oral examination is to speed up, because he or she feels nervous and wants to get it over. This is a mistake. Try to remember that rapid speech is likely to be difficult to understand.

6 Try not to lose your audience's attention

You are most likely to do this if you have not prepared yourself properly in the first place; see rule (1) above. Visual aids, e.g. diagrams, may help make your points clear and fix attention. Watch out for signs of inattention, e.g. whispering, or even yawning! Remember that successful communication is a two-way process.

SUMMARY

▷ You should be familiar with various general reading techniques and how to 'interrogate the text' – thinking and questioning as you read, as well as taking from your reading starting points for writing and for coursework. You need to know about close reading skills, including outlining, prediction, gap filling, and group comprehension.

▷ You should have noticed writing styles, including narrative, descriptive, reflective, analytical and personal, and have thought about the differences between literary and functional writing.

▷ When talking and listening remember to speak to the purpose, taking notice of your audience and circumstances.

▷ Written papers require you to follow the rules which are different for Understanding and Response, Creative Writing and Directed Writing.

▷ Oral assessment requires you to plan, be considerate, focus on the task, speak clearly, slowly and with regard to the listeners.

The courses

This chapter indicates what the English GCSE Examining Groups have in common and where there is scope for choice, and discusses assessment in the examination.

We also look at the impact of the introduction of Key Stage 4 of the National Curriculum on the English course. **Attainment targets** have been established for English (as for other subjects), i.e. objectives which set out the aspects of knowledge, skills and understanding expected of you. In English these involve speaking and listening, reading, writing and various aspects of presentation of your work.

TOPIC	STUDY	REVISION I	REVISION 2
National Criteria			
Requirements			
Assessment/marking			
Syllabus and assessment			

WHAT YOU NEED TO KNOW

National Criteria

A major aspect of GCSE is the introduction of national criteria. The **General Criteria** lay down certain rules governing the conduct of all GCSE examinations. They provide a framework for teaching and assessment in all subjects.

There are six area GCSE Boards: **EDEXCEL** (London: formerly ULEAC), the Midland Examining Group (**MEG**), the Northern Examinations and Assessment Board (**NEAB**), the Northern Ireland Council for Curriculum, Examinations and Assessment (**NICCEA**), the Southern Examining Group (**SEG**) and the Welsh Joint Education Committee (**WJEC**).

The Boards are required to draw up syllabuses which comply with the **National Criteria** for individual subjects. Syllabuses and schemes of assessment will differ, but the Boards will have some things in common, e.g. all will allow a combination of coursework and assessment by written paper. The differences between the Boards are shown in Table 2.1 and are discussed further in the criteria for English later in this chapter.

'Notice that you must be able to "communicate accurately, appropriately and effectively in speech and writing".'

What does all this mean for you in practice? Well, the National Criteria for English will have the most direct effect on your work. They concern the range of things you will be expected to do and how marks will be awarded for your work. Each of these will be discussed below, stressing new emphases which have certainly changed the way you study and the way you are taught.

First, though, how is English defined in GCSE? English is to be examined as a single subject, including some literary material, although some Boards also offer English Literature as a separate examination subject.

Requirements

There are two things of importance to notice here: the National Criteria require students to show that they can 'communicate accurately, appropriately and effectively in speech and writing'.

Reading and **writing** have traditionally been part of English examinations, and this will continue. As well as short pieces for reading comprehension, the **reading of whole works** of literature is advised. As you will see from Chapter 4, studying at least one complete work of literature is compulsory for some Boards. Your reading should cover a range of texts of different kinds:

- short stories
- novels
- autobiographies   Literary texts
- plays
- poetry

and

- newspaper articles
- advertisements   Non-literary texts
- brochures
- pamphlets

You will be tested on both 'close' comprehension of a text and more general understanding, involving some element of personal response. The multiple-choice type of objective test will still be used – see Chapter 9 for more information on this – but may not account for more than 20 per cent of the whole scheme of assessment. You will also be expected to show that you can read, understand and respond to all types of writing and develop information retrieval techniques when you study.

' "Closed" and "open" kinds of writing.'

A wide range of **writing** is also required. You should attempt pieces of writing where the subject matter, form and purpose are *given to you* ('**closed**' kinds of writing):

- letters
- reports
- instructions
- reviews
- newspaper articles

and where the subject matter, form and purpose are *chosen by you* ('**open**' kinds of writing):

- stories
- poems
- personal writing.

Your writing should show that you can use correct grammar and standard English, except where non-standard forms are appropriate, e.g. in dialogue or direct speech in conversation, in a story where the narrator uses a more relaxed style, and so on.

Writing pieces of *different lengths* is also required. The average piece of examination written work is reckoned to be 400–500 words, but much longer pieces of topic work, or sustained narrative, will be encouraged for coursework.

'You have to take an Oral examination.'

Oral Communication is seen to be an essential part of skill in the use of the language. This involves *talking* and *listening*. If you think about it, what you write communicates nothing unless there is a reader, and what you *say* needs a *listener*. An important area of English studies is officially recognized in the examination.

You will have opportunities to show that you can express yourself clearly and listen responsively, and adapt your style of speech to suit the listener/s and the purpose. The following list gives situations where these skills are needed:

- group discussion
- paired chat
- interview
- debate.

Later chapters will take each of these general areas and explain in detail how you can prepare for the examination, either with the help of your teacher or on your own.

▷ **Assessment/ marking**

Assessment in English must match the attainment targets and programmes of study set out in the Key Stage 4 criteria for English.

Schemes of assessment will vary from examining board to examining board, but all must involve the following:

▷ Assessment must be positive: schemes of assessment should allow candidates to show as fully as possible what they can do, and will either include a variety of papers, or a variety of tasks within papers or coursework.

▷ Assessment of Oral Communication is compulsory, and a candidate must achieve at least Grade 5 to have a grade in English recorded on the certificate.

▷ In each scheme of assessment:
Attainment Target 1 (Speaking and Listening) must be weighted at **20 per cent**.
Attainment Target 2 (Reading) must be weighted at **40 per cent**.
Attainment Targets 3–5 (Writing, Spelling and Presentation) must be weighted at **40 per cent**.

▷ Each scheme of assessment must include a terminal examination. The weighting of the examination must be at least **60 per cent**.

▷ Coursework (half Attainment Target 1 and half Attainment Targets 2–3) must be weighted at not more than **40 per cent**.
NB The terminal examinations will have at least two levels – Foundation and Higher.

Each of these requirements will now be discussed more fully.

Assessment must be positive

For English there are two ways of distinguishing between different abilities, while allowing all candidates to show what they can do. The *first* is to set everyone the same task (e.g. writing about a personal experience or discussing a painting) and then to allow for differences of treatment or approach. The *second* is to set what is called a 'stepped question' with several parts in ascending order of difficulty, each part carrying a separate mark. All candidates should be able to succeed with the early parts of the question.

Stepped question

'What are "stepped" questions?'

A **stepped question** might be set on a passage concerning the wreck of a passenger liner, and have the following parts:

Question 1   Which three events warned passengers that the ship was in trouble?   (3 marks)

Question 2   From the statements made by the captain and first mate, how far is there evidence of mistakes made by members of the crew?   (5 marks)

Question 3   Imagine you were a passenger on board at the time of the disaster. Using only ideas in the passage, write an account (in about 200 words) of your reactions to events as they occurred.   (7 marks)

Notice that Question 1 asks you to give only facts from the passage; the second part (Question 2) asks you to make a judgement, based on information given; and the third (Question 3), which asks you to write an imaginative yet accurate narrative, gives you the most scope.

The grade descriptions for written English in the **National Criteria** indicate the different demands placed on candidates. A *low* pass grade requires candidates to show that they are capable of 'understanding and conveying information at a straightforward level' and can 'show sufficient control of the written language to communicate effectively, despite some weakness in spelling, punctuation and the construction of complex sentences'. The *middle* grade requires skill in 'understanding and conveying information both at a straightforward and at a more complex level' and 'writing in paragraphs, using sentences of varied kinds and exercising care over punctuation and spelling'.

However, *all* candidates should be given opportunities to show their abilities to

▷ understand and convey information clearly
▷ understand facts, ideas and opinions and present them in an orderly way
▷ consider information and select what is relevant
▷ describe what is felt or imagined
▷ recognize implied meanings and attitudes
▷ understand the ways in which language changes according to circumstances
▷ paragraph, spell, punctuate and construct sentences accurately.

Assessment of oral communication

Though compulsory, oral English is assessed separately. English is graded by a seven-letter system from A to G (with an 'Ungraded' category), and Oral Communication by numbers from 1 to 5 (with an 'Ungraded' category). If you achieve the lowest grade or better in both, the two grades are shown together on the certificate, e.g.

C3 (Grade C in English and 3 in Oral Communication).

Otherwise, a grade in English or Oral Communication is not shown on the certificate.

'What must I do for a pass in the Oral?'

The **National Criteria** state what you should be able to do to achieve a pass in Oral Communication. You should be able to

- understand and convey straightforward information
- present facts, ideas and opinions in an orderly sequence
- choose and comment on spoken and written material relevantly
- describe your experience in simple terms, and express what is felt or imagined
- recognize the difference between fact and opinion or attitude in discussion
- vary your way of speaking according to the situation and the listeners
- speak so as to be heard and understood, with an appropriate manner, and at a suitable speed.

Attainment targets

AT1 Speaking and Listening
You should be able to express a point of view clearly and convey information and ideas to others appropriately, contributing to group discussion.

AT2 Reading
You should show that you can read a variety of literary and non-literary texts drawn from different cultures and times (i.e. some pre-twentieth-century writing) and communicate your response as well as show an awareness of style.

AT3 Writing and ATs 4–5 Presentation, Spelling and Handwriting
You should be able to write about your experiences and feelings; show that you can discuss factual matters or give your opinions in a suitable style for readers and one which is grammatically correct, with correct paragraphing, sentence structure, punctuation and spelling. Clear and legible handwriting will also be taken into account.

Terminal examination

The examination will consist of written papers at different levels. There will be at least two levels: Foundation Level and Higher Level. Some boards will also offer an Intermediate Level examination. Your school or college will decide which is the most suitable level for you.

Coursework

It is recommended in the **National Criteria** that there should be a combination of assessment by coursework and by final examination. Some of the work must be done while a teacher is present, and the arrangements under which the work was done, and the time spent, must be noted. This is called working under 'controlled' or supervised conditions.

'Working under "controlled" conditions ...'

The requirements mentioned above apply to coursework as well as to written examinations, so you should bear these requirements in mind as you work throughout the year. Your class teacher or tutor will help you to choose the pieces of coursework to submit for assessment (the number will depend on the percentage of coursework being offered). These pieces should normally be handwritten, although some groups allow all but the controlled conditions piece to be done on a word-processor. Photocopies, diagrams, etc., may be included, if their source is acknowledged. You may have worked through earlier drafts and at least one of these should be attached to the final effort, along with any comments made by your teacher or tutor.

All the pieces should be put together in order in one folder, with your name and the date the work was done clearly written on each piece. The folder should have

- a front sheet, listing the work it contains
- dividers, separating the creative from the critical work.

It will be marked by your teachers, and your progress throughout the course assessed. Work done by pupils in your school or centre will be considered by your own teachers to make sure that everything is marked to the same standard. Then the assessed work will be compared with work in other centres, to ensure that the standards are comparable and reliable across the whole country.

Table 2.1 Comparison of English GCSE syllabuses

Group	Papers	Length or description of papers	Course-work	% of marks
London	Paper 1: Coursework Folder	2 sections: Speaking and Listening (3 units) Reading and Writing (4 units)	✓	40
	Papers 2 and 4: Reading and Response (Two tiers)	2 hrs	–	30
	Papers 3 and 5: Writing and Reading (Two tiers)	2 hrs	–	30
MEG	Papers 1 and 3: Non-Literary and Media Texts (Reading and Writing) (Two tiers)	2 hrs	–	30
	Papers 2 and 4: Literature (Reading and Writing) (Two tiers: Standard and Higher)	2 hrs	–	30
	Coursework Folder	5 pieces of written work; record of oral work; record of texts studied	✓	40
NEAB	Paper 1: Reading	2 hrs	–	30
	Paper 2: Writing, Spelling, Handwriting, Presentation (Papers 1 and 2 have two tiers)	2 hrs	–	30
	Paper 3: Coursework Folder	3 oral pieces; 2–3 written pieces	✓	40
NICCEA	Paper 1: Reading and Writing Literary material (Two tiers)	2 hrs	–	30
	Paper 2: Reading and Writing Non-literary material (Two tiers)	2 hrs	–	30
	Coursework Portfolio	4 pieces on reading and writing 4 oral pieces		40
SEG	Written Examination: version 1* Reading, Writing and Presentation OR	2–2½ hrs	–	60
	Written Examination: version 2 (each version has two tiers)	1¼–1¾ hrs	–	60
	Coursework Folder	1,500 words and selection of oral work	–	40
WJEC	Paper 1: Reading and Writing Literary	Tier 1 (1½ hrs)		60
	Paper 2: Reading and Writing Non-Literary	Tiers 2/3 (2 hrs)		
	Coursework	Oral Reading (2 units)	✓	40

*pre-released on set theme

From Table 2.1 you can see that the various syllabuses offered by the Groups differ, though all require at least 40 per cent coursework assessment and also examine Oral Communication. We shall consider the distinctive features of each in turn.

Table 2.2 shows you the grading system of *levels* used for GCSE since 1994 and how they relate to the previous system of *letter* grades.

Table 2.2
Grading levels
for GCSE

GCSE grades used up to and including 1993	GCSE levels used now		
A	10		
	9		
B	8		
C	7	7+	
D	7−	6+	
E	6	6−	
F	5		
G	4		
U	3		
	2		
	1		

The ten levels are used for assessing coursework, but the letter grades A–G are used for the final GCSE award. There will be an A* (a super-A) grading for those achieving the equivalent of a Level 10.

We now look in rather more detail at each GCSE Syllabus.

▷ **Syllabus and assessment**

London

Paper 1: Coursework folder
There are *two* sections.

1 Speaking and Listening component with teacher's record of assessments. This should include *three* assignments, covering talk to explain, describe, narrate; talk to explore and imagine; talk to discuss and persuade.
2 Reading and Writing components. This should consist of *four* units of writing
   • personal and imaginative work
   • work reflecting diverse cultures and traditions
   • work based on a play by Shakespeare
   • work based on a prose work by an author published before 1900.

The folder should contain 1,500 words approximately.

Papers 2 and 4: Reading and writing
This consists of response to pre-released material which will be twentieth-century prose, poetry and non-fiction. There will be *three* questions

▷ two based on close reading
▷ one of writing to inform, explain or describe.

Papers 3 and 5: Media texts (unseen)
There will be extracts to give candidates' writing context focus and support and they will be given *three* questions

▷ one will be assessed for reading
▷ two will be assessed for writing to
   • argue, persuade, instruct
   • analyse, review, comment.

MEG

Paper 1: Non-literary and media texts – reading and writing
There are *two* sections.

Section A   Specific questions on non-literary texts, including analysis of style.

Section B   Tasks to elicit a broader response to texts, e.g. a piece of sustained writing for a specific audience.

Paper 2: Literature – reading and writing
There are *two* sections.

Section A   Pre-released text for critical/personal evaluation.

Section B   Broader, thematically based tasks to elicit a creative, imaginative response.
Candidates may take Standard Tier (Levels 4–7) or Higher Tier (Levels 5–10).

Coursework folder
The folder must contain evidence to show

▷   the range of reading undertaken by the candidate
▷   evidence of evolving written work through drafting
▷   the study of language
▷   the study of whole works of literature, including Shakespeare.

There should be *five* pieces of written work, including one handwritten by the student, a record of oral activities which covers most of the assessment objectives attempted during the course and a record of texts studied during the course should be included.
NB Candidates taking both English and English Literature may submit one common folder.

NEAB

Paper 1: Reading
There are *two* sections.

Section A   This will require responses to the *close reading of prepared texts* (distributed six weeks before the examination). The texts will relate to one theme, e.g. People and Environment, *in common with the syllabus for English Literature*.

Section B   This will require responses to the *close reading of unseen texts*. Questions will be structured to allow candidates in each tier to show appropriate abilities for the target levels. (This paper is common to Paper 1 of English Literature.)

Paper 2: Writing, spelling, handwriting and presentation
There are *two* sections.

Section A   There will be a choice of tasks which will require presenting text for specific audiences. The content will be based on pre-released materials.

Section B   Candidates will be asked to write imaginatively and/or about their own experiences. The paper will be tiered to provide differentiated stimulus material. The pieces of writing will be assessed for spelling, grammatical structures, punctuation, handwriting and general presentation.

Coursework folder
The folder should include *two* sections.

Section A   Teacher summary of oral work from several points in the course.

Section B   *Two to four* pieces of written coursework.

NB Candidates taking both English and English Literature may submit one piece of work in common for both.

NICCEA

There is only *one* syllabus: *two* written papers and *three or four* pieces of written coursework.

Paper 1
Comprehension, including creative response to a literary prose passage.

Paper 2
Functional or practical writing, and comprehension based on non-literary material.

Oral communication
Assessed coursework, including a range of assignments from the following areas: personal response, response to literature, non-literary and media texts, exploration of spoken language, relaying information, persuasive argument, collaborative talk.

SEG

Written papers

- ▶ **Version 1** Part 1: Reading and response to pre-released material.
  Part 2: Writing and presentation based on the same material.
- ▶ **Version 2** Part 1: Reading of unseen material.
  Part 2: Writing and presentation based on fresh stimulus material.

NB There are two levels for Part 2: Foundation Level and Higher Level. Extra reading time will be allowed to candidates taking Version 2.

Coursework folder
There are *three* parts.

- ▶ Teacher-assessed oral work
- ▶ Personal writing
- ▶ Writing in response to literature: 1,000–1,500 words.

Candidates should include evidence of skills in information retrieval, in drafting, editing and proofreading, and in knowledge of language.

WJEC

Paper 1: Reading and writing – literary
There are *two* sections.

Section A   Reading of literary material will be tested through structured questions.

Section B   Writing skills will be tested by two tasks, the first linked to Section A.

Paper 2: Reading and writing – non-literary
There are *two* sections.

Section A   Reading of non-literary material will be tested through structured questions.

Section B   Writing skills will be tested by two tasks, the first linked to Section A.
Presentation will be assessed on the evidence of both papers.

Coursework folder
There are *three* sections.

Section A   Speaking and listening: assessment will be based on the best work in a range of situations and with various audiences, including work in pairs, small groups, in larger groups and at least providing evidence of the following:

- communicating to an audience
- developing understanding through talk
- collaborating.

Section B   Reading: *two* assignments are involved. One will be based on the study of a whole work of literature; the other may be based on literature, or a non-literary or media text.

Section C   Writing: *two* pieces should be submitted. One piece should be imaginative writing; the other should be transactional (i.e., an article, leaflet, report or letter). There should be *evidence of the overall writing process – planning, drafting and editing.*

SUMMARY

- You should know the National Criteria and be clear about what you will be asked to do.
- You should understand how marks will be awarded for your work: that assessment is positive, also how tasks set match the ATs. You should have some understanding of coursework assessment, including oral, and what is required in the final examination.
- You should have picked out the requirements of the examining board with which you are involved.

Chapter 3

Importance of the topic areas

▷ **GETTING STARTED**

Most of the remaining chapters of the book deal with fifteen special topics relating to GCSE written English and Oral Communication. All the topics have some relevance, whatever course you are taking, and some are especially important. The purpose of this chapter is to help you decide *which* chapters and topics are most useful for the papers you personally will be taking, and the coursework you will be submitting.

TOPIC	STUDY	REVISION 1	REVISION 2
London			
MEG			
NEAB			
NICCEA			
SEG			
WJEC			

WHAT YOU NEED TO KNOW

Table 3.1 gives an overview of which chapters and topics are relevant for which exams.

Table 3.1 Which chapters are relevant for which examinations

Chapter and topic	London	MEG	NEAB	NICCEA	SEG	WJEC
4 Knowledge about language	✓✓	✓✓	✓✓	✓✓	✓✓	✓✓
5 Spelling, handwriting and presentation	✓✓	✓✓	✓✓	✓✓	✓✓	✓✓
6 Individual oral	✓✓	✓✓	✓✓	✓✓	✓✓	✓✓
7 Group oral	✓✓	✓✓	✓✓	✓✓	✓✓	✓✓
8 Researching and writing up	✓	✓	✓	✓	✓	✓
9 Case study: preparing an assignment	✓	✓	✓	✓	✓	✓
10 Reading comprehension	✓✓	✓✓	✓✓	✓✓	✓✓	✓✓
11 From reading to writing	✓	✓✓	✓✓	✓✓	✓✓	✓✓
12 Summary	✓	✓	✓✓	✓✓	✓	✓✓
13 Writing narrative	✓	✓	✓	✓	✓	✓
14 Writing dialogue	✓	✓	✓	✓✓	✓	✓
15 Persuasive writing	✓✓	✓	✓	✓✓	✓	✓✓
16 Descriptive writing	✓	✓	✓	✓	✓✓	✓
17 Responding to a stimulus	✓✓	✓✓	✓	✓	✓✓	✓✓
18 Personal writing	✓✓	✓✓	✓	✓	✓✓	✓✓
19 A sample coursework folder	✓	✓	✓	✓	✓	✓
20 Checking and correcting	✓✓	✓✓	✓✓	✓✓	✓✓	✓✓

(✓✓ = mentioned as compulsory, or of special significance in syllabus)

Some chapters obviously apply to *any* examination you may take: all require a range of examination techniques, such as careful reading, note-taking, planning your time, and many more matters that are discussed in Chapter 1. Also, it is always important to write in an appropriate style, paying some attention to accuracy of expression: Chapter 5 is concerned with this. In written examinations it is wise to leave time to check and correct your work. How does this apply to written coursework, though? Should you submit work for the examination which has been corrected by your teacher or tutor? Chapter 20 looks at these matters.

Three other chapters also deal with topics that are important because they are part of the syllabus for all Groups and courses. You will be assessed for your speaking and listening abilities as one of a group and, most likely, individually and as one of a pair, therefore Chapters 6 and 7 will be important to you. Researching and writing up an assignment is a key part of coursework activity and Chapters 8 and 9 will help you with this, as will Chapter 19. All courses require candidates to read and understand a passage and respond in writing – so Chapter 11 will also be important.

To explain Table 3.1 further, and give some more information, each Board's syllabus will now be looked at briefly. Details of the options offered by the Boards are given at the end of Chapter 2.

▷ London   *Paper 1: Coursework folder*   *(40%)*

There are *two* components of the Coursework folder.

Section 1   (20%)
Section 1 is the *Speaking and Listening* component. The teacher's record of your *three* best assessments throughout the course will be included here. You should have done work which shows that you can

▶ express what you have felt and imagined
▶ understand facts, ideas and opinions
▶ show an awareness of listeners and choose an appropriate style
▶ communicate a personal response to something heard or read
▶ discuss and consider others' written or spoken language.

Section 2   (20%)
Section 2 is the *Reading and Writing* component. There should be *four* units

▶ personal and imaginative work
▶ work reflecting diverse cultures and traditions
▶ work based on a play by Shakespeare
▶ work based on a prose work by an author published before 1900.
One unit must be handwritten.

Whole texts must be studied for the second, third and fourth units.

Papers 2 and 4 Terminal examination: Twentieth-century prose, poetry and non-fiction (pre-released material)   *(30%)*

There will be *three* questions:

▶ *two* based on close reading of the prepared material, showing interpretation of content, language and presentation
▶ *one* a writing task, requiring candidates to inform, explain or describe.

Papers 3 and 5 Terminal examination: Media texts (unseen)   *(30%)*

There will be *three* questions:

▶ *one* on reading response to unseen passages
▶ *two*, based on the passages, to argue, persuade and instruct, and also to analyse, review and comment.

NB For both papers there are two levels: Foundation and Higher Level. In both papers spelling, handwriting and presentation will be assessed.

▷ **MEG**   *Paper 1: Non-literary and media texts – Reading and writing*   *(30%)*

This paper is of two hours' duration and will be in *two* tiers: *Standard* and *Higher*. Candidates will be given tasks based on non-literary texts and asked specific questions about linguistic effects, style, sense of audience and presentation. Also there will be an opportunity for a broader response: a sustained piece of creative writing.

Paper 2: Literature – Reading and writing   *(30%)*

A booklet with pre-release extracts will be sent to schools by the beginning of the summer term. Tasks will be based on this material – both critical and imaginative/creative.

At the Higher Tier, candidates should show an awareness of attitudes towards language, show a wide range of suitable vocabulary and a personal style, and good level of accuracy.

Each paper will include assessment of spelling, handwriting and presentation.

Coursework folder   *(40%)*

Your folder must contain up to five pieces of your best written work, including one hand-written by you, a record of the oral activities on the course and the assessment; a record of the texts you have studied throughout the course. There should be evidence of the reading you have done on the course, including whole works of literature and Shakespeare. There should be some evidence of language study and of work evolved through drafting and revision to its final form.

The **terminal examination** will consist of two 2-hour papers.

▷ **NEAB**   *Paper 1: Reading*   *(30%)*

There are *two* sections.

Section A

Here you will be asked *to respond to questions on an anthology of prepared texts* which will be given to centres about six weeks before the examination. The texts, which will cover different periods and styles of writing, will relate to one theme (e.g. Experience of School), changing every year of the examination. You will have chances to read and discuss the material but you will not know what the questions are until the examination date.   **(15%)**

Section B

Here you will be asked *to respond to questions on an anthology of unprepared texts*.

(15%)

(This paper is the same as Paper 1 NEAB English Literature.)

Paper 2: Writing, spelling, handwriting and presentation   *(30%)*

There are *two* sections.

Section A

Here you will be asked to write about some factual matter, giving your ideas and opinions.

(10%)

Section B

Here you will be asked to write imaginatively about your experiences. There will also be assessment of spelling, handwriting and presentation.   **(20%)**

Both papers will be set in two tiers, and you will be entered for one at the appropriate level:

▶   *Tier P:* Texts from Shakespeare, and twentieth-century literature.
▶   *Tier Q:* Texts will include compulsory pre-twentieth-century literature work/s.

Coursework folder   (40%)

Your folder will show evidence of work of *two* kinds:

▶   *Oral work:* This will give a description of your work in speaking and listening, and
    samples from *three points* in the course.   (20%)
▶   *Written work:* There should be two to four pieces of your written work, depending on
    length, of your own choice, including literary and non-literary material.   (20%)

▷ **NICCEA**   The examination consists of *two* compulsory written papers and written coursework.

Paper 1: Reading and writing – literary

Section A
This is a comprehension test, set on a prose passage from works of literature.

Section B
This involves imaginative writing based on the texts in Section A.

Paper 2: Reading and writing – non-literary

This has two questions, one needing functional or practical writing, and the other a comprehension test on non-literary material.
NB Both papers will be set in two tiers: Tier S and Tier T. Each paper will include assessment of spelling, handwriting and presentation.

Coursework folder

The folder (three or four pieces) should cover three elements:

▶   response to reading a variety of texts, including one of the plays of Shakespeare
▶   creative or imaginative writing
▶   functional or transactional writing.

Oral coursework will be assessed on a candidate's ability to listen and speak in a variety of formal and informal situations, preferably where more than one pupil is involved. The following six kinds of talk should be attempted:

▶   describing and/or expressing feelings about a place, person or experience
▶   relaying information
▶   persuasive argument – recognizing and expressing opinions
▶   collaborating – starting a discussion, stating a problem, commenting on how a discussion is going and reaching an agreed conclusion
▶   speculating – putting forward ideas about what might happen
▶   roleplay.

The *four* best assessments should be included.

▷ **SEG**   *Written papers*

There are *two* versions of written papers.

Version 1
This is based on an anthology of material sent to candidates about eight weeks before the examination. The anthology will have a theme (e.g. Outsiders) and be a collection of passages from plays, poems, graphics and so on. Candidates will have an opportunity to discuss the material but will not know the questions until the examination.

Part 1   Reading response to the material, in the anthology.   (30%)

Part 2   Direct questions and other written response, which may involve directed writing such as a pamphlet, advertisement, newspaper article.   (30%)

Version 2

As above, except that the material will be unseen. Candidates will have fifteen minutes' extra reading time at Foundation Level and half an hour extra time at Higher Level on these papers.

NB There are two levels for Part 2: Foundation Level and Higher Level. Each paper will include assessment of spelling, writing and presentation.

Coursework folder

There are *three* parts.

1   A selection of teacher-assessed work in speaking and writing which should include some of the following: a response to reading a work of fiction; an individually planned activity of your own choice; a collaborative group activity; a task involving pairs inter-acting; a task focusing upon talk about language use and appropriateness.
2   Personal writing including description, narration, based on experience, and so on.
3   Response to literature including more than one genre and whole works of literature. Candidates taking Levels 7–10 should include some pre-twentieth-century works.
      Include some of your drafts, and edited or proofread work (you may include draft-ing done on a word-processor), as well as something to show your skills in information retrieval and your knowledge about language. The latter could be something on the development of language in children, the language of persuasion and argument, lan-guage in the media, bilingualism, the historical development of language and language in the classroom or workplace.   (40%)

▷ WJEC   *Written papers*   (60%)

There are *two* written papers, each 1½ hours long at Tier 1, but 2 hours long for Tiers 2 and 3.

Paper 1: Reading and writing – literary

Section A   Reading literary material, e.g. a story, drama or poetry, and answering set ques-tions.   (30%)

Section B   Two writing tasks, one linked to the material in Section A, the other with freer choice.

Paper 2: Reading and writing – non-literary

Section A   Reading non-literary material, e.g. an advertisement, newspaper report and answering set questions.

Section B   Two writing tasks, one linked to the material in Section A, the other of freer choice, but probably directed to a particular type of reader and for a particular purpose.
                                                                                    (30%)

NB On each paper spelling, handwriting and presentation aspects will be assessed.

Coursework folder   (40%)

There are *three* sections.

Section A: Speaking and listening

Here samples of oral work that you have done during the course should be included, with your teacher's evaluation. There should be an example of your work in a pair (e.g. problem-solving), in a small group (e.g. discussing a topic) and in a larger group (e.g. addressing the class). Your work should show that you can speak effectively to an audience, collaborate with a fellow student in discussion, and develop ideas through talking them over.   (**20%**)

Section B: Reading

There will be *two* assignments here: one based on the study of a complete work of literature; the other may also be literary but may be a non-literary or media text.   (**10%**)

Section C: Writing

There should be *two* pieces of work here: one an imaginative piece (e.g. a story, a drama script, a poem or group of poems) and one a transactional piece (e.g. an article, a report, a leaflet or a formal letter). You should include some material to show the writing process (e.g. a draft which has been edited).   (**10%**)

SUMMARY

You will have found information about each group syllabus.

London • Twentieth-Century Prose, Poetry and Non-Fiction (pre-released material)
  • Media Texts (unseen)
  • Coursework Folder: Speaking and Listening
                          Reading and Writing

MEG • Non-Literary and Media Texts: Reading and Writing
  • Literature: Reading and Writing
  • Coursework Folder: Speaking and Listening
                          Reading and Writing

NEAB • Reading
  • Writing, Spelling, Handwriting, Presentation
  • Coursework Folder: Speaking, Listening, Reading, Writing

NICCEA • Reading and Writing: Literary
  • Reading and Writing: Non-Literary
  • Coursework Folder: Reading, Writing, Speaking, Listening

SEG • Reading Response and Writing (pre-released material)
  • Reading Response and Writing (unseen material)
  • Coursework Folder: Reading, Writing, Speaking, Listening

WJEC • Reading and Writing: Literary
  • Reading and Writing: Non-Literary
  • Coursework Folder: Speaking and Listening
                          Reading
                          Writing

Knowledge about language

▷ GETTING STARTED

For the purposes of GCSE, English should not be defined too narrowly. This chapter is as much about appropriate expression as correct grammar, spelling and punctuation. Most of us have a range of forms of English that we are able to use and our 'linguistic manners' subconsciously suggest to us which is the right form; there would be considerable difference between a report of an accident you might make in court as an eye-witness and how you would describe it among friends and family.

Among the many forms of English there is one form that is generally considered to be the most 'correct'. This is **Standard English.** It is important for all who speak or write in English to be able to use this form, when appropriate. This is because it is universally used for official communications. In the examination you will be expected to show that you can adopt different styles, and this will certainly include expressing yourself in Standard English.

Among the skills to be assessed are the ability to

▷ show a sense of audience, and an awareness of style in both formal and informal situations

▷ exercise control of appropriate grammatical structures, conventions of paragraphing, sentence structure, punctuation and spelling in writing.

TOPIC	STUDY	REVISION I	REVISION 2
Adopting an appropriate style of writing			
Drafting to improve style			
Adopting an appropriate style of speech			
Correct grammar			
Paragraphing			
Punctuation			

▷ WHAT YOU NEED TO KNOW

▷ **Adopting an appropriate style of writing**

You would probably be surprised to read in an essay on 'Visiting Friends' part of a telephone conversation like this:

'Good afternoon, John. I was hoping I might visit you this afternoon, at three o'clock.'
'Good afternoon, Bill. Yes, it will be quite convenient for you to call at the time you suggest.'

You would feel it was very stilted, and that people don't really talk like that. Bill and John would be more likely to say something like this:

'Oh, hello John, it's Bill. Look, I'd like to pop round for a while this afternoon, all right? About three?'
'OK, Bill. I'll see you then.'

On the other hand, you would be equally surprised to read in a pamphlet 'Succeeding in an Interview' these sentences:

'You must let them know you are well up in things that are going on. Don't get in a flap and go on about how much money you will be paid.'

Something like this would be more appropriate:

'Try to show that you are interested in current affairs. Keep calm, and avoid asking about the salary.'

'Develop a sense of style'

It is very important for the examination that you should be able to write in different and appropriate styles. But how is a sense of style to be developed? Mainly by wide reading and practice in writing.

Table 4.1 Categories of writing

Expressive (examples)	Referential (examples)	Literary (examples)	Persuasive (examples)
Conversation	Discussion essay	Descriptions	Advertising
Dialogue	Explanation	Drama	Editorials
Diaries	News article	Essay	Lawyers' speeches
Invitation	Problem-solving	Film script	Public speeches
Joke	Proving a point	Folklore	Sermons
Letter	Report	Novel	
Personal writing	Summary	Poetry	
		Short story	
		TV script	

There have been many attempts to describe and classify different types of writing. One model, given in a simplified version in Table 4.1, describes a range of styles in written English from the most informal **Expressive writing** (the sort of writing you might do if you kept a diary, or wrote down an incident from your own life) to the more formal **Referential writing** (reports, essays, summaries, and so on). There is also another very important kind of writing, **Literary writing** (imaginative writing that has a definite pattern or way of being organized, as in stories and poems).

In school, you will almost certainly have plenty of opportunity in different subjects to do referential writing but much less to do literary writing. English coursework will give you the opportunity to do both.

Take your writing seriously as a craft at which you can get better. Sometimes, try out your own ideas very roughly at first, in draft form, and then work at the draft, rewriting, reshaping and improving your first attempt until you are more satisfied with it. You can put both the draft, or drafts, and the finished piece in your coursework folder, so that the *way* your story, poem, description, report – whatever it is – has grown is clear.

▷ **Drafting to improve style**

Here is the first draft of a piece of literary writing by a student. She was describing Garrard's, a famous jewellers in London.

> I visited Garrard's jewellery shop in Regent Street in London. There were three floors each with a large selection of precious gems made up as rings, necklaces and brooches. There were lots of diamonds, of course: solitaires, some were cut square, some round, some oval as well as loose stones. In the room with sapphires there were sapphire and diamond rings, and clusters of sapphires, diamonds and pearls. Another room had rubies in necklaces and tiaras. Next, there were pearls in earrings, and bracelets with pendants. There were also lots of semi-precious stones. I really enjoyed visiting Garrard's.

After discussing this with her teacher she decided that it was rather generalized and confusing. She chose to paragraph the piece differently, to describe the shop, floor by floor, concentrating at each level on a different type of jewel until she reached a climax at the top. Read the second version, now. I think you will agree that it has much more impact.

By including both pieces in her coursework file she could show how the writing had evolved and improved in craftsmanship.

> Garrard's, Jewellers to H.M. the Queen, is a beautiful shop in Regent Street, in London; it has several rooms full of precious gemstones and pearls.
>
> The Diamond room has solitaires by weight in various cuts. There are square cuts, oval cuts in ring setting, sparkling round cuts, and also loose stones.
>
> The Sapphire room has large cut sapphires with diamonds, single sapphire earrings, Princess Di sapphire and diamond rings, plus sapphires with pearls and diamonds.

(continued)

> *The third room specializes in rubies. There are blood-red rubies in delicate necklaces; special cut rubies, and you can even buy a ruby and pearl tiara.*
>
> *The fourth room shows pearls: drop pearl earrings in many settings; pearl and diamond-encrusted bracelets with matching pendants.*
>
> *Then you come to the final room: opals, topaz, jade, onyx – a semi-precious heaven!*

Most authors of published works make several drafts and revisions of their first attempt. The chapter you are reading now has been through this process!

More advice on different kinds of writing is given in Chapters 12–19.

▷ Adopting an appropriate style of speech

'Correct' speech, like 'correct' writing, is not something fixed. Consider the following remarks made by someone within the space of an hour to his employer, a colleague, and his wife:

'All right, Mr Hammond, I'll collect it on my way home. I know Richard Hobbs & Co.'

'Got to run an errand for N.H., and pick up a parcel from Dirty Dick's.'

'I got landed with collecting a parcel from Hobbs' for Old Nick.'

The remarks are in different styles, but each is an example of effective communication. The second and third cannot be considered incorrect. It is clear from these examples that how we speak depends on the person we are addressing and the circumstances at the time. Even in familiar, everyday situations, our way of speaking changes without our noticing it, or thinking about it. But at school, you will be asked to speak in a variety of situations, some of which may be new to you. Also, samples of your talk will be assessed. There is no need to be anxious or self-conscious about oral coursework but it may be wise to be a little self-critical and also to take any opportunity that arises to take part in as many kinds of oral work as you can. In this way you will be practising and improving your skills. How to do this is really what Chapters 6 and 7 are about. One or two general matters will be mentioned now, because they directly influence the way we talk.

The first concerns the size of the audience. Discussing something with *one* other person is very different from talking in a *group*, and even more different from addressing the *whole* school.

Five main styles of talk have been identified, each depending on the size of the audience:

▷ **intimate:** one to one – very private and personal
▷ **casual:** one person to one or two friends in relaxed chat
▷ **consultative:** small group discussion
▷ **formal:** one person to larger group, or one to one where there is a difference of status between the talkers
▷ **frozen:** one to very large group or one to one where one of the speakers has very high status.

Most of the talk you do for GCSE English will be *consultative*, won't it, with perhaps some *formal* talk, too. Try not to talk in a *frozen* style, even if you feel nervous!

As your audience becomes larger you will probably feel less confident and so your speech will become more formal and standard in form. Talking to a friend, you can leave a good deal unsaid, because you know he or she is likely to respond. It is much more difficult to judge how much a really large group will be able to understand and sympathize with what is said. In your efforts to be audible and clearly understood you will almost certainly speak more slowly, put points more simply or even repeat them several times and in different ways.

'There's no need to be a smooth talker!'

Remember that if 'correct' talk is to be understood as talk appropriate to the situation, it will not normally be a continuous stream of perfectly formed sentences. It has been said that 'to "er" is human': natural speech is full of hesitations, pauses, repetitions, ums and ahs – and ers! To have a reputation as a 'smooth talker' is not enviable because the talk sounds too perfect to be sincere. In a prepared short talk you may well speak more carefully and formally than in a group discussion, but each way of speaking will be 'correct', in the sense that each is natural and suits the occasion.

▷ **Correct grammar**

'Correct' grammar, then, is all part of the 'good linguistic manners' referred to. In fact, most of us have a good knowledge of the English grammatical structures used in speech, acquired through long practice from our first use of words in infancy. It is possible to make occasional mistakes, but for those with English as a first language it is not so very usual. The grammatical structures of speech and writing, though, are not the same. To help us when we speak we have *non-verbal* aids, such as gestures or changes of expression. We can also change our *tone of voice*, speak *more quickly or more slowly*. Finally, we have *someone to interact with*: if what we are trying to communicate is not being understood by the listener, we can rephrase, try another arrangement of words, and so on. None of these things is normal in written English. The grammar of written English tends to be more formal and disciplined. If you write just as you speak you will find that this can be inappropriate and therefore considered 'incorrect'.

Below are some of the **common mistakes** made by pupils in written English examinations.

Confusing collective nouns

This mistake is easily made because it seems logical that a number of people or things should take a plural verb. Sometimes, though, the people or things are a group, and then a singular verb is needed.

To take an obvious example: *class*. The class is made up of quite a few pupils, but also exists as a unit, such as 5B or 2A, therefore it is singular:

> The *class* finishes at four o'clock, and the pupils go home then.

The following groups of words behave in a similar way:

▶ **groups of animals**: e.g. herd, pack, flight, etc.
▶ **numbers, weights and measures**: e.g. dozen, ton, yard.

Confusing noun and verb forms

Sometimes the noun and verb have the same, or a similar form, and then they are easily confused.

Take *to affect*, *to effect* and *to have an effect*.

To affect means to influence; to effect means to bring something about and the resulting change is the effect:

> Television *affects* the lives of all of us; often the *effect* is educational, entertaining, informative and therefore good, but it can *affect* behaviour to make some people antisocial, leading some critics to talk of it *having a bad effect*.

Collect a glossary of these words, and learn not to muddle them.

Confusing subject and object

Everyone knows that the personal pronouns I, he, she, we and they are the subject of the sentence, and me, him, her, us and them are the object – but in usage they are sometimes confused:

> My sister and **me** agreed to meet *them* at the station, so my friend came with *us* and *we* three set off as arranged.

This should read

> My sister and **I** agreed to meet *them* at the station, so my friend came with *us* and *we* three set off as arranged.

A variant of this mistake occurs with the relative pronouns *who* and *whom*:

> The burglar *who* stole my stereo equipment recently disposed of it at a car boot sale, and the buyer to **who** he sold it had eventually to hand it over to the police.

This should read

> The burglar *who* stole my stereo equipment recently disposed of it at a car boot sale, and the buyer to **whom** he sold it had eventually to hand it over to the police.

Confusing tenses

This is particularly common in very long sentences where the writer forgets his or her original intention and keeps changing the tense of the verb:

> Every Sunday we would get up early, shower and have our breakfasts, do the washing up, get out the car and then we rush to the local market where we look at all the antique stalls. We bought all the paintings we liked and we used to bring them home and brushed them off with a soft brush.

Double negatives

Remember that two negatives make a positive. An instance of disregarding this error was made by a civil servant who produced a form for members of the public needing help with loft insulation. The first question was

> Is your loft not insulated?

Most claimants answered 'No', i.e. they denied that their loft was not insulated, meaning that it was. So they were disqualified from receiving the grant. The form was recalled and the troublesome question was changed to

> Is your loft insulated?   Yes/No

False agreement

Here a singular verb is often used with a plural subject – or the other way round – and pronouns get muddled too:

> It was a raw evening. No one seemed to be about. Everyone was huddled up inside their homes by the fireplace.

instead of

> It was a raw evening. No one seemed to be about. People were huddled up inside their homes by their fireplaces.

Here is another example:

> At an interview one should always be punctual and they should look presentable.

which should read as follows

> At an interview one should always be punctual and one should look presentable.

Incomplete sentences

When writing quickly it is easy to leave out an essential part of the sentence, which often includes the verb. There are some occasions when this would be perfectly appropriate: an example (known as **elliptical sentence**) would be in a dramatic scene, where tension was being built up:

> He paused and strained to listen. An intruder!

'Basic errors to avoid'   You could easily justify the exclusion of a verb in the second sentence. It speeds up the action and makes the situation seem more tense. But take the following example: the omission of the verb forces us to go back, re-read and still feel unsatisfied:

> I hate getting up on Monday mornings. It is not so bad in summer but in winter, when temperatures end up at extremely low levels and there is ice on the window panes and swirling mist outside. The alarm clock rings at about half-past seven and I sleepily stop it.

Indefinite articles

Is it 'an hotel' or 'a hotel', 'an hour' or 'a hour'? Many people are unsure. The rule to remember is that 'an' is used before a vowel and a silent 'h', 'a' is used before a consonant and a sounded 'h'.

She took *an hour* to complete *an easy* task.

but

She took *a train* to get to *a Heavy* Metal Concert.

Misrelated participles

In this case, a participle, intended to qualify one noun, is placed beside another noun in the same sentence. This leads to confusion:

I could hear music coming from a radio floating out from the shore.

would be better as

I could hear music floating out from the shore, coming from a radio.

Wrong idiom

The fault often involves a muddle over a misheard phrase, not usually seen written down:

You should *of* known about it.

instead of

You should *have* known about it.

Sometimes, the muddle can be quite amusing:

My mother came in and cleared out all my clutter in one *foul* swoop.

instead of

My mother came in and cleared out all my clutter in one *fell* swoop.

Misusing prepositions

English prepositions don't have easy rules, and it is difficult to know sometimes which one to use. Take special notice of the following, as they are frequently confused:

▶   Use '*compare to*' when you judge one thing against another:

The Cézanne exhibition drew huge crowds *compared to* the previous show at the gallery.

▶   Use '*compared with*' when you compare something lesser to something greater:

The pyramid I visited was small *compared with* the Great Pyramid at Giza.

▶   Use '*different from*', not '*different to*':

The packaging was *different from* the style I'd been used to.

Possessives and contractions

This mistake is a contender for being the most commonly made of all. We all know that adding the letter 's' shows possession in the noun:

This is the cat's food. The cats' chorus disturbed the neighbourhood.

However, the possessive pronouns hers, ours and yours do NOT have an apostrophe:

I have a record of *yours*. You lent it to me ages ago; in fact we have had it so long that we thought it was *ours*.

Note that the possessive pronoun *its* is spelled with the same letters as the contraction *it's*, but *only* the second has an apostrophe:

It's obvious that I will pass the driving test because *its* route is one I know so well.

▷ **Paragraphing**

There is no rule of thumb here: paragraphs should relate to the organization of what is being communicated. Each new idea or stage of development needs a new paragraph. One paragraph extending over dozens of pages has been known, as in James Joyce's novel *Ulysses*, but this was appropriate because it was used for the flow of a woman's thoughts, as she lay in bed.

Young writers sometimes have the uneasy feeling that new paragraphs should occur every ten lines or so. This may often be a convenient way of breaking up the text but it is not a rule. Paragraphing should be logical.

Compare the following examples from a pamphlet 'Succeeding at an Interview':

Young people are often criticised for being slow and unenthusiastic. The first impression is the most important impression you give to the interviewer. Check your appearance. Is your hair in place? Are your shoes as clean as you can get them? Are your finger-nails clean and tidy? The smallest detail is an important detail. Watch how you put your attitude across.

Interviews can take anything from ten minutes to half an hour. The longer interviews are designed to get to know the real you!

You must let them know you are well up in things in the real world. You know what's going on in current affairs.

Tell them about your interests and hobbies incorporating that you get on well with people, so getting to know the other staff shouldn't be too difficult. Let them know you will be committed to your job.

Having a mind of your own matters – do not copy what parents and friends have told you to say. Speak your mind, but do not be rude.

There are five paragraphs. The first paragraph concerns first impressions; the second, the likely length of an interview; the third advises you to show that you can keep up with current affairs. So far, the arrangement may seem rather 'bitty' – too many short paragraphs for comfortable reading – but it *is* logical. The last two paragraphs are less well arranged, though: ideas about hobbies, staff relationships and work commitments jostle for attention. The final paragraph 'tails off' with after-thoughts.

A better version might run as follows:

Paragraph 1
Young people are often criticised for being slow and unenthusiastic. The first impression is the most important impression you give to the interviewer. Check your appearance. Is your hair in place? Are your shoes as clean as you can get them? Are your finger-nails clean and tidy? The smallest detail is an important detail. Watch how you put your attitude across.

Paragraph 2
Interviews can take anything from ten minutes to half an hour. The longer interviews are designed to get to know the real you!

Paragraph 3
You must let them know you are well informed about the real world, and know what is going on in current affairs. Also, tell them about your interests and hobbies, indicating that you get on well with people, so getting to know the other staff shouldn't be too difficult.

Paragraph 4
Make it clear that you have a mind of your own, and are not just repeating what your parents and friends have told you to say. Speak out, but don't be too assertive. Show that you have thought about this particular job for yourself, and will be committed to it.

▷ **Punctuation**

Punctuation in the twentieth century has become less heavily used in writing than it used to be a hundred years ago, chiefly because of the growth of modern business technology, and the need for speed in communication. Even so, some punctuation is basic, and your ability to punctuate will be assessed in the GCSE examinations.

'Putting in the right stops.'

The use of **full stops** to mark the ends of sentences is essential but examination candidates have been known to write whole stories of four or five pages without any stops to pace their work, apart from an occasional comma. The reader of the story then has to work very hard to make sense of it:

> That evening I was working late, it must have been about seven-thirty when I finally walked out through the office doors, it was a dark wet dreary winter's night the sky was overcast and snow was already falling, the view before me was very grim and bare the car park was empty and so was the street beyond nobody was about there was not even anyone waiting at the bus stop they must all have gone home by now I thought.

Putting in normal punctuation marks makes a great difference here:

> That evening, I was working late. It must have been about seven-thirty when I finally walked out through the office doors. It was a dark, wet, dreary winter's night; the sky was overcast and snow was already falling. The view before me was very grim and bare: the car park was empty, and so was the street beyond. Nobody was about. There was not even anyone waiting at the bus stop. 'They must all have gone home by now,' I thought.

Let us consider the function of the **commas** in the extract. The first comma gives the reader a slight pause, to take in when the action happened:

> That evening, I was working late …

Next, commas are used to separate adjectives in a list

> a dark, wet, dreary winter's night …

and, a little further on, to separate balanced clauses

> the car park was empty, and so was the street.

Finally, we have a comma to separate thought from action:

> 'gone home now,' I thought.

Note that, although this comma ends a sentence of inner thought, the main sentence continues with 'I thought', so a comma and not a full stop is needed.

These are the main uses of the comma. The main function of the full stop, of course, is to mark the end of a sentence.

As well as commas and full stops you will notice three other punctuation marks in this extract: the semi-colon, the colon and inverted commas.

The **semi-colon** here offers a longer pause than a comma, and breaks up quite a long sentence:

> It was a dark, wet, dreary winter's night; the sky was overcast and snow was already falling.

The **colon** introduces a comment or further explanation. Here we are told of a view, then, after the comma, more information is given about the view:

> The view … was very grim and bare: the car park was empty …

The **inverted commas** here indicate thought rather than speech:

> 'They must all have gone home by now,' I thought.

Apart from failing to put these basic stops in punctuation, the error most commonly made is confusion over setting out direct speech, and what to do when writing dialogue in a play. The rule to remember about the layout of **direct speech** is that *each speaker's words begin on a new line.*

All the remarks of an individual speaker are enclosed in inverted commas, even if they continue after the reporting clause (he called):

> 'Hello!' he called. 'May I give you a lift?'

Notice that each remark is punctuated like a normal sentence.

Finally, a word of advice about the **dash**. Don't overuse it, but here its use is quite dramatic and effective:

> 'Hello!' – a cheerful voice brought me back to the present. 'May I give you a lift?'
> 'Oh, yes please. I was just wondering whether there would be any public transport on such a dreadful night.' I had never been more relieved to see my next door neighbour as when I climbed into the car.

The simplest procedure to adopt, if this were *dialogue in a play*, would be to *dispense with quotation marks altogether*:

NEIGHBOUR   Hello! May I give you a lift?

YOUNG WOMAN [*relieved*]   Oh, yes please. I was just wondering whether there would be any public transport on such a dreadful night.

[*She climbs quickly into the car.*]

Always try to be consistent in setting out dialogue.

If you have more problems with punctuation there are some helpful textbooks – see 'A Step Further'.

▷ A STEP FURTHER

Here are some titles of books which will help you to learn more about some of the matters discussed in this chapter:

Carey, G.V. (1971) *Mind the Stop*, Harmondsworth: Penguin.

Cripps, C. (1986) *Catchwords: Ideas for Teaching Spelling*, Cambridge: Cambridge University Press.

Cripps, E. (1997) *Longman English Tips Book*, Harlow: Addison Wesley Longman.

Crystal, D. (1988) *Rediscover Grammar*, Harlow: Longman.

SUMMARY

▷ You should know the different categories of writing: expressive, referential, literary and persuasive.

▷ You should be aware of the need to adopt appropriate styles of speech and of the five types of talk: intimate, casual, consultative, formal and frozen.

▷ You should have brushed up your grammar if you have any weaknesses in the following: confusing collective nouns, confusing noun and verb forms, confusing subject and object, confusing tenses, writing with double negatives, with false agreement, in incomplete sentences, or muddling indefinite articles, using misrelated participles, using the wrong idiom, misusing prepositions, and making errors with the possessive form of words.

▷ You should be thinking about improving your paragraphing.

▷ You should be thinking about improving your punctuation.

Spelling, handwriting and presentation

GETTING STARTED

The National Curriculum for English at Key Stage 4 sets out Attainment Targets for Spelling, Handwriting and Presentation.

These are treated for assessment purposes as integral parts of the writing tasks which you undertake for GCSE.

This chapter shows how you can prepare for and aim to reach these targets effectively.

TOPIC	STUDY	REVISION 1	REVISION 2
Spelling			
Handwriting			
Presentation			

All Examining Boards assess for spelling, handwriting and presentation as part of the Writing components. The assessment represents 10 per cent of the total mark, so you cannot afford to neglect any of them.

▷ **WHAT YOU NEED TO KNOW**

▷ **Spelling**   Candidates must demonstrate in their writing that they can spell common words. **(AT4–5: 1)**

The chief objective is that you can 'exercise control over spelling'. The degree of skill required depends upon the level you are taking, but achieving good marks here is not a matter of spelling *every* word correctly. You need to do the following:

1   Spell common words right **consistently**. Avoid writing the same word in several different ways, e.g. 'conceit', 'conciet', 'conceet'; avoid this especially if the word is printed for you on the question paper!

2   Use a vocabulary of some **complexity**. Obviously, a candidate who 'plays safe' and writes in a very basic style, using only simple words that he or she knows how to spell, does not deserve more credit than one who writes more ambitiously, trying out more difficult vocabulary and making some mistakes in doing so. Misspelling common words, e.g. 'freind' instead of 'friend', is more serious than making errors in words which you do not often see written down, e.g. 'sureptitous' for 'surreptitious'.

3   Aim for **accuracy** for most of your spelling, and notice how words look when written down, even though the same groups of letters often sound different when spoken, e.g. 'sign' and 'signature'.

4   Aim for **intelligibility**. If you regularly make errors that leave your reader struggling to understand, then your spelling is getting in the way of clear communication.

Useful practical approaches

English is not a regularly phonetic language and such rules as can be given for spelling are not practically very useful for people with major spelling difficulties. The process by which we learn to spell is a complex one. People have different ways of remembering spellings: some have strong visual memories and can 'see' the word vividly in the mind, or write it down to check whether it 'looks right'; others rely more on the sound of the word. One thing that has been definitely established is that attempts to learn lists of words by heart out

'Spelling hints.'

of context is unproductive for most spellers. It is better to concentrate on words you mis-spell in your own writing. A simple technique has been suggested for improving spelling and it can be adopted by anyone. You look up the word in a dictionary, then turn the book over and try to reproduce the word. If you cannot find it in the dictionary, ask someone who knows the word to write it down on a piece of paper for you. Look again if you are doubtful, until you are sure you have remembered it correctly, but never copy it. Once you have written a version you feel is right, make a final check in the dictionary, or on the piece of paper. This process can be remembered by the simple expression LOOK – COVER – WRITE – CHECK.

There are, however, some groups of words which it is helpful to know, and there are some rules which work well. Here are the most useful.

Words that are spelled alike but sound differently

Spelling with **au**

sound	(au)	(o)	(a)
	assault	because	aunt
	author	cauliflower	draught
	caught	restaurant	laugh
	pause		
	sauce		

Spelling with **ua**

sound	(w)	(ua)	(ai)	(ā)	(o)
	acquaint	annual	quake	guard	qualify
	dissuade	continual	quaver		quantity
	equal	gradual			squabble
	equation	punctual			squat
	equator				
	persuade				

Spelling with **ch**

sound	(ch)	(sh)	(k)
	bachelor	machine	ache
	detached	schedule	anchor
	ditch	niche	architect
	hitch		chemistry
	pitch		choir
	quench		chorus
	rich		scheme
	which		scholar
	wrench		school
			schooner

Spelling with **sion**

sound	(sh)	(zh)
	admission	confusion
	discussion	diffusion
	expression	occasion
	omission	persuasion
	permission	provision

spelling with **gh**

sound	(f)	(g)
	cough	aghast
	draught	ghastly
	enough	ghost
	laugh	ghostly
	rough	

Words that sound alike but are spelled differently

Spelling with **e** *and* **ee**

concede	exceed
precede	succeed
recede	proceed

Spelling with **ie** *and* **ei**

achieve	ceiling
believe	conceit
field	deceit
niece	perceive
piece	receipt
retrieve	receive

Spelling with **ce** *and* **se**

advice (noun)	advise (verb)
device	devise
practice	practise

Spelling with **or** *and* **our**

corridor	armour
doctor	behaviour
error	colour
exterior	favour
interior	honour
motor	humour
senior	labour
superior	rumour
visitor	vigour

Spelling with **ant** *and* **ent**

concordant	crescent
defendant	dependent (adj.)
dependant (noun)	independent
nonchalant	superintendent

Silent letters

Remember to include the following silent letters:

b	bomb	dumb
	climb	lamb
	comb	limb
	crumb	numb
	debt	thumb
	doubt	tomb
g	consign	gnat
	design	gnaw
	foreign	resign
	gnash	sign
k	knack	knit
	knee	knock
	kneel	knot
	knife	know
	knight	
p	pneumatic	psychiatry
	pneumonia	psychology
	psalm	receipt
w	wrap	wring

wreak wrist
wreck write
wrench wrong

Useful spelling rules

Spelling compound (joined) words
Rule: never add or take away a letter at the join.

dis + agree	disagree	
mis + spell	misspell	PREFIXES
un + necessary	unnecessary	
soft + ness	softness	
peace + able	peaceable	SUFFIXES
speech + less	speechless	
over + take	overtake	
under + achieve	underachieve	COMPOUNDS
with + hold	withhold	

*Spelling **ie** and **ei** words*
Rule: i before e, except after c when the sound is 'ee'.

achieve	but	perceive
retrieve	but	receive
piece	but	deceit

*Spelling words which end with **ce** and **se***
Rule: the noun takes a c; the verb takes an s

advice (noun)	but	advise (verb)
device	but	devise
practice	but	practise

*Spelling words which end with **y** + suffix*
Rule: when adding a suffix after y, change y to i

early	but	earlier
happy	but	happier
try	but	tried

*Spelling words which end with **e** + suffix*
Rule: when adding a suffix after e drop the e

acquire	but	acquired
declare	but	declaring
hope	but	hoping

Spelling words which end with a consonant + suffix
Rule: words that end with a single consonant double it before a suffix with a vowel, but not before a suffix with a consonant

forget	but	forgetting
refer	but	referred
travel	but	traveller
forget	but	forgets
refer	but	refers
travel	but	travels

*Spelling words with **ful** or **full** + suffix*
Rule: When -full is added, drop one l, unless the ending is -ly

helpful	but	helpfully
restful	but	restfully
truthful	but	truthfully

Spelling words ending with l + suffix

Rule: When -l words have a suffix added, drop one l

all	+	so	also
all	+	though	although
all	+	together	altogether
well	+	come	welcome

If you get to know these rules, and persist with the LOOK – COVER – WRITE – CHECK procedure, then your spelling will improve.

Student's answers

Here are two examples of writing by candidates in the examination: one at Foundation Tier and one at Higher Tier. Read them through carefully, try to spot the spelling errors, and then decide what mark out of 10 was awarded.

Candidate A

> *Even tho I'm her father it dosent atall seem like it. We never speak or discus anything. Her behavure has changed. She just sits there, dosent say anything, writing in that book and looks at us in suprise as if we have done something wrong. She's mody and dosent apreciate nothing. Sometimes she looks at me in disbelieve. I don't know why.*

Candidate B

> *My mate Mel. I had never met anyone like Mel and I probably won't meet anyone like her again, not for a long time, anyway. She is so laid back she's almost horisontal, but she still manages to succeed in everything she does and she'll probably carry on being successful for the rest of her life. Mel can laugh at everything and anything. She would sit through entire lessons making jokes, gosiping, basically keeping her friends in constant hysterics, and she still managed to achieve As and Bs in exams, although she seemed to pay no attention.*

Examiner's comments

The first candidate was awarded 3 and the second 8 out of 10. Both have written lively pieces, which communicate quite well. You hardly notice the two errors (horizontal, gossiping) in B, but you tend to trip over the errors (though, doesn't, at all, discuss, behaviour, surprise, moody, appreciate, disbelief) frequently in A, even though you can still understand the content.

The examining board's criteria for these mark bands were:

3   A range of simple words will be used and often spelled correctly, but there will be a fair number of errors overall.

8   Candidates will spell correctly almost all words used, including some borrowed from other languages. Their errors will be fairly infrequent.

I hope that you agree that marking here is positive, and in the spirit of rewarding candidates who communicate stylishly, with a fair degree of accuracy of spelling, but not penalizing those who write more simply and have more problems with spelling too harshly.

▷ Handwriting

Candidates must demonstrate in their writing that they can write legibly and present finished work clearly and attractively.

(AT 4–5: 2)

No one will assess you on the style of your handwriting, so do not despair if you do not write in elegant italics, or in a perfectly formed style. It is **legibility** that matters. True, you probably associate illegible handwriting with badly formed letters, but actually some very neat, small, closely spaced handwriting is difficult to read, too (see Figure 5.1).

Take comfort in the thought that examiners read hundreds of scripts, and can decipher almost anything. In short, most candidates need not worry too much about handwriting in GCSE; all, though, may learn something from the following advice.

Figure 5.1

> I'm not sure if I should get hysterical, running around, trying to find them, or if I should just assume that I'll find them eventually and not to worry. They probably didn't want to be nothing anyway. I hardly spoke. What was that? Sounded like an owl. They always seem so powerful for some reason. I don't know why. I have always wanted to stare down on an owl. Just for the sensation. I don't know if I'd be able to do it. I hate catching people's gazes. Look down, down. I don't understand why everyone feels they need to look into your eyes when they pass you on the street. Of course if I'm noticing this, I must do it too. It feels like they are looking deep into me (and god knows I cannot deal with that.... did I use 'god''s name in vain again?), even if only for a brief fleeting moment. Can they tell I'm screaming inside? I would love to scream on the outside. Breaking glass. Burning fields. God, I want to scream. Julian Schnabel must scream a lot. His artwork is so angry. Resist, resist. The squalid pavement often has an artistic quality. The textures, the shapes, the colours. Does anyone else ever notice this? Sometimes I can stare into the fibers of clothing for hours. Carpets are also quite nice. When I stare too long, I swear I can see cells. Swirling and vibrating.

Useful practical approaches

▷ If your teachers, parents and others regularly tell you that they cannot read what you have written, then you need to do something about it.

▷ Try practising for half an hour every day, using lined paper and writing double-spaced, forming your letters more carefully.

▷ Try larger writing and leave more space between your words.

▷ Avoid large loops (*ascenders* and *descenders*) in your writing.

▷ Do not write over words. If you make a mistake, cross the word through and write it again clearly as the next word.

▷ Do not write over erased (whitened) patches.

▷ Do not write entirely in capitals.

▷ Use a fountain pen or real-ink pen rather than a ball-point pen.

Obviously, many people now rely on printouts from word-processors for a good final effect, but that will not help you in the terminal examination, nor for at least one piece of coursework. If you take notice of some of the tips above, you should do well enough. Examiners know that everyone's handwriting deteriorates when writing 'against the clock' and especially over the last few pages of a script.

Student's answers

Just to encourage you, here are two handwritten pieces of coursework. Figure 5.2 is written in capitals and arranged in columns, to simulate a newspaper article. Figure 5.3 is a neatly handwritten profile, representing an article in a weekly magazine.

Figure 5.2

> GEORGE CAROL, THE TOP EXPERT IN NASA STATED THIS MORNING THAT "THERE SHOULD BE NO DOUBT IN THE CORRECTNESS OR VERITY OF THIS MESSAGE WE HAVE RECEIVED – IT IS CLEAR AND REAL! THE UFOS USED ESPERANTO AS THEIR WAY OF COMMUNICATING WITH US. THEY SEEM TO BE FRIENDLY CREATURES BUT MOST PROBABLY ON A HIGHER CIVILISATION LEVEL THAN THE HUMANS. THAT IS ALL WE CAN SAY NOW."
>
> THE COMPUTERIZED PHOTO-GRAPH SENT WITH THE MESSAGE "...SHOWS CREATURES VERY SIMILAR TO HUMANS." MAYBE NOW THE OLD SUSPICIONS OF UFOS INFILTRATING THE EARTH BY BEING "DROPPED HERE" WILL BE PROVEN RIGHT.
>
> HOWEVER, THIS IS NOT THE FIRST THAT THE EARTH HAS BEEN CONTACTED. IN FACT THE ARCHIVES HAD PROVED IT THAT THE USA HIGHEST POLITICAL AND STATE CIRCLES WERE FULLY AWARE OF THE EXISTENCE OF E.T. LIVING CREATURES. PRESIDENT ROOSEVELT, REAGAN AND BUSH HAVE ALL SIGNED AGREEMENTS WITH NASA THAT "...SUCH DISCOVERIES AND CONTACTS SHOULD BE KEPT SECRET IN ORDER NOT TO ALARM THE WORLD."

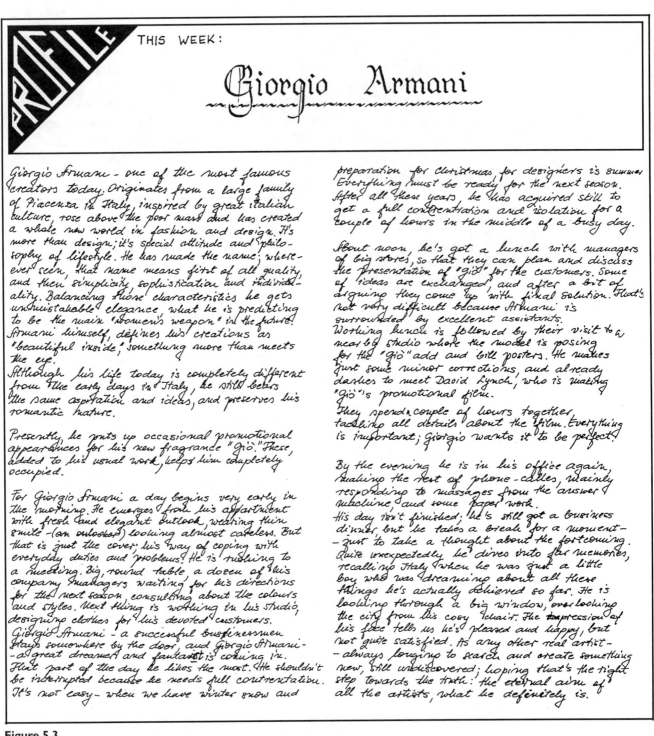

Figure 5.3

▷ **Presentation**   Candidates should be given opportunities to produce writing which is varied in form, purpose, audience. They should engage with the writing of diaries, letters, reports, accounts, reviews, newspapers and promotional materials … they should learn to plan their writing and its communicative success, consider its features in relation to its presentation impact – including layout.

(AT 4–5: 2)

Useful practical approaches

Titles and headings
It is usual to give pieces of your own composition **titles,** which are underlined, or may be capitalized.

Headings occur in two contexts.

Headings are used **to subdivide longer stretches of work**. In an extended piece of course-work, you may use subheadings (short side-headings) such as have been used in this chapter, to divide up the text and make it easier for the reader to tackle. For example, dates were needed as subheadings in this question from a recent paper:

Imagine you are Rachel's mother. Write a series of 3 entries from your diary.   **(London)**

Headings are also used **to present an article for the media**, i.e. newspaper or journal. Sometimes the stimulus material given to you is in such a form, and often you will be asked to produce something in a similar style in your answer. Here are some questions of this type from recent papers.

Imagine you spent a day … on the banks of the Thames. Write your diary entry for that day. Describe what you did, anything you found and how you felt.   **(SEG)**

Many people feel that too much rubbish is left lying around, both in our towns and countryside. Write an article for a newspaper suggesting ways in which the problems of rubbish could be dealt with.   **(London)**

'A Weekend of Hell'. Imagine that you do not get on with your neighbours, and you keep a diary describing your problems with them. Write your diary entries for a Saturday and Sunday.   **(MEG)**

Your school has just staged a very successful pantomime. As one of those involved, you have been asked to write an article for the school magazine about the production. It should be lively, interesting and properly organised.   **(NICCEA)**

Every place has its own atmosphere. Write an article with this title, for a newspaper or magazine.   **(SEG)**

Write an article for a newspaper or magazine on men who try to be helpful around the house.   **(SEG)**

Writing an article: presentation aspects

Headlines   Articles in newspapers often have big, attention-catching features. **Banner headlines** are the width of the article. Here is a good example from a student's work:

T   H   E   C   U   L   L   I   N   G   F   I   E   L   D   S

Sub-headlines divide an article into information bites (see Figure 5.4).

Figure 5.4

their true descent... bring forth the parties of suspicion.'
At this, a priest, Friar Lawrence, stepped out voluntarily and said that he was the prime suspect!
'I am the greatest, able to do least, yet most suspected, as the time and place do make against me, of this direful murder.' Although everyone was surprised, the Prince kept everything under control and told this priest to continue: 'Then say at once what thou dost know in this.' This priest was openly distressed but told quite clearly the

against the wishes of Lord Montague and Lord Capulet, he carried this out because he knew how much Romeo and Juliet loved each other.

Exiled
However, fortune seemed to be working against the couple for that very afternoon (Monday), Romeo was exiled from Verona because he had slain Tybalt Capulet, Juliet's cousin. Romeo's friends had been surprised when he had refused to respond to Tybalt's provocative remarks and instead said that he loved Tybalt,

Figure 5.5

> There are many alternatives to animal experimentation, either for cosmetics or drugs. Some of these methods such as population and clinical studies, have recently been used successfully for years and some methods have been developed recently with advances in scanning and computer technology.

Bridging capitals   These draw the eye of the reader into the text of the article (see Figure 5.5).

Capitalization   As well as the main headline, capitals can be used for impact elsewhere.

Bold print   The opening is usually bold.

Varied type size and font   Large type is often used to start an article, then type decreases in size as the article continues. Newspapers use various types of fonts in one article for greater impact and to highlight the key ideas in the piece.

Writing a diary entry

Here you need a subheading with the day's date, and short paragraphs for the entry.

> Tuesday, 20 May, 1997
>
> I really can't think what has come over Rachel these days. She won't answer when I speak to her, stares at me as if she doesn't know me, and then goes out slamming the door. Her father and I have tried to give her the best of everything, and this is how she repays us.

> Wednesday, 21 May, 1997
>
> I am going up to school to discuss Rachel's behaviour with her Form Tutor tomorrow. Maybe he will be able to throw light on what is upsetting her.

Writing a leaflet or poster

Here bold, capital lettering for the key information and a clear layout are essential, as well as carefully written, well-spaced paragraphs.

> ▷ A **poster** may just have a list of key points.
> ▷ An **information leaflet** will have carefully staged points, in the correct order, the most important coming first, and it will probably end with an address or telephone number which the public may contact for further advice.

Here are some questions of this type from recent papers:

> Write an advice sheet for parents of fourteen year olds to reduce truancy.   **(NEAB)**

> Write a leaflet for Year 7 pupils (11 year olds) giving advice on how to cope with bullying.   **(London)**

> Write a poster with a list of five things which people might avoid doing to help give endangered animals a better chance of surviving.   **(London)**

> Write a leaflet supporting a wild-life conservation scheme for endangered animals.   **(WJEC)**

Writing a letter

The Boards often ask candidates, as part of the Writing paper, to produce a letter. This may be of varying degrees of formality, and each will need a different form of presentation. Here are some questions of this kind from recent papers.

> Write a letter from Pamela to [her friend] Kate, apologising for what happened at the party.   **(MEG)**

> Write Sarah's first letter to her mother, written a week or so after she has left home. The main purpose of the letter is to try to heal the wounds opened by their last conversation.   **(MEG)**

You are a secondary school teacher taking a trip to one of the places described in the booklet [information given on the paper]. Write a letter to the parents of your pupils, giving them information about the day. **(NEAB)**

Imagine you are a parent of a pupil at the school. You have become very concerned after a recent Parents' Evening, and after listening to what your child has told you. Write a letter to the head teacher, making your feelings known, outlining the problems and suggesting how the school could be improved. **(NICCEA)**

Write a letter to a close friend who wishes to visit you. Let your friend know what he/she can expect to find and what your feelings are about where you live. **(SEG)**

Write a letter to a friend telling him/her about life on the farm with your aunts. **(London)**

▶ **Personal letter**
You need the following features:

	20 Riverine Road, Broadstairs	(private address)
	Tuesday, May 20th	(optional date)
(casual opening) Dear Kate,		
. . . .		
. . . .		
. . . .		
	Best wishes,	(informal conclusion)

▶ **Consultative letter**
You need the following features:

	20 Riverine Road, Broadstairs CT9 2TE	(full address)
	20 May, 1997	(full date)
(semi-formal opening) Dear Mr Travis,		
. . . .		
. . . .		
. . . .		
	Yours sincerely,	(semi-formal conclusion)

▶ **Formal letter**
You need the following features:

	20 Riverine Road, Broadstairs CT9 2TE	(full address)
	20 May, 1997	(full date)
(very formal opening) Dear Sir or Madam,		
. . . .		
. . . .		
. . . .		
	Yours faithfully,	(formal conclusion)
Head Teacher, Bromsgrove Secondary School, Margate, Kent, CM8 3TE		(full address of recipient)

Student's answer

Here is a **diary entry**, written in response to the London question listed above.

Monday, 19th, '97 (June).

Today Rachel is unwell so she did not go to school. I asked Rachel if she would be OK to stay at home while I go out to do the shopping. She says 'Yes, sure.' So I came back and found the house in a mess – food, drink, everywhere. Rachel decided to have a picnic in the house. I thought she was grown up from the Little MisBehaving she used to be.

Friday, 23rd '97 (June).

After a whole week she said something to me. I did feel a bit guilty for telling her off for messing up the house because she felt ill. She need not have sulked for so long, though.

Wednesday, 28th '97 (June).

Oh, she really gets to me sometimes, and one day I will tell her who she is and who I am to her face. Rachel's father doesn't do or say anything when she is behaving like that to me. He will say 'She is my love … ly daughter. Let her be.' Don't ask me how many times I've heard that. I can't face them any more and I only wish that he would know that but it looks as if he doesn't. He comes in from work and acts as if we're a happy family, but he knows as well as I know that it isn't working out for us and Rachel!

Examiner's comments

This candidate has written the dates as subheadings, indicating the diary form, though they are rather odd in sequence. In terms of presentation this does give the immediate impression of a personal diary and so is appropriate for this question.

Student's answer

Here is a **personal letter**, written in answer to the London question above.

Glebe Farm,
South Lyme Fen,
Lincolnshire
12 June, 1997

Dear Julie,

Hi, how are you? I hope things are all well with you and that you're enjoying your holiday. At the moment I'm at my aunts' farm, as you know. The weather has been quite good, and their company is as refreshing as ever.

I never realized that older people could be such fun or as silly as them, you know. The other day, when Aunt Elspeth was sleeping, Auntie Grace persuaded me to play a trick. We crept into the room and tied Aunt Elspeth's feet together with a red ribbon in a big bow. She wasn't half mad when she woke up and tried to move!

But funnier than that is when we milk the cows. I can do it really well now, except when I'm laughing. Both aunts sing so loudly and out of tune, both saying she doesn't know where the other gets the idea she can sing! I'm sure that all the surrounding farms can hear them. I'm so glad they can't see them, though. Auntie Grace runs around slapping the cows on their rumps, and then she chases them into the fields!

Uncle Craig is very busy 'working'. I'm not allowed to disturb him, especially when he's typing. I only see him at meal times in the morning and evening, although he did make an exception and joined us for afternoon tea when the neighbours visited. Aunt Elspeth and Auntie Grace made me wash and put on neat clothes, while they ran around like headless chickens baking cakes and pastries and things. The whole house was cleaned especially, and we used the best crockery, too, all because the daughter had married a rich city lawyer, and a greedy one, too. By the time he'd finished eating most of the food, he had crumbs and icing round his face and stuck in his moustache.

Well, I've got to finish now, it's time to go to bed and I must get up early in the morning to help milk those cows. Write to me soon, and tell me how your holiday is.

Take care,

Love from,
Jessica.

Examiner's comments

This is an excellent personal letter. It has an appropriate address, greeting and conclusion. The content is interesting, amusing and does relate quite closely to the set material. Style is casual, much as you might use when writing to a good friend, but does not become too intimate or close to slang. The candidate has remembered that this is a letter for the examiner as well as for a personal friend. She has managed to combine the two audiences well – a tricky task.

Student's answer

Here is an article, written for inclusion in a coursework folder (Figure 5.6).

Figure 5.6

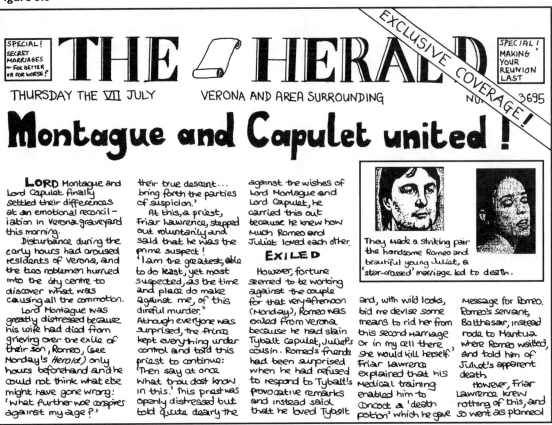

Examiner's comments

This has excellent presentation: capitals for the headline, bold print, good spacing, short, readable paragraphs and an illustration – it can be read in a minute or two. This is very effective layout and good communication.

 A STEP FURTHER

Though tedious, regular spelling practice can be helpful. Try working half an hour every day at groups of words you know you get wrong. As well as the advice in this chapter, *Longman English Tips book* and other recommended spelling books there is also computer software such as *Spell-It 3* (ABLAC), *Spelltime* (EDISK), *Language Plus* (AVP) and many others.

Handwriting *does* improve if you are concentrating on it, and write carefully on a regular basis. One way of doing this is to keep a diary and write a short entry every day in your best handwriting. You will find that there will be some 'carry over' from this to the writing you do most of the time, in more hurried conditions.

Get into the habit of looking for good practice in respect of presentation. You will find many striking examples in newspapers and magazines.

SUMMARY

▷   You should know the ATs for Spelling, Handwriting and Presentation.

▷   You should understand the importance of being able to spell words of some complexity consistently, accurately and intelligibly.

▷   Practical approaches to spelling, including words which sound differently but are spelled alike, which sound the same but are spelled differently, words with silent letters and some useful spelling rules were outlined.

▷   You should consider ways of making handwriting legible, clear and attractive.

▷   You should know ways of setting out your work: using headlines and titles, bridging capitals, capitals, bold print, various types and sizes of font.

▷   Layouts for articles, diaries, leaflets and letters were explained.

Individual oral

▷ **GETTING STARTED**

Assessment in Oral Communication is compulsory for all GCSE candidates. According to the **National Criteria** (5.2) 'the interactive nature of listening and speaking cannot be demonstrated solely by reading aloud or delivering a talk'. However, these do have 'a useful role to play in the assessment of the spoken language' by providing 'contexts for the interview and/or discussion in which both listening and speaking are to be assessed'.

LONDON	MEG	NEAB	NICCEA	SEG	WJEC	IGCSE	TOPIC	STUDY	REVISION 1	REVISION 2
	✓					✓	Talk about personal experience			
	✓	✓	✓	✓			Read and/or discuss a text			
✓		✓				✓	Give an individual talk			
✓	✓	✓	✓	✓	✓	✓	Describe or inform about something seen or read			
✓			✓				Informal roleplay			
✓				✓	✓	✓	Hypothesize and speculate			
				✓		✓	Talk about language use			

There is considerable diversity in the approaches of the different Examining Boards.

London

This syllabus assesses competence in *three* areas, chosen from the following list:

▷ individual talks
▷ roleplay
▷ problem-solving
▷ group discussion.

These areas of competence may be shown in coursework discussions.

MEG

For **MEG** a range of activities is expected from the following list:

▷ giving a personal account of something
▷ reading aloud
▷ play-reading
▷ pupil in conversation with teacher or tutor
▷ giving instructions to others for a task
▷ giving a description or information about something heard or seen
▷ giving a talk to a wider audience.

NEAB

For **NEAB** assessment should cover

▷ discussion in pairs
▷ small group discussion

> whole class discussion
> talk about texts read
> talk to a variety of audiences.

NICCEA

For **NICCEA** assessment will be by observation of the candidate's ability both to listen and to speak in a variety of situations, ranging from the formal (e.g. a prepared talk) to the informal (e.g. a group discussion of a book). A range of tasks is offered for the examination in the form of a list, from which candidates choose *four* tasks:

> reading a text aloud
> formal interview
> formal presentation of information: description, relaying information, persuasive argument
> formal roleplay (e.g. as news-reader)
> small group discussion of a particular subject
> problem-solving in small groups
> informal roleplay (e.g. as a narrator)
> hypothesizing and speculation.

SEG

For **SEG** assessment will be through coursework, but each candidate must attempt work in the following categories:

> a response to reading a work of fiction
> an individually planned activity of the pupil's choice
> a collaborative group activity
> a task involving interaction of pairs
> a task focused on discussion about language use.

WJEC

WJEC requires

> best achievements in paired talk
> small group talk
> communicating to a wider audience
> collaborating on a task
> developing understanding through talk.

There is a very wide range of oral work that can be offered as part of the examination. This chapter will be concerned, then, chiefly with **individual oral work** and the next will concentrate on **group oral** situations.

▶ WHAT YOU NEED TO KNOW

Candidates must demonstrate in conversation, discussion ... that they can

> recount personal experience, views and feelings
> share and experience views and ideas
> use language to inform and explain
> plan and take part in group presentations
> show an awareness of how spoken communication varies according to situation, purpose and audience.

(AT1: 1–5)

Whatever form of *individual oral work* you are engaged in, there are certain basic principles to bear in mind.

Audible and intelligible speech

First, you must be **audible** and **intelligible**: no talk is successful unless it can be clearly heard and understood. Speak fairly loudly and a little more slowly than usual. Suppose, for example, you are asked to read aloud something which is given to you. You will have time to read through the material quickly, if it is unseen. It may however be something you have prepared. In the first case, try to read as if reading to someone you know well, using your voice to make the meaning as clear as you can. In the second case, bear the following advice in mind. Choose a passage

- of an appropriate length (usually between 250 and 500 words but check with the syllabus to make sure)
- that you think will interest the listener
- that has a shape and is complete in itself, such as an episode from a story or an article from a newspaper.

'Can they hear you at the back?'

If you feel you can handle it, you could consider choosing something with emotional impact – amusing or tense. Avoid a lengthy introductory stretch of narrative; you can always give a brief explanation yourself to start with. Whatever you choose, discuss it with your teacher or tutor.

When you have found something you are comfortable with, you can practise reading it to a friend. Don't do this too often, or your reading will have an over-rehearsed, unnatural effect.

Response to others

The **second** principle to remember is that, whether you are talking with your teacher, an external assessor or among a group of people, a vital part of communication is that you **respond to the other people present**. Of course, it is easiest to do this well if you are relaxed and can behave naturally. This may not always be possible, especially if you are talking about something fairly formally, e.g. giving a talk you have prepared beforehand to someone you aren't very familiar with. Whatever the situation, it is essential to appear friendly but polite. Show that you are engaging in the activity with a sense of its importance but not so stiffly that the talk becomes what is sometimes described as 'frozen'. Given the opportunity, begin by introducing yourself and what it is you are going to talk about. Even if someone else is involved, in an individual oral it is *your* talk that is being assessed and you will need to show that you can sustain a conversation or a lecturette and not 'dry up'. If you do, don't worry. The assessor or others present will want to put you at your ease and start you off again.

Avoid using simple 'yes' or 'no' answers; try to interest the listener and genuinely want to tell or teach him or her something. You are responsible for how the talk goes. If you think in this way, you will be careful to interest and involve the listener.

If you are giving a *prepared* talk, try to have plenty of material ready and know it well. You can then answer any questions that are put to you. As long as you keep to the main area of discussion there is no reason why you should not talk about your own experience of whatever is the topic of conversation. You will talk with more warmth and fluency if you are personally involved.

Well-organized talk

A **third** important matter (and another aspect of intelligibility) is that a prepared talk should be **well organized**. This is particularly important if you are, say, giving a lecturette or relating information about something seen or heard.

In the case of a lecturette, you can choose to talk about something you feel you know quite well, or can research effectively, and will enjoy. You will then be more likely to hold the attention of the listener. Also choose a topic which has some breadth or depth and then decide how you can plan it clearly. A good plan involves thinking of five or six main points that you would like to make. This will probably be sufficient for the average length of a formal talk – about five minutes. Do not write out the whole talk as a continuous piece and then read it aloud. This will result in a much duller performance.

'Planning matters.'

Remember that you need to interact with your listener and to do this you must address him or her directly. It is a good idea to have a set of cards and make brief notes such as a heading and one or two details, e.g. date, statistics – small things that you may not feel confident you will remember. Keep these very brief – just enough to see at a glance. You may want to illustrate the points you make with more visual or aural aids. You may want to show a map or diagram – if so, make them big and clear.

If you are going to do some sort of practical demonstration, practise beforehand until you are confident that you don't make mistakes that will worry you and your audience. When you have finished your talk, don't just relax. Keep your attention on any questions asked and try to answer as fully as you can. Remember, you will almost certainly know a good deal more about the topic than the listener!

Again you could consider choosing something with emotional impact – amusing or tense for example – provided you feel you can cope with the topic and situation. Avoid a lengthy introductory stretch of narrative (you can always give a brief explanation yourself to start with). Whatever you choose, discuss it with your teacher or tutor. The right choice of passage is, of course, very important, if your oral work is to be a success.

USEFUL PRACTICAL APPROACHES

The following speech situations are some of those which will be used for assessing individual oral work:

1   Reading aloud
2   Holding a conversation
3   Giving a talk
4   Giving instructions.

Reading aloud

As you read new stories or non-fiction material throughout the year you could keep a note of any passages which you like and think would be suitable for **reading aloud**. Then you will have plenty to choose from.

Consider the following passage from George Orwell's *Animal Farm*:

> June came and the hay was almost ready for cutting. On Midsummer's Eve, which was a Saturday, Mr Jones went into Willingdon and got so drunk at the Red Lion that he did not come back till mid-day on Sunday. The men milked the cows in the early morning and then had gone out rabbiting, without bothering to feed the animals. When Mr Jones got back he immediately went to sleep on the drawing-room sofa, with the *News of the World* over his face, so that when evening came, the animals were still unfed. At last they could stand it no longer. One of the cows broke in the door of the store-shed with her horns and all the animals began to help themselves from the bins. It was just then that Mr Jones woke up. The next moment he and his four men were in the store-shed with whips in their hands, lashing out in all directions. This was more than the hungry animals could bear. With one accord, though nothing of the kind had been planned beforehand, they flung themselves upon their tormentors. Jones and his men suddenly found themselves being butted and kicked from all sides. The situation was quite out of their control; they had never seen animals behave like this before, and this sudden uprising of creatures whom they were used to thrashing and maltreating just as they chose, frightened them almost out of their wits. After only a moment or two they gave up trying to defend themselves and took to their heels. A minute later all five of them were in full flight down the cart-track that led to the main road, with the animals pursuing them in triumph.
>
> Mrs Jones looked out of the bedroom window, saw what was happening, hurriedly flung a few possessions into a carpet bag, and slipped out of the farm by another way. ... Meanwhile the animals had chased Jones and his men out on to the road and slammed the five-barred gate behind them. And so, almost before they knew what was happening, the Rebellion had been successfully carried through: Jones was expelled, and the Manor Farm was theirs.
>
> For the first few minutes the animals could hardly believe in their good fortune. Their first act was to gallop in a body right round the boundaries of the farm, as though to make quite sure that no human being was hiding anywhere upon it; then they raced back to wipe out the last traces of Jones's hated reign. ...
>
> Then they filed back to the farm buildings and halted in silence outside the door of the farmhouse. That was theirs too, but they were frightened to go inside. After a moment,

however, Snowball and Napoleon butted the door open with their shoulders and the animals entered in single file, walking with the utmost care for fear of disturbing anything. They tiptoed from room to room, afraid to speak above a whisper and gazing with a kind of awe at the unbelievable luxury, at the beds with their feather mattresses, the looking-glasses, the horsehair sofa, the Brussels carpet, the lithograph of Queen Victoria over the drawing-room mantelpiece. They were just coming down the stairs when Mollie was discovered to be missing. Going back, the others found that she had remained behind in the best bedroom. She had taken a piece of blue ribbon from Mrs Jones' dressing table, and was holding it against her shoulder and admiring herself in the glass in a very foolish manner. The others reproached her sharply, and they went outside. Some hams hanging in the kitchen were taken out for burial, and the barrel of beer in the scullery was stove in with a kick from Boxer's hoof, otherwise nothing in the house was touched. A unanimous resolution was passed on the spot that the farmhouse would be preserved as a museum. All were agreed that no animal must ever live there.

(George Orwell, *Animal Farm*)

The passage is of a suitable length, interesting, with a definite beginning and end and concerns a rather dramatic episode in the book: the capture of Manor Farm. There are points where the *pace* of the narrative changes and as a reader you would want to go *faster* and *louder* – for example, 'The next moment he and his four men were in the store-shed with whips in their hands, lashing out in all directions' – and *stress the verbs* in a crescendo which shows the furious reaction of the animals – 'flung themselves', 'butted', 'kicked' – working to a climax with the flight of the men and the animals 'pursuing them in triumph'.

Another major change in mood – and as a reader you would want to try to bring this out by reading more slowly and quietly – occurs with the entry by the animals into the farm buildings: 'Then they filed back to the farm buildings and halted in silence outside the door of the farmhouse. That was theirs too, but they were frightened to go inside.' Another place where a slower more emphatic reading would help to stress meaning might be the last two sentences of the extract.

Certainly, it would help to have read the whole novel to know that this is not just an animal story, but a fable, with something ironic to say about human beings and society. To know this would help you to read the extract with the right tone, perhaps showing the indignation of the animals. You could also answer questions. Suppose you were asked why you thought George Orwell had written this story, or how you could explain the animals' action in burying the hams? This extract would be a good passage for reading aloud.

▷ Holding a conversation

This is probably the easiest part of the oral work to prepare, because it is what we do all the time. You might list topics that you would like to talk about to the assessor, who will be your teacher or an examiner. The following list of suggestions offers a starting point – you should certainly be able to talk about most of them:

- ▶ Myself and my interests
- ▶ My family and home
- ▶ My school or work
- ▶ What I do in my leisure time
- ▶ Books I have read
- ▶ Films and TV I enjoy
- ▶ Hobbies
- ▶ Travel
- ▶ Sport
- ▶ Music
- ▶ Fashion
- ▶ Food I enjoy
- ▶ People I know
- ▶ My local town or village
- ▶ Items in the news.

▷ **Giving a talk**   There are as many subjects for a prepared talk as there are readers of this book, of course. Turn back to the list in the previous section and write down topics you would like to research. Next, break down your topics into five or six short headings:

FASHION
Making my own clothes (*Title*)
Where I get ideas/Choosing patterns and materials/Stages in making/Reactions when garment is first worn (*Sections of talk*)

ANIMALS
Keeping tropical fish
How to get going/Choosing fish/Keeping the tank healthy/ Feeding/Breeding

SPORT
Long-distance running
How I became interested/Training/Sports events/Where I go from here

MUSIC
Playing the drums
How I became interested/Basic skills/Practice/Playing with others

Of course, this is only one way of arriving at a title and plan for your talk, and there are many others. Whatever approach you use, it is very important that the talk is well planned. Note that you will be allowed only a limited time to speak – say five minutes, usually.

▷ **Giving instructions**

'Passing on information to a friend.'

It is surprising how hard it can be to explain something that you think you know how to do, to someone else who has had no experience of it, in a way that makes it really clear to them. If you have not attempted this before, try an experiment. Explain to a friend how to operate a simple appliance, e.g. to make a cup of coffee with an electric percolator. You will find out how easy it is to overlook basic steps and get the stages of the process in the wrong order.

Alternatively, you could give instructions for doing a job you are familiar with, e.g. issuing books in the school or college library. However well you know the task, it is best to check the instructions very carefully.

▷ **QUESTIONS FOR ORAL WORK**

The following are examples of the kinds of task that you might embark upon for individual oral work.

▷ **Question 1**   *Relaying information from a tape*

You listen to an educational or informative tape, and while doing so make notes on a note-sheet given you. Then you tell some other pupils what you have learned about the subject of the tape. What you say is recorded.

Here is a transcript of a topic about spiders:

There are over 23,000 different kinds of spiders and over 600 of these are found in Britain.

Spiders are not insects. All insects have six legs but spiders have eight. Also, insects have three parts to their bodies: the head, thorax and abdomen. Spiders have only two parts. The head and the thorax are merged into one part to which the legs are attached. Another difference between insects and spiders is that the young of spiders emerge from their eggs as slightly smaller versions of their parents. As they grow, they split their skins and shed them. Insects on the other hand pass through a number of different stages of development before attaining their adult form. One final difference between insects and spiders is that a spider has no wings or feelers and there is always a pair of poison claws in front of the mouth.

Most spiders rely mainly on their senses of smell and touch. Spiders are very short-sighted, they detect their prey by smell and not sight. They have smelling bristles on various parts of their bodies, but the sense that counts for most is that of touch. A spider does not usually, for example, see a fly that gets caught in its web. It feels the vibration caused by its struggles.

With most kinds of spiders the female is able to spin silk. Spiders' silk consists of numerous strands which are woven together like rope or cable. Spiders have glands capable of making several different kinds of silk. The pattern of the silk strands is changed to suit the purpose for which the spider is spinning the silk. For example, there's one kind of silk for trapping insects, another for use as a cable along which the spider can run to catch its prey, another for use as parachutes or balloons on which the spider may go sailing through the air, and so on.

Nearly all spiders make webs. The most obvious use that the spider makes of the web is to catch prey. There are many different kinds of webs. Some upright and others horizontal, some like tents and others like domes. The orb web of the garden spider is one which is particularly attractive.

In the next part of the exercise you will hear of how the garden spider builds her web.

These are notes made by a fifteen-year-old student; the subheadings relate to the main points on the tape.

---

1   *The numbers of spiders*
          over 23,000
          600 in GB
2   *How spiders differ from insects*
          insects 6 legs – 3 parts for body
          s. 8 legs – 2 parts (merged)
          no metamorphosis – split skins
          insects have stages of development
          no wings, feelers but poison claws
3   *The spider's sense of smell and touch*
          s. sighted
          relies on touch
          smelling bristles on parts of body
          feels insect on web
4   *The spider's silk*
          female spins
          like rope
          glands make different kinds
          trapping, a cable
          parachutes
5   *The spider's web*
          to catch prey
          vertical, domes, tents
          orb-web of garden spider

This is a transcript of the student's report:

ASSESSOR   *OK.*

PUPIL   *There're over twenty-three thousand types of spiders in the world, and six hundred of those are found in … Great Britain. Spiders aren't insects there're several differences, insects have six legs, whereas spiders have eight legs and spiders only have two parts of the body. The first two par … the first part is merged, to the second part. Insects have three parts of the body the head the thorax and the abdomen. And spiders go … don't go through a metamorphosis. They em … are born a small image of their parents and they … as they grow they split their skins, whereas insects go through definite stages of development. In … insects have wings, but spiders don't and spiders do … do not have feelers either but in front of their mouth they have poisoned fangs. Spiders are very short sighted and they rely a great deal on their sense of touch. For instance, if there's an insect who's on a spider's web, the spider would not see it but would feel it, feel the s … the insect moving on the web. They have, also smelling bristles on various parts of their body. Only the females spin silk and, silk is made up of different materials spun together like rope. And the spiders' glands make various different kinds of s … silk for trapping, t … to make parachutes so they travel, or, or cable for instance so they can slide down on their webs. A spider's web is primarily used to catch prey, but it is many different*

(continued)

> shapes vertical, domes, tent, horizontal. The prettiest webs are probably those of the garden spider, which is an orb web.
>
> ASSESSOR   OK. Thank you.

Tutor's comments

The pupil's notes were good: brief and organized under subheadings. She could see at a glance the information she needed to keep going when giving her talk. Normally, there should be an introduction, e.g. 'I'm a pupil at school, in Year 11, and I'm going to give you some general information about spiders.'

This is very fluent – the small hesitations and repetitions are normal in speech – and it is very well organized. She followed the order of the stages of the tape exactly, and the information given was clear and comprehensive.

▷ Question 2 *Describing a process from a tape*

You listen to a taped account of the process, and while doing so look at a series of illustrations or diagrams. Then you describe the process to some other pupils, who are also shown the illustrations. What you say is recorded.

This is an account of the web-building process:

This is how the garden spider spins her web.

1   First of all, the spider carries a thread of silk between two supports, though sometimes the thread can be blown across by the wind.
2   After the first thread has been fastened, the spider spins another thread down from the middle of this thread and fastens it to a third support.
3   Then the spider runs backwards and forwards, adding more spokes to the web, and reinforcing the edges of the frame of the web, to make it stronger.
4   Next the spider starts to join all the spokes together. First of all it spins a spiral of widely-spaced threads, starting at the centre of the web and working outwards to the edge.
5   When the spider reaches the edge of the web, it turns around and comes back, spinning the threads more closely. These threads replace the first spiral, which the spider eats on its way back to the middle of the web.
6   When the web is finished, the spider will hide in its lair, ready to dash out and catch its prey when it feels a tug on the web.

The illustrations are shown in Figure 6.1.

Figure 6.1

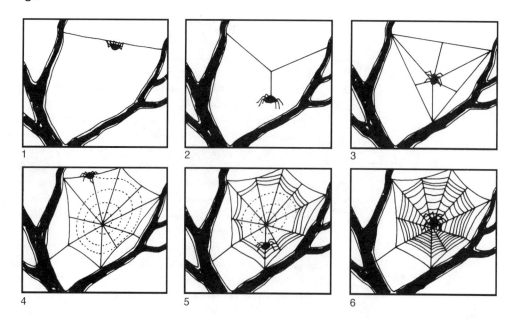

This is a transcript of the pupil's description:

> PUPIL   *Well, for a start, the spider puts one thread across the support, the supports, like that. And then from that she drops one down the middle to make a third support, and then moves in and out of these three, to make the web, well you know, make more supports, for the web. And then she starts from the middle and goes outwards in a spiral shape until she gets to the edge. Then she turns round and starts going back in. An' while she's going back in she eats the first lot, the, the spiral what she put out to start with. An' then once she gets to the middle, of all …, after going back in, she goes to the lair and waits for the prey.*
>
> ASSESSOR   *Fine, right, thank you very much.*

Tutor's comments

The pupil spoke fluently, with only a few hesitations and corrections. He had understood the process, and he mentioned all six stages, but his descriptions of four of them are unsatisfactory: such phrases as 'like that', 'from that', 'these three' are vague and he could have been more explicit. He was not altogether clear when he said 'she eats the first lot', but quickly added a bit more explanation. This is rather short. His descriptions of the process as a whole would not be intelligible without the drawings.

▷ **Question 3**   *Personal response to an article*

1   Present your personal reactions to the article 'Boys in Hospital after Drugs Cocktail' and the issues it raises to the rest of the group. At this stage, the other members of the group will listen.

2   Comment individually on at least one point raised by somebody else, and explain your own feelings on the topic.

3   Imagine that you work for one of the charities which try to help families with difficult teenagers. Using information from the article you have read and from your own personal experience, produce guidelines for parents and teenagers offering practical help to the problems raised in the article. You will need separate but complementary guidelines for parents and teenagers. Try to remain objective in your advice, considering the viewpoints of both the parents and the teenagers.

Suggested timescale:

▷   Personal reactions: 5–10 minutes
▷   Individual commentary and general discussion: 10 minutes
▷   Establishing the guidelines: 10 minutes.

Boys in Hospital after Drugs Cocktail

A 15-year-old boy was last night fighting for his life and another was recovering in hospital after they took a drugs cocktail including Ecstasy.

Eddie Ingleby and Kenneth Williams were taken ill just hours before tragic Leah Betts lost her fight for life.

The schoolboys were taken to the Queen Alexandra Hospital in Cosham, Hants, after hallucinating at their homes on Wednesday night.

Kenneth was fighting for his life in the hospital's intensive care unit while Eddie was said to be 'recovering'. Both boys are from the Leigh Park area of Havant, Hants.

Kenneth's mother, Sandra Page, described how her son returned staggering and stumbling to their home in Winterslow Drive. She said he could not speak when he arrived home and added: 'I'd like to string up whoever is responsible for this.'

Kenneth's step-brother, Carl Page, said Kenneth kept falling over and bumping into things.

He said: 'He went into the kitchen and tried buttering a plate. We thought he was just drunk. We put him to bed but he kept getting out and wanted to sleep on the floor. He got really aggressive when we went towards him.'

The family called an ambulance at about 11 p.m. and he was taken to hospital.

Eddie was taken to the hospital about an hour later, after his mother found him staggering uncontrollably around their home at Fleet End Close, Leigh Park.

Detectives in Portsmouth, Hants, warned yesterday that the drugs problem was so bad in the city that there could be 'ten Leah Betts tragedies every week.'

Drugs Squad Detective Sergeant Nigel Midgley said Portsmouth's club scene attracted many young people from around the region each weekend and drugs were widely available.

'We have spoken to both the boys, but not surprisingly they do not want to tell us what they took. We believe they took a cocktail of drugs; it's frighteningly easy to get hold of Ecstasy, amphetamines and cannabis.'

Portsmouth police estimate that the drug trade in the city is worth £13m a year.   (IGCSE)

▷ **Question 4** *Planning and speculating*

The National Lottery has been set up to provide money for charitable organizations, for sports associations and for the Arts. Some money also goes towards the Millennium Fund which will provide money for the celebration of the year 2000, in the form of a festivity or something more permanent.

Your task is to make a bid for some of this money. You must research an organization which operates at a local level and make a bid for a sum of money to fund a specific project. This assignment provides the opportunity to obtain three oral grades.

Individual

You are to provide an interviewing panel with the aims and objectives of the group which you are representing, together with a simple outline of the project and its cost.

For the oral itself, you will make an oral submission of some 4–5 minutes' duration in support of your bid. Be prepared for the panel to question you.

(**London**)

A STEP FURTHER

▷ Start making a list of things you could do for the individual oral.
▷ Find suitable passages for reading aloud and practise them with a friend or with a tape recorder.
▷ Explain a process to a friend and see if he or she can carry it out successfully from your explanations. If something goes wrong, re-evaluate your instructions.
▷ Choose one or two topics of interest to you and prepare a short talk, with a set of note-cards and audio-visual aids. Try your talk out on a receptive adult or friend.

SUMMARY

▷ What the Boards expect for oral work.
▷ How to prepare for oral work, including being audible and intelligible, responding to others present, organizing your talk effectively, practising reading aloud, conversing with an assessor, giving a prepared talk and giving instructions.

Group oral

All the examining boards expect you to submit evidence of **group oral** activities. Boards do not specify exact tasks, but here is a list of the kinds of activities you might choose from:

In pairs

▶ consider a problem and suggest a solution
▶ produce a piece of work jointly
▶ plan an event
▶ interview each other
▶ instruct another pupil in a task.

As a group

▶ discuss a text or audio or video recording
▶ talk about a topic of current interest
▶ discuss a theme explored in literature
▶ discuss possible ways of ending a play or story
▶ compare two poems
▶ play different roles in turn
▶ record a mock trial
▶ plan a TV or radio programme and record it
▶ hold a formal debate
▶ work on scripted drama, or at improvisation.

LONDON	MEG	NEAB	NICCEA	SEG	WJEC	IGCSE	TOPIC	STUDY	REVISION 1	REVISION 2
		✓		✓	✓	✓	Paired talk with peers			
	✓					✓	Paired talk pupil–teacher			
✓		✓	✓		✓	✓	Small group discussion			
	✓						Instructing others in a task			
✓		✓	✓	✓	✓	✓	Problem-solving in groups			
	✓						Whole class discussion			
	✓	✓			✓		Talking to a wider audience			

▷ **Skills involved** Group oral work may be unsupervised – pupils talking on their own – or partly directed by an assessor or teacher. Work may range from the formal (e.g. debating) to the informal (e.g. undirected group discussion). Whichever approach you choose, marks will be awarded for skills in several areas. It could be said broadly that you will need to be able to

▶ speak clearly and with appropriate pace, volume and intonation
▶ speak directly and involve a listener
▶ organize ideas effectively
▶ communicate thought and feeling with expression
▶ develop, illustrate and explain ideas, opinions and feelings

▷ respond to changes in the direction of a conversation or discussion

▷ react intelligently to new ideas and defend or modify a position, as needed.

'Four rules for oral work'

There are various essentials to bear in mind when taking part in a group discussion:

1   You cannot discuss anything capably unless you are well informed. This means having some facts, as well as opinions, ready. Research the subject well first.

2   You should show that you are able to lead the discussion, perhaps act as chairperson and direct others, as well as take your place in the group, listen to others and be receptive to their ideas.

3   You must be good humoured and courteous, and show toleration for others who may disagree with your views.

4   You should take care to speak in an appropriate manner for the occasion.

▷ Methods of preparation

Group discussion will almost certainly be part of your normal classroom work. Every opportunity that you have to work in a group, discussing, for example, a story, a poem or some topic of current interest, gives you a chance to practise your skills. In any group discussion it is not the person who speaks most frequently and most emphatically who gains the respect of the group, but the one who knows what he or she is talking about. So, if you have been told in advance what is going to be discussed, it is a good idea to make a few preparations. This may mean no more than thinking about the subject, to see what you remember about it. On the other hand, if a topic in the news is going to be discussed, you might read it up in the newspapers, or talk about it to your friends and family. Remember, too, that the reference sections of libraries contain books which give up-to-date information about a huge range of subjects, and that library assistants are normally very helpful. If you are going to be the discussion leader, it is essential for you to be well prepared, so that you can help things along by occasionally asking questions, by encouraging and stimulating remarks, and by summarizing points for the rest of the group.

Audio and video recordings can provide a valuable record of your group oral work, as they give those taking part the opportunity to evaluate their performances. They do introduce difficulties of their own, however. Both make you behave rather self-consciously: you may not be used to them. Audio recordings, of course, do not show your gestures and facial expressions, which can be a very important part of communication – but tape recorders are easy to come by and to use. Video equipment is expensive and requires special skill to operate if a good recording is to result. Its use in schools and colleges is increasing, however, and you may well find that you have access to it.

▷ Examples of group oral work

'Ideas for group oral work.'

The range of possibilities for group oral work is large, and at different times you will probably narrate, describe, expound, argue, persuade, speculate, act, and do many other things. Here are some of the activities you might be engaged in:

1   Discuss, in a small group, first reactions to a novel, play or poem you have read.

2   Record your own version of an established soap opera, or an invented one.

3   Set up your own 'Any Questions?' panel, and ask and respond to questions on topical issues.

4   Hold a formal debate on a proposition of interest to the group, e.g. 'School would be better if there were half-day attendance'
    or
    'Sixth form pupils should be given a maintenance grant, like that awarded to students in higher education'.

5   Set up a mock trial.

6   In pairs, improvise short conversations between people in a situation where they have time on their hands, e.g. in a waiting-room, at the bus stop, in a queue.

7   In pairs, work as an interviewer and as the person interviewed, e.g. a famous person in history.

8   Chair a group discussion on a topic of current interest.

9   In a group, do a prediction exercise on a text you are all reading.

10   In a group, work at a **cloze** (deletion exercise, i.e. blank filling) activity on a text you are all reading.

> ## SAMPLE DISCUSSIONS

▷ **Question 1**   *Group discussion of a text*

The following is a transcript of the beginning of a discussion by pupils who had read Alan Garner's *Red Shift*, for the first time.

B1   Well, we have decided to talk about this book by Alan Garner. Keith, what did you think?

B2   I read up to page twenty … I read to the end of the Tom and Jan section and thought 'I can't take this any more!' I just put it down and I didn't start it again until yesterday night. Then I read a bit more of the next part and I carried on and really … I really didn't enjoy it.

G1   I liked the characters on the first page. They amused me. I wasn't very sure about all the short sentences, though … I … I got to the second part. Then I was trying to think 'Were they Romans? Were they in the future, or what?' I don't think I'd have gone on from there if I'd been reading it just for myself.

G2   Well, I enjoyed it. I thought though the fact that I liked it … it had something to do with seeing it on television, some time ago. I could remember the plot and realized that it was happening in three different times and that there was a link between them. I think that did help a lot.

B1   That would be like a second experience of the book, because you'd been over it once on the television.

G2   Yes, it was.

B1   When you said you were trying to find a link, did you think there was like a key, and if you could just find it, it would all fall into place?

G2   Well, yes! But I never did find it! [*Laughter and general agreement.*]

B2   But I didn't, either. I only read on because I couldn't understand it. I thought 'I'm going to understand this the more I read', but I didn't. [*Laughter.*]

B1   When you were reading, what was happening if no meaning was coming through? [*Laughter.*]

B2   I thought 'It's going to come clear in a minute. Keep on! Keep on!' I wanted to know what was going to happen to Tom and Jan. That's what I wanted. [*Murmur of agreement.*]

G1   I thought 'It must be worth doing because we've been asked to read it.' I thought 'Great! A story to read' but when I started it, I thought, 'Wow!' [*Laughter.*]

B1   What about Tom's Mum and Dad? Do you think they were like people in real life, or not?

G1   Um, yes, especially his Mum, grumbling at him to keep his things tidy, all the time. … Yes, that was all right, but I was put off by the first piece about Roman times. You could tell from certain clues that it was Roman times, but the language they were using sort of clashed. They kept saying things like 'Come on, kid' and 'Don't push it' – more like the army today talking.

B2   I … [*pause*]

G2   Perhaps what it was saying is that ways don't change all that much – like only on the surface it changes. Wars are the same. War's always war.

Tutor's comments

There are quite a lot of good points to notice here. Let's work through a short checklist of the kind that would be used by an assessor. We shall consider the following for the speakers:

▷   Delivery
▷   Content and appropriateness
▷   Ability to respond to others' remarks
▷   Ability to convey ideas, feelings and experiences
▷   Asking and answering questions
▷   Presenting and backing up a point of view.

▶ **Delivery**   Although you can't tell this from the transcript, all of those taking part spoke loudly and clearly and could be heard easily. The laughter shows that members of the group were relaxed about the discussion.

▶ **Content and appropriateness**   All four speakers contributed to make this quite an interesting discussion, as regards content, though they had different evaluations and opinions of the book they had read. There is a good balance kept between details from the book and opinions about it. Appropriateness, here keeping to the point, was chiefly the responsibility of Boy 1. As leader of the discussion he introduced the subject and invited Boy 2 to start. When he thought the group was getting a bit stuck in the groove of what to decide about the meaning of the story he turned to something else by asking 'What about Tom's Mum and Dad …?' This enabled Girl 1 to carry on. His question about the 'clash' of language in the Roman sections of the book helped Girl 2 to articulate a really profound idea. Boy 1's role in this would be rated highly.

▶ **Ability to respond to others' remarks**   All four speakers are fairly good listeners. They took in what the others said and picked up the thread of the discussion as it unwound. Follow Girl 2. She disagreed with Girl 1, and liked the novel, even though she didn't really understand it. She went quiet for a while, but, by listening to the others, was able to contribute the final idea in this extract.

▶ **Ability to convey ideas, feelings and experiences**   The members (excluding Boy 1, the leader) are good at conveying ideas and experiences and are honest about their feelings. Boy 2: 'I thought "I can't take any more!" '; Girl 1: 'I don't think I'd have gone on from there if I'd been reading it just for myself', and later 'I thought "Great! A story to read!", but when I started it, I thought "Wow!".'

▶ **Asking and answering questions**   Boy 1, quite suitably in his role as leader, was good at asking questions to draw out the other speakers, or keep the discussion going, and move it forward, e.g. 'Did you think there was any reason for that?' The other three responded readily, though sometimes in a way that brought that line of investigation to an end, e.g. Girl 2: 'Yes, it was', and 'Well, yes! But I never did find it.'

▶ **Presenting and backing up a point of view**   It is not enough just to have opinions about what you read, you need evidence to support them. Boy 2 explained that he gave the book a fair chance ('I read up to page twenty … I read to the end of the Tom and Jan section') before he gave up and decided he didn't enjoy it. Girl 1 thought Tom's Mum was like a person in real life 'grumbling at him to keep his things tidy, all the time'. She also gave good examples she had remembered from the text of the odd language, which she couldn't see the reason for, as she read.

Altogether this was a lively and interesting discussion, in which all four participants took part ably.

▶ **Question 2**   *Roleplay paired*

Here is a transcript of two pupils roleplaying as housewives, talking to pass time while waiting for a bus:

G1   [*cheerfully*]: Hello, Eve. How are you today?
G2   [*surprised*]: Hello, Dawn. Haven't seen you for ages.
G1   I know I've been a bit ill, really.
G2   Oh – nothing nasty?
G1   No … not really. It's my knee, and Fred has been getting a bit – a bit on my nerves, you know.
G2   Oh-h-h?
G1   Um.
G2   Well, what are you doing with yourself now?
G1   Oh, well, I'm getting ready for my sister-in-law coming down. I still haven't told Fred yet; I don't think that he's going to be very pleased, you know. Doesn't like things like that.
G2   Oh, doesn't he get on well with his sister, then?
G1   [*laughing*]: We-e-ell. I don't know. She's a funny old dear, she really is. She … you know … she comes over and she sort of goes in all the rooms. She has a good nose

round. It's so bad – you have to lock all the drawers up. It's awful.

G2   You haven't seen her for a while have you? You've never mentioned her to me before.

G1   No – we don't like to mention her very much. No, poor thing. She'll get over it one day.

G2   She coming far?

G1   Um – yes. Um … Liverpool. So, you see …

G2   How's she getting here?

G1   On the train.

G2   You'll have to meet her, then?

G1   [*emphatically*]: No. I can't meet her; not with my leg. I'll have to get Fred to go. Yes. He'll have to have a day off work; he won't like that, either.

G2   No, I see. No, we don't have much trouble with relations. All ours live nearby, so they're for ever popping in and out. We never worry about them …

G1   Oh, I wouldn't like that! Well, ought to go now – no use waiting here all day.

G2   I'll wait a bit longer.

G1   See you later, then. Bye.

Tutor's comments

This is an attractive short dialogue, in which each girl sustains her role convincingly.

▷ **Delivery**   On the tape it is clear that both girls are 'in character'. Girl 1 speaks clearly but, after her cheerful opening greeting, in a tone of tired resignation, the pitch of her voice dropping at the end of each remark. Girl 2, in the role of the sympathetic friend, speaks in gentler tones, often of enquiry, with a rising note at the end of her contributions. Both show the hesitations and repetitions that are natural to relaxed speech. Both girls speak in an informal idiom, just as two housewives might, e.g. 'Fred has been getting a bit – a bit on my nerves' or 'She's a funny old dear, she really is.'

▷ **Content and appropriateness**   Both speakers talk about nothing very significant, as suits an idle chat at the bus stop, but they do manage to develop the chief topic – the sister-in-law's unwelcome visit – quite well.

▷ **Ability to respond to others' remarks**   Each follows on from what the other says remarkably well, considering that this was spontaneous roleplay. At one point Girl 2 interrupts her friend, when she hesitates, in a way that anticipates what she was probably going on to say next – at least it is a very convincing continuation: Girl 1: 'Um – yes. Um … Liverpool. So you see …' Girl 2 breaks in with 'How's she getting here?'

▷ **Ability to convey ideas, feelings and experiences**   Girl 1 conveys her situation and its problems partly by stretches of narration: 'She's a funny old dear, she really is … She … you know … she comes over and she sort of goes in all the rooms. She has a good nose round. It's so bad – you have to lock all the drawers up. It's awful!' and partly by dark hints, which are equally effective, e.g. 'No – we don't like to mention her very much' or 'I still haven't told Fred yet; I don't think that he's going to be very pleased, you know.' The role of Girl 2 is that of steady confidante, and appropriately she shows no surprise at the revelations of her friend.

▷ **Asking and answering questions**   Here, it is only necessary to do this in order to sustain the dialogue. Girl 2 asks most of the questions to draw out Girl 1 and get details of what has been happening to her. Both girls are very consistent in keeping to their questioner and respondent roles.

This is a well-shaped, convincing short dialogue, and both girls took their part commendably.

▷ **Question 3**   *Roleplay paired*

Here is another roleplay assignment for pairs, which was set for oral examination.

In this assignment you are going to consider different registers of speech. We are all aware that we change the way we speak according to the person to whom we are speaking. Thus, we speak differently to our friends than we do to our parents. We use other registers of speech when we are talking to people in authority or people we do not know very well. We are going to examine how registers of speech operate in English by roleplaying a situation which will require you to speak using a variety of registers.

Characters

Claire: a fifteen-year-old girl
Emma: her best friend
A police officer
Claire's parents

Situation

Claire's parents have gone away for the weekend, leaving her to look after the house. This is the first time that Claire's parents have left her on her own in the house, but they have decided that she is old enough and responsible enough to be trusted. Claire's parents do not want to appear over-anxious or fussy, so they have not issued her with a set of instructions as to what she may and may not do in their absence. Claire knows, however, that they would be furious if she were to have a party in their absence. Her parents are fair but strict.

Once her parents have left, Emma calls round and suggests that Claire have a small gathering of friends on the Saturday evening. Claire is not at all sure, but Emma persuades her that nothing will go wrong.

The Saturday evening arrives and about ten friends turn up. Everything seems to be going really well until there is a loud banging on the door, accompanied by drunken singing. The word has gone round about the party and Nina, a notorious troublemaker, has decided to gatecrash, bringing several of her acquaintances with her. Claire opens the door and Nina and her friends barge in, shouting, 'Let's liven things up a bit!' The resulting party is so riotous that Claire's neighbours call the police. The police arrive and tell Claire that unless the party ends immediately they will charge her with a breach of the peace. Then they leave. Claire and Emma discuss how they are going to get rid of Nina and her friends, who are by now extremely drunk. When they ask them to go home, Nina's friends respond by damaging the lounge and its furnishings. Finally, they leave.

Claire is devastated: what on earth is she going to tell her parents when they come home on the Sunday morning? She knows that they will be extremely angry because the lounge has recently been redecorated. She is also uncomfortably aware that she has let them down, and that they will find it difficult to trust her after this.

1   With your partner, roleplay the following conversations:
    (a) the conversation which Claire has with the police officer
    (b) the conversation which Claire has with Emma after the police have left
    (c) the conversation which Claire has with her parents when they come home.
    You should each play Claire at some point.
2   With your partner, discuss the registers of speech which you used in each conversation. What kind of language and expression did you use in the different situations? Why was the type of spoken English which you used appropriate to the situation?   (**London**)

Tutor's comments

These are the assessor's notes made while watching two pupils, Charlotte and Sarah, engaging in the roleplay about Claire's party.

	Charlotte	*Sarah*
1(a)	Effective as police officer, using appropriate tone of voice.	Suitably timid and apologetic as Claire.
1(b)	Both girls effective in terms of register. Sarah more confident than Charlotte. Talked convincingly as best friends.	
1(c)	Not quite convincing as parents: idiom forced and unrealistic.	Good – lively, spirited attempt to give her account of how things got out of control.
2	Both made some good general points about changing register with new role but should have mentioned more specifically linguistic aspects.	
	Both girls rather intimidated by the camera. (This was recorded on video.)	
	Score 6–	Score 6+

▷ **Question 4**   *Problem-solving paired*

Here is a transcript of two pupils working at a simple sequencing task. The speakers are trying to put in the right order instructions for planting a bulb in a pot.

G1   Oh, we've got to sort this out. What do you think?

G2   [*reading slowly from a slip of paper*]: 'Cover the bottom of the pot with the mixture'.

G1   That must be the first one.

G2   [*continues reading*]: 'Leave the shoulders of the bulb above the surface' – Oh, that's wrong. We haven't even got the bulb yet!

G1   [*continues reading*]: 'Place the pot in a sunny position' –What … where shall I put this?

G2   'Fill the pot …' Fill the pot!

G1   Oh, yes, I see. That must come next, after 'Cover the bottom of the pot'.

G2   'When the first growth appears …' Oh, no; not yet!

G1   [*thinking aloud*]: Cover the shoulders of the bulb, then fill the pot with the remaining mixture … that must be right.

G2   That 'When the plant is growing …' bit must come near the end, don't you think?

G1   [*still thinking aloud*]: How about having 'Fill the pot with the remainder of the mixture', then 'Place the pot …'.

G2   [*irritated*]: Look! We haven't even got the bulb in yet! [*Hysterical giggles from both girls.*]

G1   Oh, I've got it. Look 'Place the bulb in a central position', etc., then 'When the buds appear; water more often …'.

G2   [*excited*]: Yes, then 'When the plant is growing, support it with a cane or stick' – that goes right at the end. Yes?

G1   Yes! right! Let's try it in order, now.

G1 and G2   [*together*]: 'Soak the potting mixture thoroughly and squeeze out the surplus mixture. Cover the bottom of the pot with the mixture. Place the bulb in a central position. Fill the pot with the remainder of the mixture, pushing it down firmly, so that the shoulders of the bulb are just above the surface. Place the pot in a sunny position and water sparingly. When the first growth appears, water freely from time to time. When the buds appear water more often, probably every day. Then, support it with a stick or cane.'

G2   Good. Yes, I think that'll grow!

Tutor's comments

The girls obviously had a little difficulty working out the correct sequence of instructions. They had some fun while they were attempting it, but they could have collaborated more effectively, especially in the early stages.

▶ **Delivery** Girl 2 was the dominant partner and spoke more loudly, and at one point, aggressively: 'Look! We haven't even got the bulb in yet!' Girl 1, who spent some time in thinking aloud, tended to mutter her ideas quietly.

▶ **Content and appropriateness** In so far as the task was set for them, the content of the girls' talk was partly predetermined – there was a fair amount of reading aloud to remind themselves of the different instructions. They did concentrate on the task in hand, though this was over a fairly short stretch of time. Their speech was appropriate for the problem-solving activity they were engaged in.

▶ **Ability to respond to others' remarks** Girl 1 was not very good at responding to her partner. Girl 2 attempted to move things along but sometimes her attempts were ignored, e.g. Girl 2: 'That "When the plant is growing …" bit must come near the end, don't you think?' Girl 1 continued thinking 'How about having "Fill the pot with the remainder of the mixture" then "Place the pot …"' This resulted in Girl 2 interrupting in exasperation 'Look! We haven't even got the bulb in yet!' After the release of laughter they got down to helping each other to sort things out quite quickly.

▶ **Ability to convey ideas, feelings and experience** Rather surprisingly, the girls did not translate the stages of the instructions into their own words to help them decide on an order. Their explicit thinking was confined to remarks such as 'Not yet' or 'That bit must come near the end'. Quite a lot of their thinking was not communicated to each other. If Girl 1 had explained the lines along which she was thinking in the middle of this exchange the pair might have got on more quickly.

▶ **Asking and answering questions** Each girl asked at least one question but they tended to work out the problem independently: their questions were sometimes just to reassure themselves that they had established something that was acceptable, e.g. Girl 2: 'That "When the plant is growing …" bit must come near the end, don't you think?'

▶ **Presenting and backing up a point of view** *They began better than they went on, in this respect: Girl 2's statement about where to start ' "Cover the bottom of the pot with the mixture" ' was adopted by Girl 1 as reasonable: 'That must be the first one.' They tended to assert their views, rather than explain them or back them up, e.g. Girl 2: ' "Fill the pot ..." Fill the pot!' If they had offered reasons for their decisions, the breakdown in communication at one point would probably not have occurred.*

This was only partly successful: the girls had more difficulty with the task than they should have had, and this was because they did not tell each other what they were thinking sufficiently often.

▶ A STEP FURTHER

Watch television programmes and notice in particular how the persons introducing the discussions handle things. How well do the speakers measure up to the standards indicated in 'What you need to know' above? You might also have an opportunity to attend a live discussion, e.g. of a local issue.

Roleplay is best produced from spontaneous drama situations. Get involved in as much school or college drama as you can, or even consider joining a local drama group, if there is one in your area.

SUMMARY

▷ The skills you need for paired and group oral work: being well informed about your topic, keeping calm and in control, directing and shaping your talk, having good 'linguistic manners', i.e. using appropriate ways of talking for different listeners and occasions.

▷ How to prepare for group talk by researching your topic and using audio and video recordings were discussed.

▷ Practising roleplay.

▷ How paired and group oral work is assessed.

Researching and writing up

▷ **GETTING STARTED**

It is probable that you will at some time have been given the task of investigating a subject, and then writing an essay or extended report based on what you discovered. A piece of work of this kind may be a very suitable choice to put in your coursework folder for GCSE assessment.

The original stimulus for the work may come from your own interests, a group project, a suggestion from your teacher or tutor or an examination question. Whatever your starting point, the essential approaches are the same. This chapter will discuss these approaches in detail.

TOPIC	STUDY	REVISION 1	REVISION 2
Choosing a topic			
Selecting and refining ideas for topics			
Deciding what to find out			
Locating the resources			
Organizing and planning your work			
Using the resources			
Evaluating your materials			
Writing up the topic			
Preliminary drafts and final version			
Reading for research			
Making useful notes			
Planning a questionnaire			
Conducting an interview			

▷ **WHAT YOU NEED TO KNOW**

This section deals with the general techniques of researching and writing up a topic. There are eight main areas to be considered, and they will be looked at in turn:

'Eight rules for topic work'

▶ Choosing a topic
▶ Selecting and refining ideas for topics
▶ Deciding what to find out
▶ Locating the resources
▶ Organizing and planning your work
▶ Using the resources
▶ Evaluating your materials
▶ Writing up the topic.

▷ Choosing a topic

Part of the justification for examinations by coursework is that they give the opportunity for an individual choice of work, so do talk about things that are really important to you. After all, in the world outside school or college, writing and talking are invariably related to a purpose: if you are a police officer, you will write an account of a traffic accident because it has to go into the records and may be needed in court; as a journalist you would interview a person in the news to inform or entertain the public. Most writers have an idea of their readers, and try to satisfy them as well as to express themselves. There is no need for coursework pieces to be a series of dreary exercises. If you choose something which really interests you and which you want to tell others about, then you have taken a first step towards communicating successfully, and are likely to be better motivated during the hard-slogging phases of bringing the work to completion.

When you are doing your coursework folder, be open to ideas from all quarters, not just school. Read as widely as you can, get involved in debate with fellow students and keep up to date on current affairs and on developments in the arts and sciences. And don't forget those most popular of media – television, radio and films. At least one of the Boards (London) recommends these as sources of promising stimuli for oral coursework.

▷ Selecting and refining ideas for topics

Brainstorming

You may have quite a few ideas for writing or talking in mind but not know how to develop them. One of the best ways of doing this, apart from a discussion with your tutor or teacher, is 'brainstorming' with fellow students. In this process, key words or ideas are suggested by the members of the group, as many as possible being thought of. One member of the group notes them down as they occur – there is no need to classify them; that can come later. This is a useful stage in any project – following the maxim 'two heads are better than one'. Several persons can come up with angles and questions that you hadn't thought of by yourself, either adding to your original idea, refining it or even changing it radically. Collaboration at this stage is quite legitimate, provided the finished pieces are your own work.

'Putting heads together'

Suppose that an item in the news about football hooliganism had caught your attention and set you thinking in general about its causes and cures. A quick brainstorming session with friends might come up with the following:

group violence	European ban
macho image	police patrols
drink and drugs	youth clubs needed
TV influence	sports idols should set example
frustration at losing game	special trains
more police needed	'No drink' enforcement
unemployment	surveillance in the stands
bad facilities at grounds	video cameras
ticket touts	heavy fines
police provocation	imprisonment
crowd control	counselling
identity cards	international cooperation

I think you will agree that these are more ideas than you would be likely to think of by yourself. The next stage would be to classify these ideas as causes or cures.

Try for yourself

For each of the following topics try, preferably in a group, to produce a list of ideas by brainstorming:

Council Tax	international exchange visits
GCSE	AIDS
private health care	animal rights
Youth Employment Schemes	pollution
school trips	wildlife preservation.

Related pieces of work

'Try two different approaches'

If you are interested in a topic, it may well be worthwhile to attempt more than one piece of work on it and submit the related pieces as one unit. Suppose the topic were 'The Argument'. You might write a poem, concentrating on the emotions of the people involved, and the suppressed violence of the situation, and you might also write a story in which a husband and wife had an argument when one of them came home late.

Compare the treatment of the same piece of material in a poem and in an extract from a novel in these examples:

Poem

Discord in Childhood

Outside the house an ash-tree hung its terrible whips
And at night when the wind rose, the lash of the tree
Shrieked and slashed the wind as a ship's
Weird rigging in a storm shrieks hideously.

Within the house two voices arose, a slender lash
Whistling she-delirious rage, and the dreadful sound
Of a male thong booming and bruising, until it had drowned
The other voice in a silence of blood, 'neath the noise of the ash.

(D.H. Lawrence, *Collected Poems*)

Extract from novel

In front of the house was a huge old ash-tree. The west wind, sweeping from Derbyshire, caught the houses with full force, and the tree shrieked again. Morel liked it. 'It's music,' he said. 'It sends me to sleep.' But Paul and Arthur and Annie hated it. To Paul it became almost a demoniacal noise. The winter of their first year in the new house their father was very bad. The children played in the street, on the brim of the wide, dark valley, until eight o'clock. Then they went to bed. Their mother sat sewing below. Having such a great space in front of the house gave the children a feeling of night, of vastness, and of terror. This terror came in from the shrieking of the tree and the anguish of the home discord. Often Paul would wake up, after he had been asleep a long time, aware of thuds downstairs. Instantly he was wide awake. Then he heard the booming shouts of his father, come home nearly drunk, then the sharp replies of his mother, then the bang, bang of his father's fist on the table, and the nasty snarling shout as the man's voice got higher. And then the whole was drowned in a piercing medley of shrieks and cries from the great, windswept ash-tree. The children lay silent in suspense, waiting for a lull in the wind to hear what their father was doing. He might hit their mother again. There was a feeling of horror, a kind of bristling in the darkness, and a sense of blood. They lay with their hearts in the grip of an intense anguish. The wind came through the tree fiercer and fiercer. All the cords of the great harp hummed, whistled, and shrieked. And then came the horror of the sudden silence, silence everywhere, outside and downstairs. What was it? Was it a silence of blood? What had he done?

(D.H. Lawrence, *Sons and Lovers*)

To take a second example, something you have prepared for oral assessment may also be shaped into a piece of writing. Compare these two pieces by a student, first talking then writing about an experience recalled from childhood:

Oral (talking)

My name is Stephen – the earliest thing I can remember is standing on the doorstep waving my brother goodbye as he went off to school – well he went to school and what I did was fall down the stairs afterwards and the next day I can remember as well because I was playing with a model plane and what happened was I thought I was a pilot and I stepped forward which was deadly because – because well there was no more space to walk forward see and I fell down the stairs – and I had a bit of a headache afterwards – and the plane was a bit smashed up too so what I did was I went in the garden and I buried it and got out my soldiers

– yes it did die actually – and I smashed up another plane and used that and buried that as well you see – got my soldiers out and played with them and the two planes as if they had fought each other and blown each other up – it was quite a good game really because it was just like it was real.

Written work

The earliest thing I can remember is standing on the front doorstep, waving goodbye to my brother. When he had gone I slipped and fell; I didn't break anything, but I fell heavily. The next day I can remember well too, because I was playing with my planes on the top of the stairs and what happened was I thought that I was a pilot. So I was walking round and round, then I took a step forward, but that was silly because there was no more space to walk forward, and I fell down. When I reached the floor I had a headache, but worse, the plane was broken to pieces.

What I did next was go into the garden, crying and bury it. Then I got another old one and broke that up and buried that too. I got my soldiers to make a procession for the funeral. It was a great game. I pretended that the planes had collided and crashed in the mud, with no survivors.

▷ Deciding what to find out

You will probably know something about the topic already, and a good way of making a start is to list what you know. Then, if possible, discuss it with friends and borrow one or two books from the school or public library which treat the area generally. You should consult your teacher or tutor, too, to make sure that the subject is a suitable one, and consider any suggestions offered at this stage. After these steps, you should be able to make a first list of things you definitely need to find out and to do.

▷ Locating the resources

When you have decided what you need to find out, you will have to discover suitable sources of information. This may not be very easy, and it may help to consult again your friends and teacher or tutor. Library staff are usually very helpful, too; and it is also just possible that you might be able to do a computer search.

Suppose that you were researching the following topic: 'Acting in the Seventeenth-Century Theatre'. After a period of thinking, discussion and general reading you may make two lists along these lines:

What I know already
(a) Some seventeenth-century actors are famous, e.g. Richard Burbage, Edward Alleyn, Shakespeare himself.
(b) Boys played women's parts.
(c) Stages were often in the open.
(d) There were few costumes and props.
(e) Audiences were from a wide cross-section of the public.
(f) Puritans were opposed to the theatres and players.

What I need to find out
(a) What evidence is available of early theatres and players? Is there much good source material?
(b) Were there theatres outside London?
(c) Which were the most popular plays and players?
(d) What status did acting have as a profession?
(e) Why were the Puritans so hostile to theatres and acting?

Many of these questions could probably be answered by visiting the local library and consulting literary reference books (e.g. *The Oxford Companion to the Theatre*), dictionaries of biography, and the section of the library on theatre history. As the period is in the past, there would be comparatively little non-book material available. You might be lucky enough to have a theatre museum within visiting distance; there is, for instance, in London, at Southwark, a reconstruction of the Globe Theatre, where Shakespeare acted, including a museum and educational centre; there is also a National Theatre Museum, near Covent Garden, and the Museum of the Moving Image at the South Bank.

Alternatively, a local museum might have a section devoted to the theatre.

In contrast, consider a contemporary topic: 'Drug-Taking as a Threat to Young People Today'. Possibly, after thinking, discussing and reading, your lists of ideas might look something like this:

What I know already

(a) There are TV films and videos warning young people against drugs.
(b) Some young people have been prosecuted for drug-handling.
(c) People in the news sometimes set a bad example to the young.
(d) Drugs can kill.
(e) Some dangerous drugs are fairly easily obtained.
(f) Drug-taking can lead to crime to finance the habit.
(g) Some powerful drugs are used as medicines.

What I need to find out

(a) What organizations help and advise young people about drug-taking?
(b) What laws are there about obtaining and using drugs?
(c) What proportion of young people today take drugs?
(d) How much money does the average drug-taker spend on the habit?
(e) What are the names of the dangerous drugs?
(f) What cures are there for drug dependency?

There may be comparatively few books on the subject, so other resources come to mind: a social studies textbook or video; current news items or documentary programmes on television; centres in your area, offering information and help; stories and articles in the local and national newspapers; Stationery Office publications; information gained from friends; posters or photographs, and so on.

These two projects would require a totally different range of resources.

Now let us look at three further assignments and try to identify the range of resources needed for each.

Assignment A

Returning to the topic of football hooliganism, you will remember that brainstorming produced a long list of relevant ideas, and it was suggested that you classified these as 'causes' and 'cures'. You can now delete any that seem unimportant, or that it would take you too far afield to discuss.

Your 'cures', i.e. ways of diminishing the hooliganism, may have been:

crowd control	special trains
European ban	'No drink' enforcement
police patrols	video cameras
more police	heavy fines
youth clubs	imprisonment
surveillance in the stands	counselling
sports idols should set an example	international cooperation
special campaign	

You might start by noting down the sources of information you already know about, e.g. a TV documentary, recent articles in the press about measures taken against supporters of a team who got out of hand. Perhaps you also have a fair amount of general knowledge about this topic, being a soccer enthusiast yourself. Visits to the school library and the public library should also be worthwhile: they often have collections of non-book materials – articles or photographs – which would be helpful, and you may find something useful under 'Sociology'. If you are going to refer to particular incidents that you remember vaguely, and to the steps that were taken by the police and club officials, it will be best to make sure that you have the facts right. However, a topic of this kind may be one you can embark on fairly quickly, without any need for detailed investigation.

Try for yourself

Choose two of the above topics and decide what would be the best sources of further information about them.

Assignment B

At your teacher's suggestion, you are going to write a chapter of an autobiography for inclusion in your coursework folder. After further thought, you decide to make it a chapter comparing your expectations of the future with those of your grandmother or grandfather at your age.

The sources of information needed would be rather different from those for Assignment A. Your grandfather or grandmother would be the first source of information. He or she might well speak of leaving school at fourteen, without any qualifications, because very few school pupils took public examinations then. He or she might mention the threat of war, which in the late 1930s affected everyone's expectations, or talk about what it was like during the Second World War.

This talk with your grandfather or grandmother could lead you to the school library and the public library. What could you find out about the 1930s and 1940s, about the pre-war and war periods generally, to supplement their reminiscences?

You have already investigated the non-book information for Assignment A and found out where it is filed. Look through it again for any old newspapers or photographs of the 1930s. Also, some Sociology packs have useful information. Next, make use of the catalogues: subject first, then author index and find the right classification numbers (most likely they will be the Dewey system). Note down titles of likely books to look into further. Remember that your grandfather's memory might not correspond exactly with what the prospects really were. For a fuller picture you will need to consult the other sources. Don't forget fiction too – this is another valuable source of interesting information in a very readable form.

And now, what about your own expectations? No doubt you have discussed the future endlessly with your friends and found it difficult to be certain about the chances for yourself and your contemporaries. It might be best to ask the careers teacher about latest employment possibilities and perhaps to look at various publications by the Stationery Office and by the local authority.

Once you have all this information, your chapter would have a chance of capturing the vividness of real-life experience, and at the same time might be able to achieve a balance based on its well-researched social background.

Try for yourself

Find out about one of the following, noting what resources you would need:

▶ school memories of someone you know
▶ first job experiences of different people.

Assignment C

Suppose the complete text you have been studying is William Golding's *Lord of the Flies*. You have been asked by your teacher or tutor to chair a discussion on how the boys in the novel seem to compare with their present-day counterparts.

Your first resource is the novel itself. You should re-read as much of it as you can very carefully, especially incidents which seem to reveal character and to determine the boys' behaviour on the island, e.g. electing a leader; the death of Simon; Jack's revolt; the end of the novel.

A search in the library reveals a book about William Golding. You find out that he worked as a schoolmaster for part of his life and so knew about boys at first hand. You have heard in a literature lesson a recording from the radio where a group of critics discussed *Lord of the Flies* and gave their opinions of the characters. It has stayed in your mind and seems to you to give a good range of views with which to lead the discussion and to supplement your own reading of the text. You arrange to hear this again. Now you have enough information to enable you to undertake the role of chairperson, confident that if the discussion dries up you can get it going again: for instance, if it gets stuck in a rut you can help it to change direction. You can also open and close the occasion skilfully, giving a clear lead at the beginning and a helpful summary of the contributions at the end.

Try for yourself

Choose a novel or play you have worked on, and find out more about some aspect of it for group discussion.

▷ **Organizing and planning your work**

'Getting organized'

Organizing your work

It would be a great pity if coursework became a burden to students, the stress of taking several written papers being replaced by anxiety about keeping up with your work and making sure that you have produced enough pieces at an acceptable standard. To try to prevent this, think about getting your work organized at the start of the course. Some of the organization has already been done for you, as you are timetabled for English at school or college. Within those sessions, though, and more particularly in homework or study time on your own, you need to think about making the best use of your time. Here is some advice about getting organized.

▶ **Work steadily throughout the course.** If you postpone work and it keeps piling up you will feel worried, and possibly not do your best.

▶ **Keep a balance between study and relaxation.** You will work better if you feel fit and refreshed. Much of your work in English is creative, needing a lively, enquiring attitude of mind, so keep alert for good ideas.

▶ **Make the best use of your time.** It is easy to think you have spent an hour and a half studying, when you have actually spent about half of that panicking about what you should be doing, and wandering about making coffee and telephoning friends to see if they are panicking, too. This sort of behaviour is known as displacement activity, i.e. a way of avoiding getting down to what you should be doing. It is better to work hard for a stretch and then to have a break, knowing you have earned it. It is important to have a clear idea of what you want to do, e.g. in a weekend read four chapters of a novel; write a narrative; make notes for a project. Estimate how much time you will need, at your normal working pace, before you start.

▶ **Find working habits that suit you.** There are many different ways of studying. Despite the remarks above, you may work better with the reassurance of friends, so time spent telephoning them occasionally may in fact be time well spent. You may work better if you can discuss your task with your family. Alternatively, you may find it better if you shut yourself away in your room at home, or go to the public library's reading-room. Whatever you feel comfortable with, establish that as a working habit early on.

▶ **Cultivate business-like working habits.** It wastes time if your notes are unreadable or consist of a jumble of scraps of paper. Have a working-folder, and date what you do, even your draft pieces of work.

▶ **Understand your task.** Find out from your teacher or tutor exactly what you have to do and learn to make choices quickly. Time can be wasted making false starts. If you have a large piece of work to complete, e.g. a project, subdivide it into manageable portions.

▶ **Make use of helpful study methods.** You may be able to learn to read faster and more efficiently, to make better notes, to plan an essay more confidently. Advice about all these matters will be found later in this chapter.

▶ **Complete work as you go along.** It is an uncomfortable feeling to know that you have

left several pieces of work half-done, and so you should finish everything to your satisfaction as you go along. If you have been given poor grades for your work by your
teacher or tutor, ask if you are allowed to attempt another piece of work of a similar
kind. Remember, though, that you must not include something corrected or changed
after it has been marked. This is not allowed.

▶ **Review what has been achieved.** There may be more work ahead, but try to finish each
study session by checking what you have achieved. Did you complete the task? Did you
understand what the author was getting at? If not, decide what to do about it next time.
Some people even like to make a note of where to start when they sit down again.

Planning your work

Planning your work can be done in different ways. Let's consider the following:

▶ an outline timetable
▶ a flow chart
▶ a topic tree
▶ an outline plan for writing or talking.

An outline timetable

Some students prefer to carry this in their heads, but it can be reassuring to map out the
task to be completed in the time available. Going back to the three assignments mentioned
in this chapter, the timetable might look like this:

Assignment A (4 weeks)
Ways of curbing football hooliganism

▶ Class-time
  • Brainstorm in a group for ideas.
  • Organize the list of points in the best order.
  • Consult teacher or tutor.
  • Visit school or college library, looking especially for non-book material.
  • Make essential notes and work on rough draft.
▶ Spare time
  • Write to/visit local football club for information.
  • Watch a relevant video, if available.
  • Go through newspapers for up-to-date information.
  • Talk to friends and football enthusiasts.
▶ Homework time
  • Visit the public library, especially the reference section, and consult staff there.
  • Make further notes and write first draft.
  • Write up final version.

Assignment B (6 weeks)
Write a chapter of your autobiography in which you compare your expectations now with
those of your grandmother or grandfather at your age.

▶ Class-time
  • Make a flow chart of ideas as they occur to you.
  • Consult your teacher or tutor.
  • Visit the school or college library for useful background books.
  • Make essential notes and start work on a rough draft.
▶ Spare time
  • Talk to (and if possible record) grandparents, and collect reminiscences of their life
    at your age.
  • Sort through family photographs and documents.
  • Write to the Stationery Office for latest figures on youth unemployment.
▶ Homework time
  • Visit public library and consult the History section for background information on
    the 1930s.

- Make notes and write first draft.
- Write up final version.

Assignment C (2 weeks)
Prepare an introduction as chairperson of group discussion on characters in William Golding's *Lord of the Flies*.

▷ Class-time
- Re-read the novel and note page references to relevant places in the text.
- Consult teacher or tutor.
- Visit school or college library and get any information on Golding or the novel.
- Enquire about the radio recording heard in class.
- Make outline notes of key ideas, ideally on a card index.
▷ Spare time
- Visit local library and borrow R.M. Ballantyne's *The Coral Island* (which first gave Golding the idea for his book, and offers interesting parallels).
- Search for more information about Golding and his book in your local library or on the Internet.
- View the film version of the book, if you can obtain it or it is shown on television or in a local cinema.
▷ Homework time
- Check through your cards and get them in the best order.
- Run through your introduction and if possible record yourself. Play back recording and listen to it critically.

A flow chart

A *flow chart* shows the main relationships of the ideas involved in a topic but leaves the final choice and order of ideas open. You take a fairly large piece of paper, and write the topic in the centre. The main ideas are arranged around it, then subordinate ideas written under the main ones. The relationships of the main ideas are shown by putting arrows from one group to the next. You can experiment with various links and cross-connections, until you are satisfied that you have the best arrangement. Figure 8.1 shows an example, by a student, of a flow chart for Assignment B.

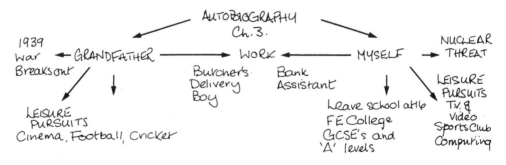

Figure 8.1 A Flow Chart

A topic tree

This is a helpful way of planning a piece of work which requires a logical structure. You draw a tree, the trunk corresponding to the topic, the branches to the main related ideas, and extensions to subordinate ideas. By this means you can see immediately the whole outline of your thinking from the main theme, through the major branches of the argument, to the subsidiary parts. It would be a good approach to take for Assignment A, after you had made a list of ways of curbing football hooliganism. It might look something like Figure 8.2.

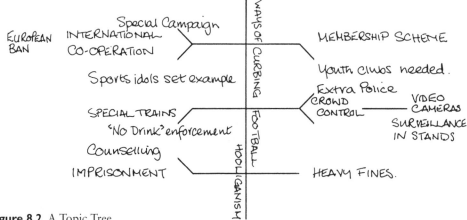

Figure 8.2 A Topic Tree

An outline plan for writing or talking

You will be invited to do a wide range of kinds of writing and talking for GCSE English coursework, and each type of work – summaries, reports, persuasive speeches, advertisements, poems, stories, plays – will have its own structure. Whatever you attempt, spend some time before you start, thinking of how you hope to:

▶   Begin
▶   Develop the work through stages
▶   Conclude.

▷ **Using the resources**

By now you will have decided on your topic area and will probably have a list of questions to which you want to find answers. You will have decided too the most likely sources of information. The next important principle is to be as business-like as possible in using your resources. Even if you find yourself facing a mountain of potential material, streamline your enquiries so that you collect a manageable amount of data, but try not to sacrifice balance and accuracy in doing so.

When gathering information from books, there are different styles of reading for different purposes. Make sure that you can vary your reading pace, and the way you read, for maximum efficiency (techniques for doing this will be explained in the section on 'Useful Practical Approaches' below). In order to remember what you have read you will need to make meaningful notes that will reconstruct the material for you when you return to them later; this will also be explained in the next section.

Information gathering from non-book sources uses a variety of skills, including listening carefully, observing and responding, asking well-focused questions, and so on. You may make notes from these experiences, but in a different way from the notes you make when you read. The following section also contains advice about making notes, formulating questionnaires and conducting interviews.

'Seeing someone else's point of view'

In your encounters with print, film and people you should remember that the facts you are looking for will often be presented to you subjectively. You have to allow for another's point of view, or bias, and take that into account. Of course, you yourself have biases, and these may get in the way of your fully understanding the material. It is a good idea to talk over your topic with as many people as possible: this is where several heads can be better than one. On the other hand, your own personal involvement can be an advantage: if you are sincerely concerned about an issue it will be clear to readers, and they will find what you write or say more convincing and persuasive.

Gathering information can be very rewarding, though often it is time-consuming and hard work. If you are to do justice to the efforts you have put in you should remember the following advice:

Don't ...

(a) rely chiefly on your memory
(b) forget to record titles of books, authors' names, page references, etc.

(c) write notes on scraps of paper

(d) leave notes incomplete

(e) leave it to the last minute to find photographs or other visual aids to fill out your topic

(f) forget to list sources of information, or do so in random order.

Do ...

(a) collect information and make notes accurately

(b) date each of your pieces of work and keep them in order

(c) record full details, especially author, title and date of publication, for books you use

(d) finish each piece of work, if possible, before going on to the next

(e) keep notes in one folder

(f) collect photographs and other non-book material as you go along

(g) make a list of all sources of information and check to see that it has been worked through.

▷ **Evaluating your materials**

When you feel you have obtained enough information to answer the questions on your list, you will have built up a body of material that will have to be structured and evaluated.

Let us look at an example 'A proposal to install speed humps in Bridge Lane, and local reactions'.

Here is a simple timetable for a project to be completed within three weeks:

A proposal to install speed humps in Bridge Lane, and local reactions

Class-time

(a) List what you know.

(b) Consult teacher or tutor and discuss with friends.

(c) Visit school or college library, choose relevant book and non-book material.

(d) Distribute questionnaire, if necessary.

(e) Make essential notes or flow chart and work on first draft.

Spare time

(a) Visit site and take photographs.

(b) Obtain and consult map of the area.

(c) Contact local newspaper office for the latest developments.

(d) Talk to local residents.

Homework time

(a) Write to local council and other associations involved.

(b) Visit public library, especially the reference section, and consult staff there.

(c) Make further notes and start writing up first draft.

(d) Write up your final version.

Your materials might now include the following:

▷ notes based on a guide to the area, and other notes based on a book about householders' rights

▷ three questionnaires completed by school friends

▷ some notes on documents you were shown at the Council offices

▷ three photocopies of parts of books on local authority administration

▷ two letters from local residents

▷ notes on interviews with local residents

▷ a photocopy of a map of the area.

You now decide to review your original list of things you had to find out, supplement it with other questions, and put all the questions in order, ready for writing. The revised list might look like this:

▷ What is the general character of the area around Bridge Lane?

▷ What are the traffic problems affecting Bridge Lane?

▷ What is the case for installing speed humps?

▷ What are the objections to installing them?

▷ Who and what is the highway authority?

▷ Does it have the power to install the humps, despite any objections?

▷ What do local people think?

▷ How do matters stand at present?

You indicate which of your materials give information relating to each of these questions, e.g. Question 1 – map, books, photographs; Question 2 – questionnaire, Council documents, interviews, maps, and so on.

Finally, you decide to give some attention, before getting down to writing, to how reliable your materials and sources of information are. The guide to your area and the book on householders' rights are presumably all right, although the latter is several years old. Your notes on the Council documents will have to be used, but you may not be sure how well you really understood the documents. Most of the people you interviewed clearly favoured the humps in Bridge Lane, although one or two overstated their case.

Now you are ready for the final stages:

▷ Prepare a final plan, with each of your sections or paragraphs decided upon.

▷ Reorganize the contents of your folder, so that material relating to each part comes in order. (If your topic is small-scale, you can number pieces of material instead.)

▷ Write the first draft of the topic.

It doesn't seem so formidable, does it, now that you have broken it down into stages?

▷ Writing up the topic

You should now be in a position to write up. Begin with the introductory paragraph. Go on with a series of sections, corresponding to the questions on your final list, referring to your materials as necessary. End with a concluding paragraph. The result will probably not satisfy you when you read it through, and you may have to revise it more than once before reaching a final version. Add any items, such as charts or maps you wish to include, a title page, and perhaps a contents page and a book list. Put the work in a clean folder or plastic envelope, with your name on it.

Here are some notes which may help you:

1   **Presentation**   Your work will make a favourable first impression if it is neatly written, well spaced out, and has diagrams that are well drawn and positioned. The work should be kept in a clean folder or plastic envelope.

'How to begin writing up'

2   **Style**   Try to write the project in an appropriate style – probably Standard English – but there may be a choice; if you are writing for a special audience, that will influence the way you express your ideas, e.g. information on drug addiction as a general article, in contrast to a pamphlet for young people.

3   **Section headings**   Unless the project is very short, it will help your readers to find what they are interested in if you begin each section with a subheading. The subheadings can be based on the questions in your final list: the road humps project might have sections headed 'Introduction', 'Bridge Lane and the surrounding area', 'The problem of speeding in Bridge Lane', 'The case for installing road humps', and so on.

4   **Title page**   This should give not only your title, but also (unless you are given other instructions by your teacher) the course for which the work is being submitted, and the date of completion.

5   **Contents page**   It is easy to look through a short piece to find any part one wants, but a contents page can be helpful with a longer project.

6   **Book list**   If you refer to several books in your project it is a good idea to list them alphabetically by author at the end. Give the author's name, the title, and the place and date of publication. A book list can also be called a 'bibliography', and this is the word to use if you want to include items which are not books, such as newspaper articles.

Let us now look in more detail at the various stages involved in writing up your work. Here are some examples of student work on the various stages.

Beginnings

These can be difficult. Beginnings should catch the attention and interest of the reader, and take him or her to a point from which the work can grow. Consider the following openings by students in their coursework.

One inch high in the bathroom

One day I was sitting in the bath when a strange feeling came over me and the water suddenly hit me in the face. … I had shrunk!

I certainly had because the bath seemed like a gigantic shiny white mountain, with me drowning in the lake in the middle. I was bobbing up and down swallowing great mouthfuls of soapy water, although of course they can't have been that big when I was only 1 inch high. I was not a very good swimmer, so by the time I reached the plug chain I was quite out of breath.

Now I was faced with another problem: how was I going to climb the plug chain? Because the chain was made of silver balls joined together. I scrambled up the first few balls with some difficulty but the next lot seemed easy. I must have developed a certain 'knack', but I don't think I could do it again.

Examiner's comments

This is a very successful opening because it makes you read on. You want to know whether the plug chain is scaled and what happens next. The writer has sustained the one-inch-high idea well, with comparisons of the mountainous bath and the bathwater lake and the huge silver balls of the plug chain. All this is very compact, taking only two short paragraphs.

Why I intend to stay on at school

The temptation of leaving school to earn some money is very great in my case. Nearly all the friends I have got have left school, and are earning fairly good wages for people who have just left school. My parents give me as much pocket money as I could expect, but I am still restricted in some ways. If I got out to a disco, that soaks up quite a bit of money, and if I need, say, a shirt I have to save up for a couple of weeks to get it. This is a prominent reason in my mind against staying on.

Examiner's comments

The writer here seems to have difficulty starting. The style is repetitious and a bit awkward. One objection to staying on at school is raised and several illustrations given. It is not clear where the argument will lead, as it seems to be marking time.

Our unpredictable weather

Summer is always a time of year when it is the warmest in Britain. The lovely lush meadows with bright coloured flowers covering the fields like a patched quilt. The humid air makes the movement of all life slow as the gleaming sun burns down on you. The delicate winds sway the grass like a swinging pendulum, rippling across the meadows, and the smell of the wonderful vegetation all around acts like a soothing drug, relaxing you completely.

Examiner's comments

The opening of this descriptive piece is promising. There are some well-observed details, 'the delicate winds swayed the grass like a swinging pendulum' as well as some rather well-worn phrases, e.g. 'fields like a patched quilt'. The pace is very slow. It could be argued that this is appropriate, as the writer says the humidity made 'the movement of all life slow'. You wonder, though, if the description will continue like this and become too static and therefore dull.

Development

The stages of **development** in a piece of work depend largely on the type of coursework it is. It is often worthwhile to experiment: the order you first thought of may not necessarily be the best. Let's consider ways of developing material for four different purposes:

- ▶ Planning an argumentative piece
- ▶ Planning a summary
- ▶ Planning a narrative piece
- ▶ Endings

Planning an argumentative piece

When setting out an **argument**, you may intend on the one hand to offer a balanced discussion of an issue, or on the other hand to argue all out for one particular side. You could proceed on the basis of a set of headings, as in the following:

(a) This discussion is about ...
(b) Some people think that .../There is some evidence that ...
(c) But others think .../However evidence can be shown to prove that ...
(d) You yourself may feel that both ...
(e) And I am offering evidence for both/I should like to persuade you that ...

You could use these actual phrases or similar ones at the openings of paragraphs, in a piece of written work. If it were a talk, you could make a set of cards with the phrases written on them to help you keep track of where you were going, and any facts or figures that you thought you might forget – but keep your notes brief. No one speaks effectively with his or her head buried in notes!

Here is an example of a piece of student's work; it is in fact the continuation of 'Why I intend to stay on at school' (p. 77).

Perhaps people would say to me after making this statement 'Why don't you get a Saturday job?' I answer this by giving the reason that Sunday is nearly always taken up by my main hobby Angling, week nights by homework and evenings out, and I like Saturdays to have a long rest in bed, and a leisurely day. But I would sacrifice my Saturdays if making money really made me feel I had to leave school.

Of course, the main reason for staying on is more exam. passes, bringing a better job and more wages. But my main reason is my hoped for career as a chartered surveyor. The chartered surveyor profession demands five years' training. There is a training scheme of five years, and you must have one 'A' level and four G.C.S.E.'s at the least to start it. This is my target if I fail to succeed in my greatest objective. That is the main reason for staying on. If I obtain two 'A' levels, instead of one I can start a different training scheme with a BSc degree as the target which, of course, is much better. The latter scheme only involves three years' training. The other two years I would have to wait until I had completed the five years necessary, could be taken up by a temporary job with an estate agents (which is also counted as training but in fact is not).

In both cases at the end of five years I would obtain membership of the Chartered Surveyors Royal Institute and could get a job as a surveyor almost anywhere.

To obtain my hoped for career, I must stay on, and so I have definitely decided against leaving now.

Examiner's comments

After raising in the opening paragraph the question of whether to leave school, the student goes on to give reasons against that course of action. He deals with what turns out to be a point of lesser importance (more money now), and goes on to give his main reasons for staying on – his hoped-for career in surveying and the steps needed to realize it. The final one-sentence paragraph is all that is needed to demonstrate that a clear decision has been reached. The piece is matter-of-fact, but effectively argued.

Planning a summary

Your starting point for a **summary** will usually be a body of information or a collection of data which you have to re-present succinctly from a particular point of view and for a specified audience. Although there is scope for individuality in a summary, there are always a number of key ideas you need to include, as well as some minor supporting ones. The main thing to do is to reproduce the appropriate part of the material briefly in your own words, without distorting the original. It is well worth experimenting with different ways of organizing the piece until you are satisfied that you have explained all relevant aspects of the topic clearly and effectively.

Try for yourself

Read the passage on the following page, and then follow the instructions. using different material for each part.

Suggestions have been made occasionally that the age of admission to school should be raised to six, and the infant teacher shortage in some parts of the country may soon make such a course of action necessary.

Staff shortages recently compelled one local authority to arrange that children becoming five during a term were accepted for half-time education only. How did the hundred parents involved in this scheme react to the arrangements? A questionnaire was sent to them asking whether they thought that half-time education in the first term for their child had been (a) advantageous; (b) harmful; (c) neither. There was a hundred per cent response and only two parents felt that the arrangement had been harmful. Twenty-one thought that it was not really either advantageous or harmful; the rest said that there were considerable advantages in the arrangement.

Typical of the majority were the following comments from parents: 'I think having to attend just the mornings may have been a contributing factor to her easy acceptance of school. It helped her to get used to a routine and gave her confidence in herself.' 'He has enjoyed school from the start and I think this is because of half-time education at the beginning of his school life.' 'Most children have never been away from their mothers before and it is a very big thing for them. I hope this arrangement will continue so that they get used to returning home after only a few hours at first ....'. 'I believe half-time education is a very good thing for a five year old who has been used to freedom. A long school day is tiring for them when they begin.' The head teachers of the schools at which this scheme was tried out were enthusiastic about it. One of them reported a high rate of attendance for children in the reception class, above average for children in their first term. Another mentioned that the children always appeared bright and lively.

Here is a possible solution to some of the problems that beset education. Staffing would be easier, and part-time teachers could also be used to greater effect: by working with the same group of children half the day only, they could give their pupils the security of one teacher. Most important, there are clear signs that the children would benefit from a more gradual introduction to full-time schooling.

NOW
Write a letter from the head teacher of one school adopting this system to the parents of the children concerned, stating the decision that has been taken and reasons for it, and saying that they will be invited to respond to a questionnaire on the matter after the end of term. The letter (excluding address, etc.) should not contain more than 85 words, should be in an appropriate style and should begin and end as follows:

```
                                   Church Street Infants' School,
                                   Wolchester
                                   Bucks.
                                   6 June 19--

Dear Parents,




                                   Yours sincerely,

                                   H. A. Smith (Head teacher)
```

ALSO
The head teacher reported to the Parents' Association on the results of the questionnaire. Write two paragraphs from the report stating (a) the advantages that parents found in the scheme and (b) the advantages that the head teacher found. Your report should not contain more than 100 words.

Here is a student's attempt at this piece of work.

> *Church Street Infants' School*
> *Wolchester*
> *Bucks.*
>
> *6 June 19—*
>
> *Dear Parents,*
>   *This coming term we are starting mornings only schooling for our rising fives and this will affect your child.*
>   *As you may know we are still suffering staff shortages and this arrangement will enable your child to have the security of the same teacher throughout the term. We feel also that it will be beneficial for your child to be introduced gradually to school life. After this term normal schooling will continue and we will invite your response through a questionnaire.*
>   *Yours sincerely,*

Extract from head teacher's report:

> *As many as 77% of the parents said that the scheme had been beneficial, with a further 21% expressing neither approval nor disapproval. Only 2% were against. A typical comment from parents pointed out that their child had more confidence, got less tired and enjoyed school more. The majority of parents, then, approved of the scheme.*
>   *I, myself, in company with the staff, also found it worked well: the children involved seemed always bright and lively and we had a higher attendance rate than is normal in the Reception Class, though there may be difficulties next term when the children face full time school attendance.*

Examiner's comments

In the *letter*, notice that the student has started with the head's main point, then given detailed reasons for it, whereas in the *report* the opposite approach has been taken: the head teacher first gives the findings of the questionnaire, then the general judgement: 'The majority of parents, then, approved of the scheme.' He goes on to offer a *balanced* view of the scheme, from the point of view of himself and the school staff. The summary is slightly over the required word-limit, but the main points have been included without confusion or changing the emphasis of the original information. The style of the piece is formal, it is appropriately paragraphed and accurately expressed.

Planning a narrative piece

Narrative, by definition, follows chronological order, because that is the way our everyday experience happens to us. Think of how you tell your family what sort of day you had. You do not give every detail, but unless you tell it in an orderly sequence no one will be able to follow.

The same applies to the narrative parts of the stories you write, but a story does not have to begin at the beginning and work through to the end. It may be more effective to vary the time sequence. Consider the following possibilities:

▷ Flashback – interrupting the main narrative to go back to significant earlier incidents.
▷ Prediction – looking forward to future happenings.
▷ Two sides of the truth – describing the same events from the point of view of two different characters.
▷ Repeated sequence – ending as you began, sometimes with a slight variation, to stress some aspect of the story.

Here is the continuation of 'One inch high in the bathroom' (p. 77). It is an example of simple narrative, although, of course, a very imaginative piece.

> *Once at the top of the bath mountain I looked down at the soapy water which seemed miles away. It made me feel quite dizzy so I decided to have a rest on the sponge. But this was very difficult as it was three times my height. I eventually got up there but just as I looked up, I nearly fell off again when I saw a great yellow, hard thing peering down at me. It was the duck scrubbing brush. It must have been, but it seemed to have white trees for legs. I scrambled up the trees onto the duck's back with difficulty when it fell down into the bath, with an almighty thundering splash!*

(continued)

> *I climbed slowly up the chain again and sat down to think. 'What if I would always be like this from now on? What had made me so small? Was it something I ate? Let me see, what did I have for dinner – ham and salad. No! I'd eaten that hundreds of times. But what about that new paté Mum had bought? Yes – that must be it.'*
>
> *I was really very worried, on the verge of tears. So would you have been if you had been in my place at that moment. I got up, consoling myself by saying, 'I expect it is just a dream'.*
> *But it wasn't …*

Here is an example of a piece where the time order is more complex.

> *The child screamed on, face contorted and scarlet under its sun-hat, in the blazing heat.*
> *'She's frightened. She's frightened of the water'. Around her the golden ocean of sand shimmered and heaved, treacherous, while eager hands tried to tug her from her haven and force her to place one foot on the uncertain ground …*
> *'Lynn!' her mother hissed. 'You're next. Go on up.' The heat in the concert hall smothered her, like a hand over the mouth.*
> *She was frightened, so frightened. Before her the golden linoleum-covered steps to the rostrum shone and heaved as she sat, unable to move a foot.*

This is a convenient point to mention the distinction between **literal writing**, where the words have their usual meaning, and **figurative writing**, where imagery and poetic devices are used. Here is the continuation of 'Our unpredictable weather' (p. 77).

> *Time passes quickly as you are taken aback by the sheer effect of great outstanding beauty, like turning on a light in a dark sinister room and suddenly seeing the true room, with an elegant picture of a loving relative mounted proudly on the wall, and a vase of golden daffodils on a table beneath. The time had edged on and the light was being dimmed. The warmth around me had gone and the wind started to pick up. The sky above had turned a lighter grey and herds of bulging blackened clouds were moving in above.*
> *Suddenly, the sky was darkened as clouds closed over the sun. The warmth and brightness had gone and the dull coldness had come. It was as if it was the turn of the dark evil to have his say. The clouds in the sky were gathering rapidly, bunching up, filling any holes of light. The black army of clouds seemed to march slowly across the sky, looking down, with the chance to let out and attack. The light was poor and the valley had gone dark. Only silhouettes of buildings could be seen with darkened trees, as though life had been taken from them …*

Examiner's comments
The first extract uses a simple narrative technique and does so rather amusingly. The second begins with a vivid flashback to the writer's childhood, and the third uses careful detail as part of the description, but also uses figurative expression, developing very well the idea of darkness and evil in the scene. This adds a dramatic element and prevents the rather monotonous developments we might have predicted from the opening.

> *Try for yourself*
>
> Choose a theme for a narrative and write it in two different ways, using a literal approach on the one hand, and a more figurative approach on the other. See which you prefer.

Endings
Endings can be as problematic as beginnings! Sometimes students exhaust their invention before the end, and, feeling that they must conclude in some way or another, repeat in a sentence what they have explained much more fully already. This is a fault common in argument and summary. Try to keep for the conclusion an idea that you haven't used before, preferably one that makes a comment on the whole issue.

Let us look at the endings of the three pieces mentioned above.

Ending to 'One inch high in the bathroom'   The writer did not take an easy way out. Her story ended as follows:

> *'I expect it is just a dream'. But it wasn't …*
>
> *I hauled myself over the edge of the jar and fell 'splish!' into some cold cream. It was awful. Never in my life have I experienced such a messy incident. As I scrambled to the edge of the bowl and fell headlong into the bath again I felt strange. I couldn't see my legs. It had been VANISHING CREAM! But dimly a blurred outline returned and … yes … it was a BIG outline. I was actually NORMAL again.*
>
> *At that moment my elder sister came in and told me off for using her cream. She said I was a stupid girl when I told her what had happened but then I don't expect anyone will believe me, do you?*

This keeps the mystery going right up to the end and leaves it unresolved. The reader is invited to participate by the final question, and the ending is left open.

Ending to 'Why I intend to stay on at school':

> *To obtain my hoped for career, I must stay on, and so I have definitely decided against leaving now.*

This conclusion is short and to the point. It tells you for the first time that a firm decision has been made.

When writing narrative, the thing to avoid is developing the plot to a point where you see no way out. An ending like 'Then I heard Mum's foot on the stairs and she called "When are you going to get up to go to school?" I realized it had only been a dream!' will irritate most readers and leave them feeling let down. Before you start, think how you can resolve your story in a satisfying way.

Ending to 'Our unpredictable weather'   Concluding descriptive writing can be just as difficult. Sometimes writers just stop, and finish with a short personal comment, e.g. 'Dusk was coming on and we wearily made our way home.'

The writer of this extract does adopt this approach, but with a difference:

> *At last I trudged home, wet as a drowned rat and in an awful mood. Opening the soaked wooden gate I saw that all the flowers had dropped in the storm and there was a stream of water running down the path. As I stood on the grass my foot became embedded in the ground; the earth was water-logged and my foot was submerging.*
>
> *Once indoors I changed my saturated clothes and sat by my bedroom window, looking out at the dark silhouette of the hills against the grey storm clouds. I was warming up now and in a dry place at last, out of the soaking wet.*
>
> *The storm had ruined a lovely day and I was beginning to wonder whether it was summer after all.*

▷ Preliminary drafts and final version

So far we have looked at the various stages of beginning, developing and ending a piece of coursework. Here we look at the progression from a first, preliminary draft to a final version of your coursework project.

Preliminary drafts

'Try drafting'

When you have gathered your ideas, collected your information, brainstormed and/or tried a flow chart or topic tree, you'll be ready to write fluently. Sometimes it is necessary to ask students to complete a piece of written work 'straight off' in class or for homework, but this is rather uncommon. Recent thinking about the writing process suggests that good writing usually evolves through one or more stages. If you are writing in rough, letting your ideas flow freely, you can go back and improve the arrangement of working and check spelling and punctuation. You may be using a word-processor, and all this can then be done quickly and easily. When you have written a draft, try to set it aside for a few days, and then read it critically, as editor rather than as author. If you are able to consult your friends, teacher or tutor, this should be done while the work is still at the draft stage. You can then incorporate suggestions from others. Once the work is finished and assessed, though, you must not alter it. You may include drafts of work with the final version in your coursework folder.

Here is the beginning of a pupil's first draft of a story:

> *Mandy had just received her exam. results and after reading them she was disappointed that she had failed all of them. She was not so bright, but her school record was good and she always worked hard. Just before the exams. she was under pressure and she had problems which made her fail her exams. Now Mandy had to return to school and redo her exams. in six subjects which would be taken in January.*
>
> *First day of term in the Lower Sixth Mandy went to see the Head Mistress who was disappointed that she had not even got one pass. She encouraged her to work harder and concentrate very hard. Unfortunately, Mandy did not take one word in, it just came out the other ear. She was not interested in studying and just felt like relaxing.*

Compare the final version

> *It was the first day of term in the Lower Sixth year. Mandy hardly had time to say hello to her friends and talk about the holidays before she had an appointment with Miss Temple the headmistress, that she didn't look forward to at all.*
>
> *In the holidays, she had received her examination results and had been disappointed to find that she had failed all the exams. She did not think of herself as very clever, but her school record had always been good and she had always worked hard. What more could she have done? Just before the exams., too, she had been under pressure with personal problems and that had not helped. She felt really discouraged.*
>
> *She tapped on Miss Temple's door and in response to a quiet 'The door is open' walked in. Miss Temple began talking in an encouraging way: 'Work harder ... make up your mind ... try to concentrate hard ... put that behind you ...' It was what she had expected but she found that she was not listening; she was distracted by two girls laughing outside the window. No, she was no longer interested in studying; she just felt like relaxing.*

Examiner's comment

As you can see, the content within the paragraphs has been rearranged, and extra detail has been added to bring the scene in the head mistress's office to life, and we are given Mandy's thoughts directly. The time sequence moves from the present to the past, and back. Some errors have been edited out. Altogether, this is a more interesting and more accurate opening.

When you are checking your own work, underline words whose spelling you are unsure about and use a dictionary. A rough guide to punctuation is to read through what you have written aloud. Punctuation should help to pace the work: a full stop for a long pause, commas or semi-colons for shorter pauses. Your teacher or tutor should help you with other forms of punctuation. Paragraphing should be logical and follow the development of the piece. There is no rule which says you must start a new paragraph every ten lines or so!

The final version

You will want your **final version** to be as accurate and readable as possible, so bear the following points in mind:

- ▶ The work should be written clearly, or typed where this is allowed.
- ▶ It should be dated and have a title.
- ▶ It may be easier to follow if it is divided into sections with subheadings.
- ▶ Illustrations and diagrams should be clear and neat.
- ▶ Titles of books should be underlined.
- ▶ Quotations should be displayed or in inverted commas, with the source given at the end.
- ▶ If a list of references or books used is included, it should be complete, accurate and in alphabetical order according to authors' names.

These rules are mostly easy to understand, but something extra might be said about **quotations**.

Long quotations should be *displayed*, that is, *set apart from* your own text.

Simon seems to be different from the other boys, on a more spiritual plane. He likes to go off to the jungle by himself to reflect:

> Simon dropped the screen of leaves back into place. The slope of the bars of honey-coloured sunlight decreased; they slipped up the bushes, passed over the pale candle-like buds, moved up towards the canopy and darkness thickened under the trees. Within the failing of the light the riotous colours died and the heat and urgency faded away. The candle-buds stirred – their green sepals drew back a little and the white tips of the flowers rose delicately to meet the open air.
>
> (William Golding, *Lord of the Flies*, p. 155).

Short quotations may be incorporated in your own sentences in *inverted commas*, the source being then put in brackets. For example:

> The set of rules established is challenged by Jack in his bid to become leader:' "The rules!" shouted Ralph, "You're forgetting the rules." ' (*Lord of the Flies*, p. 87).

When quoting poetry, you should reproduce the line arrangement exactly as it is in the original:

> Button to chin
> Till May be in;
> Cast not a clout
> Till May be out
>   (*Traditional*)

USEFUL PRACTICAL APPROACHES

There are several skills, referred to in the earlier sections of this chapter, that will be explained here. Their use should help to make the task of researching, planning and writing a piece of topic work quicker and easier.

▷ **Reading for research**

The first skill is **reading for research**. You can read in different ways for different purposes, and some ways are quicker than others:

1. **Skimming**: a quick look through a book to get a general impression and decide whether it is likely to be useful. The title page, contents, blurb, pictures or diagrams, and a few pages might be looked at.
2. **Scanning**: a quick look along certain sections of the text to find particular details or blocks of information, e.g. to find all the names of seventeenth-century actors.
3. **Intensive reading**: a slower, sometimes a word-for-word read, where you concentrate on the meaning of the text, and perhaps pause to question or think about it.
4. **Reflective reading**: a reading where you respond fully in thought and feeling to the general content.

'How to size up a book.'

If you are about to use a book for the first time, you should not plunge straight into the middle of it, but do a little preliminary 'sizing up'. The blurb should not be trusted. The date of publication should always be noticed. (Is the book out of date? When was it last revised?) How is the author described on the title page and cover? How well known is the publisher? An author's preface should never be entirely ignored: it will tell you something about the book, and often something about the author, too. How detailed is the index? Does the bibliography contain some books you didn't know about?

One special area of reading is worth mentioning separately: interpreting tables or charts, and, in general, statistics. Here you are given facts and have to interpret them yourself, remembering to take into account all the factors which are relevant. For example, in a report on children's reading, the statistic was given that 40 per cent of boys aged fourteen-plus said that they did not read books for pleasure. This caused alarmist headlines to some reviews. Yet the next table given stressed that nearly 50 per cent of the same group said that they read between one and three comics and periodicals a week. It is a matter of interpretation what difference you feel the second table makes to your views of boys' reading. Is it less valuable to read periodicals or comics than to read books? Are books read in school for study purposes never pleasurable? You should question what you read, not just take it on trust, and preferably modify your ideas in the light of each new piece of information.

▷ **Making useful notes**

The second important technique is **making useful notes**. Making notes is an individual matter, but some general advice can be offered:

1 **Be orderly**: don't get your notes in a muddle.
2 **Be brief**: there is no point in rewriting the information in your own words (paraphrase): this is time-consuming, and liable to lead to error. It is better to quote anything important exactly, and note lesser matters by a phrase or two.
3 **Be flexible**: you may find it convenient to add something to a note later, e.g. a further fact, a cross-reference or a comment. If this is likely to be so, leave plenty of space for additions.

'Be orderly! Be brief! Be flexible!'

Making notes from films, television or radio is less easy. If you are trying to write you may be distracted from what is being shown, or from following the finer points of argument. It is better to involve yourself in the experience first, and write up your impressions immediately afterwards. Alternatively, jot down quick points as the programme proceeds, and go over them, expanding and correcting them as soon as you can afterwards, preferably in consultation with someone else who has also been listening or viewing. They will almost certainly have noticed things you haven't.

▷ **Planning a questionnaire**

The third technique is **planning a questionnaire**. A questionnaire can be a useful means of gathering information from a group of people. Questionnaires take time and care to construct, so before writing one it may be worth asking yourself whether there is a better way of getting the information you want. An ideal questionnaire has to give you information that is clear and correct, in a form you can use, and, to assist the people filling it in, there should be no questions that will cause them to hesitate and wonder what is meant. Also, you should avoid loaded questions, which show bias, e.g. 'Do you honestly prefer school lunches to sandwiches?', and long, complicated questions, e.g. 'Would you prefer a two-course hot meal to sandwiches or a bag of crisps and an apple for lunch?' Don't try the patience and goodwill of those you hope to answer your questionnaire by making it extremely long.
Here are a few basic ideas to bear in mind when drawing up a questionnaire:

(a) Keep the questionnaire short.
(b) Keep the questions short.
(c) Make the wording of instructions simple.
(d) Make questions specific, not vague.
(e) Make sure that the meaning of each question is clear (not ambiguous).
(f) Place the questions in the best order.

▷ **Conducting an interview**

A fourth technique concerns **conducting an interview** with somebody. There are three stages to consider.

Before the interview

Ask permission of the person or persons concerned well ahead. Let them suggest a convenient time. Give them some idea of what you are trying to find out, so that they will have time to think about it. Plan a list of basic questions that you really want to ask and make them as specific as possible.

During the interview

'Improving your interviewing technique'

Take a partner who can jot down notes, leaving you free to ask questions and devote your attention to the person being interviewed. You can also both discuss what happened, later. If you want to make a tape recording of the interview, ask permission first, and remember that it may make the person you are talking to self-conscious and less spontaneous. Make sure that any electrical equipment you use is in working order! Take your prepared questions with you and start with them. You will probably get a good deal of extra information, too, so try to keep a balance between what you want to learn and what the interviewee wants to tell you. Thank the person concerned and offer to let him or her see a copy of your project when it is finished.

After the interview

Discuss what took place with your partner. Write it up while it is still fresh in your memory. If you have made a recording, transcribe the parts of it that you think you definitely want to use. Acknowledge the help of the interviewee in your project, and send a brief letter of thanks.

Suppose you were interviewing a very old lady about what she remembers of your locality from her childhood. You may have a list of basic questions, something like the following: 'Where were you born?', 'What was the local school like, when you went there?', 'Who lived in the old cottages in Mill Lane?', 'What do you remember about the tradespeople here?', 'What sort of things did you do in your spare time, before there was television?', 'What jobs were there for boys and girls, when they left school?' Almost certainly, you would get a great deal of fascinating information in answer to these few questions if you were friendly, tactful and patient.

► SUGGESTIONS FOR COURSEWORK

Topic work will obviously vary enormously. However, all Examining Boards require some evidence of non-literary as well as literary study. Some specify that one whole work of literature should be studied. (Work that results from reading literary texts will be considered fully in Chapter 11.) Most Boards ask that some work should be in an 'open' situation, i.e. where the form, readership and purpose of the writing are chosen by the candidates, expecting that some of this will lead to several kinds of informative writing – reporting, persuading and expressing opinions.

This gives an opportunity to include topic work.

Here is a selection of suitable topics:

1 Write a pamphlet informing members of your class of the dangers of taking drugs.
2 Plan the curriculum of your ideal school.
3 Trace your family tree and tell something of the history of your ancestors.
4 Compare transport in your area as it must have been in the late nineteenth century to how it is today.
5 Discuss the difference between job prospects now and in your parents' youth.
6 What is good and what is not-so-good about commercial television?
7 Find out what kind of Youth Club teenagers in your area would prefer, and plan a suitable scheme to provide one.
8 Investigate the history of some well-known building or landmark in your locality.
9 Plan a field trip to investigate the environment in a part of the country that you know well.
10 Investigate a conservation project in your area.

Before reading further you should choose one or two of the topics above and spend a short while outlining your own plan for an answer, in each case. Most of the topics offer scope for quite small-scale pieces of writing, as well as extended and researched pieces of work.

▷ **Coursework task 1**   *Write a pamphlet informing members of your class of the dangers of taking drugs.*

Student's answer

Drugs

Here are some facts about drugs that you should know. Drugs are various things; some of their names are cocaine, heroin, cannabis, crack, speed and ecstasy, and there's others as well. Some times doctors prescribe drugs when you're not well, but these drugs are medicines which make you well again.

Once you take drugs you can get addicted to them. You would do anything just to get drugs; you would do things which you wouldn't have even dreamed about like leave your family, steal, or even kill a person.

People who drink tea or coffee can also be addicted to it (tea/coffee). Although drugs like cocaine, heroin and cannabis are illegal, people smuggle them into countries for greed, because for a small amount of drug, you get a high price.

People that take drugs are usually in the age group of about thirteen to forty-five. They take drugs if they are depressed or under pressure. This could be because they are unemployed, they have no security, family, etc. …

At first you think you'll just have a taste to be like some of your friends, but that taste leads you to become a drug addict. You think you can control yourself but gradually it takes over your life. Drugs cost you your health and looks. Remember in the end the drug is the one that gains by killing YOU!

Tutor's comments

This piece of writing is informative and persuasive. The information given is helpful and correct, though limited in range. The work is clearly paragraphed, though there might be better ways of arranging some of the ideas, e.g. the warning about addiction in the second paragraph is weakened by the renewed information about non-addictive drugs in the third. This serves to distract the reader. The writer wavers between a detached approach ('People that take drugs …') and a direct form of address ('Once you take drugs you can get addicted to them'). The latter is by far the more effective style in this persuasive piece, as the writer realizes. The final paragraph is written exclusively in this 'button-holing' style and works well. She finishes particularly strongly: 'Drugs cost you your health and looks. Remember in the end the drug is the one that gains by killing YOU!' Expression is not perfect, but one is left with a memorable warning, forcefully emphasized by the use of capitals for 'YOU', and the final exclamation mark.

Tutor's answer

Drugs – The dangers!!

I want to tell you about drugs – the facts and the dangers.

First, here are some facts you should know. There is a wide variety of substances grouped under the term 'drugs'. Some are prescribed by doctors; when you react well to these they are relatively harmless. They are medicines to make you better. Some you take every day yourself for enjoyment or refreshment, like tea or coffee. Did you know that even these drinks are stimulants and, in excess, can lead to addiction? Some drugs, though, are definitely harmful.

Here are the names of some of the harmful drugs: crack, speed, ecstasy, cannabis, cocaine and heroin. These are all addictive, though heroin is the most destructive. Once you take these drugs you will quickly become dependent on them. You will do anything to get them, even things which you would not have thought possible a year ago. Some addicts, for example, leave their families, steal or go so far as to kill to get drugs.

Of course it should not be easy to get these destructive drugs. They are illegal. People smuggle them into Western countries for greed, because they know that for a very small quantity of cocaine or heroin, they can get a high price. They do not think about the higher price paid by their victims: indignity, pain, suffering, perhaps a life of crime, even death.

If you take these drugs you are likely to belong to a particular age-group; from as young as thirteen to about forty-five. You will turn to drugs if you are depressed, or under some kind of pressure. This could be because you are unemployed, or have no family, no security.

At first, you may think you will just have a taste, to be like some of your friends. That taste can lead you to drug addiction. You may think it won't happen to you. You may believe you can control yourself, but gradually drugs will take over your life. Drugs can cost you your looks, your health, your job and your family. Remember, in the end, you can be the loser. Drug addiction can win by killing you.

▷ **Coursework task 2**

Plan the curriculum of your ideal school

This might be partly based on what you already know – your own school curriculum, partly on research done from finding out about other schools' curricula, and probably quite a lot on what you imagine would be ideal. There has been much discussion about the National Curriculum. One starting point could be to sketch out a timetable. Think about getting a balanced curriculum, first, in terms of how you as a pupil would experience it; second, of meeting the basic educational requirements of every pupil; and third, in terms of offering variety and interesting options. Your true 'ideal' curriculum may well have to be restricted because of a realistic appraisal of necessary and obtainable resources: staffing; finance for books, laboratories, cookery, craft or sports facilities; art equipment, etc. After sketching out your ideas, discuss the differences between what you would really like and what seems possible.

▷ **Student's answer**

The school I'd want to go to would probably be freaky and not boring. I'd want it to be big with about three halls and three activities blocks. As I like doing athletics a lot, I'd like there to be teams and competitions every month. And mainly sports like swimming, football, American (not rugby), baseball – mostly boys' games and far less of netball as I'm quite boyish. Red, black and yellow is the colour of the uniform I'd like, because it would mix well, better than the dull colours, green, brown, etc. There would be five lessons a day because school will start 9 o'clock and finish 5.30 p.m.

My timetable would look like this.

Monday	Maths	Music	3 lessons of P.E.		
Tuesday	Maths	English	Fashion Design		Typing
Wednesday	Computers		W. Processing	Maths	English
Thursday	3 lessons of P.E.			Swimming	Computers
Friday	Music	Computers	Maths	English	Fashion Design

That would be my ideal picture of a timetable. The teachers would be average age, around 25 to 35. Mostly men because they're more strict. Punishment mustn't be from jumping off Waterloo Bridge to standing on the rails in Waterloo Station.

Tutor's comments

This piece of work shows the pupil's clear sense of priorities; she likes sports, so there would be plenty of time devoted to them on the timetable. She is also realistic about the need for a balanced curriculum: the basics, Mathematics and English, are there, as well as practical skills, such as Typing and Computing. Another aspect of balance is the provision of time for the Arts: Music and Fashion Design are represented. The sample timetable is clearly drawn up. Given that the pupil has thought out her ideal school curriculum quite well, it is a pity that she didn't enter more fully into a discussion of its advantages and disadvantages. The day seems to be very long, for example, but we are given no reasons for this. Would there be no homework in the evenings to compensate, perhaps?

Organization of the piece could have been better: details of the timetable are mixed in with more personal references – the colour of the uniform, for example. The paragraphs are short, but then this is a small-scale piece of writing.

There are some attractive examples of individuality, e.g. the humour 'Punishment mustn't be from jumping off Waterloo Bridge to standing on the rails in Waterloo Station'! The confession that the writer is 'quite boyish', and would prefer a 'freaky' school, is individual and appealing. These touches enhance the writing considerably. On the whole, the tone and style are appropriate – fairly formal, but also with a strong individual point of view. There are some errors, e.g. starting a sentence with a conjunction 'And mainly ...', instead of joining it to the last sentence; finishing a sentence lazily with 'etc.' However these errors do not seriously impede communication. The piece, though lively, is rather short and underdeveloped.

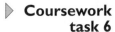

Coursework task 3

Outline answer

Trace your family tree and tell something of the history of your ancestors.

The obvious starting point is what you know: a sketch of your family tree, as far as you can fill in the details. Next, what you need to know and could try to find out would be apparent from the gaps in what you had drawn. The first source of information would be older relatives, then family records. If you were very lucky there might be a Family Bible, with names written inside the covers. There could well be old documents – birth, marriage and death certificates, old letters, and so on. At the very least there should be photographs. If your family had lived in the same area for many years, you could ask at your parish church, or at the Public Records Office, where records going back to the nineteenth century are kept. Once you had gathered your material, you could follow some of the sorting, planning and writing up methods suggested in this chapter.

Coursework task 4

Outline answer

Compare transport in your area as it must have been in the late nineteenth century to how it is today.

A starting point here is what information you can gather about modern-day transport. You could make two lists – Public Transport and Private Transport – then gather facts about local trains and buses, also the availability of cabs, and estimate the number of private cars per head in your road. A similar parallel list for the nineteenth century would look very different. In the first would be horse-drawn buses, main line trains and, if you lived in London, the beginnings of the Underground (the Metropolitan line was begun in the nineteenth century, for instance). There may be a Museum of Transport in your area and the local newspaper, if it were founded early enough, may have information and pictures of older forms of transport.

Organizing your piece of writing would provide opportunities to bring out the great changes within less than a hundred years by contrasting sections or paragraphs.

Coursework task 5

Outline answer

Discuss the difference between job prospects now and in your parents' youth.

Adults at home could provide you with what you need to know about earlier job prospects for school-leavers, and the current scene is one you probably know well. With this topic there would be a need for careful evaluation: it would be easy to overstate your case or become personally involved in a way that might distort the facts.

Coursework task 6

Outline answer

What is good and what is not-so-good about commercial television?

This question clearly asks for your opinions, so that you would be free to air your own likes and dislikes about commercial television, or even to support one side of the proposition heavily. You should allow some time, though, for considering the other side, since both are represented in the question. Two lists would be a likely starting point: the 'Good' and the 'Not-so-good' aspects. You would need to consider how wide your discussion should range: should it concentrate on programmes or the commercials themselves? What about other forms of commercial television, e.g. cable TV? These choices would need to be made early on in your planning.

Quite a lot of what you would need could come from your own viewing and past experience, as well as from the opinions of friends and family. There are also books and articles available about audience figures, and so on, that could be researched for a larger scale project.

▷ **Coursework task 7**

Outline answer

Find out what kind of Youth Club teenagers in your area would prefer, and plan a suitable scheme to provide one.

This topic would need some consumer research from the start. You would have to draw up a questionnaire, or interview as many teenagers as you could to canvas opinion and preferences. If your scheme is to be realistic you would also need to consider your area very carefully, e.g. what about location – is there a place that could be acquired for premises? What about the authorities? Could the local church or the local council help? There are some important large issues to sort out before you begin with any detailed consideration of the clubhouse furnishings! Altogether, though, this could be a worthwhile and quite extensive piece of work.

▷ **Coursework task 8**

Outline answer

Investigate the history of some well-known building or landmark in your locality.

The advantage of this topic is that you could begin with some definite source material. Any landmark or well-known building is likely to have been recorded either in local history books or a town guide. It may have its own visitors' information sheet. There will be old photographs and you can take your own. There may be a guide or local person who could tell you a great deal about the monument or landmark. One danger here could be that there was so much information, so well written down that, in making notes, without meaning to do so, you could lose your own style and copy someone else's – even copy part of the texts themselves. Guard against this. Always make notes in your own words: you may miss some details, but they have the advantage of providing a fresh and individual view.

▷ **Coursework task 9**

Outline answer

Plan a field trip to investigate the environment in a part of the country that you know well.

A field trip involving even one person requires a good deal of careful planning, and much of it would depend on the location chosen. An advantage of writing on a place that you know – perhaps that you have visited with the school – is that you would have accurate details to rely on. This topic lends itself to being planned in sections: *Before the Trip* – deciding the route, means of transport, what to take, and so on; then *During the Trip* – observations to make, unexpected happenings, timing the visit, arrangements on site, and so on; and finally *After the Trip* – return journey, records to make, etc.

▷ **Coursework task 10**

Outline answer

Investigate a conservation project in your area.

If you choose this topic it is likely that you will be interested in conservation and possibly involved in a project already. The range of possible projects is vast as each has its own concerns and problems. There are many organizations, including enthusiastic local groups, to supply information. One strength of this topic is the opportunity it gives both for detailed recording of what is to be preserved as well as for showing an individual or group enthusiasm for the importance of saving what we have from the past.

▷ A STEP FURTHER

Get into the habit of reading critically other people's attempts to convey information. Collect a selection of pamphlets on a topic in which you are interested, or cuttings from newspapers. You will notice that they tend to obey certain rules. For example:

1   **Material is set out clearly.** There are headings, side-headings, wide spacing, paragraphs of varied lengths, and so on. Compare articles from two newspapers on a topic of current interest and see how the layout differs and what this tells you about the readers the papers expect to be addressing.
2   **Information is carefully staged and sequenced.** Try rearranging your own ideas when draft writing, to see which is the best order.
3   **Clarity of expression is important.** Try to say exactly what you mean.
4   **Conciseness can be important.** Many forms of communication to inform are very much to the point – they don't waste words.

You should be able to learn from how others go about instructing and informing. Remember, though, that your own way of presenting ideas is distinctive, and can add interest and quality to your communication as long as you do not distort the facts.

SUMMARY

▷   You should know how to choose a topic wisely and select and shape your first ideas by brainstorming and group discussion.

▷   You should be aware of the differences between talking and writing.

▷   You should know how to use source materials for research, both book and non-book sources such as questionnaires and interviewing, as well as reading, evaluating argument and making useful notes.

▷   There was advice on how to plan your time and how to work to a routine.

▷   There was information on writing up research, taking special care with openings, developments and conclusions, and with presentation and scholarly aspects such as including contents, headings, and book lists.

▷   You will have discovered how to put forward convincing arguments, to write summary and narrative.

9 Case study: preparing an assignment

> **GETTING STARTED**

The great advantage that you have when submitting coursework, instead of doing written papers, is *time*. No piece of work in your folder needs to have been written against the clock, except perhaps occasionally when you are working in supervised conditions. In GCSE oral work, too, you will normally be allowed plenty of time to prepare work which will be assessed.

Having more time has a number of advantages.

In **written work**, you can

▶ note down first thoughts
▶ think about and order first thoughts
▶ obtain any information and supporting material needed
▶ write a draft
▶ develop the draft
▶ edit and correct the draft
▶ decide on the type of presentation required
▶ make a final fair copy.

In **oral work**, you can

▶ decide on a subject to talk about
▶ obtain background information to help sustain a discussion subsequently
▶ prepare any necessary aids
▶ practise talking (but there are dangers here)
▶ take part in the final talk
▶ perhaps record it.

One difference between preparing written and oral work is that it is difficult to spend too much time improving the first, whereas over-preparation may damage the second – but this will be considered more fully below. It is assumed throughout the chapter that you will have researched anything you are working on, if that is necessary, *before* reaching the stage of presenting it finally to an audience, whether readers or listeners. How to go about this *research* is discussed fully in Chapter 8.

TOPIC	STUDY	REVISION 1	REVISION 2
Noting down first thoughts			
Ordering first thoughts			
Writing a draft			
Improving the draft			
Editing and correcting the draft			
Deciding on the type of presentation required			
Making the final fair copy			

> ## WHAT YOU NEED TO KNOW

Whatever kind of writing you are attempting, whether it is setting out arguments of your own, summarizing other people's ideas, communicating to others your response to something you have read, or inventing a story or poem, the way you approach it will depend very much on your own personality. Your individuality will show particularly strongly in your **first thoughts** about what you are attempting; however different the finished piece may be from where you started, you should try not to lose the freshness and vitality of the beginning. But liveliness of mind and good ideas are no excuse for careless or half-thought-through pieces of work, so the various **stages of preparation** are necessary, and well worth the effort, because you will want your work to be the best you are able to create and communicate.

> ## Noting down first thoughts

Of course, it is very convenient if your good ideas for coursework come to you when sitting, pen in hand, in front of a clean sheet of paper, but usually this does not happen. It is more likely that your ideas will come to you from the stimulus of talking among friends, or with a teacher or tutor; they may even come when you are on a bus. But whatever the circumstances, try not to lose these ideas. Hold them in your mind and think around them, so that they develop greater cohesion, until you can discuss them with someone or start straight away on a draft.

You may, though, prefer to keep a notebook and to jot down ideas. Many authors have done this: John Milton, the poet, wrote out a long inventory of the titles of poems he intended to compose, and I myself once, in a rare bout of creativity, took up a pen and wrote down 56 titles of novels I hoped to write – when I had some spare time; but I haven't actually started on any of them yet!

Let us take a particular example of the way a piece of writing might evolve. Turning over the pages of a daily newspaper, you read the following:

SEARCH FOR LONG-LOST LOVE

Mr Wilfred Reynolds, a seventy-two-year-old retired manufacturer, is hot on the trail of his war-time sweetheart, a former nurse called Angela Carter. Angela, he says, was beautiful, with a pale oval face, blue eyes, and a mass of golden hair, and she was as good as she was lovely. Mr Reynolds has placed advertisements in all the national newspapers in order to find her, and intends to leave her a fortune in his will.

It stays in your mind. Intriguing, isn't it? It poses so many questions. Why has Mr Reynolds waited for over forty years before looking for Angela? Will she still be beautiful and good? What has her life been like since they parted? If he finds her, how will she react to his reappearance? You revolve these ideas in your head for a while, and then forget Mr Reynolds and his problem.

Shortly afterwards, in school or college, you are asked to write a short story. Then you have a good idea: why not a story about Mr Reynolds and Angela, his long-lost love? You pick up a pen and write Lost Love. Then you underline it: <u>Lost Love</u>. You have your title. And it's a good one: it gives some clue to the story that will follow, but it doesn't give much away. Will it be a happy or a sad story? Will the love lost be found or not? You begin to get enthusiastic, and search through your memory for what you can recall of the article, still with pen in hand. You jot down:

> Mr. William (?) Reynolds
> Angela – fair, with blue eyes
> The War
> Newspapers
> Wants to leave her all his money.

It was only half a minute's work, but your short story has begun.

▶ **Ordering first thoughts**

For many people this is often the most important stage in the process of composition, because it is here that the communication takes its essential shape. However much you develop the piece of work later, the first way of seeing it rarely becomes entirely lost. In our example above you were given the form, a **short story**, but if that had not been so you might now be thinking of a poem, a play – or even a piece of investigative journalism, where you pose as a reporter researching the case. The original stimulus, the newspaper article, offered several possibilities. But you have no problem in this case, as you have been asked to develop your first thoughts, as you jotted them down, into a short story.

You find your piece of paper and look again at what you wrote, then you make one or two changes:

Lost Love
Mr. Wilfred Wright
Angela – fair, with blue eyes
Wartime romance
Wants to leave all his money to her
Newspapers – advertises in

You can't remember whether the man's name was William or Wilfred; you decide it was Wilfred. Oh, but if he is a real person you probably should change the name. What about Mr Wilfred Right, as Angela's 'Mr Right'? You decide this is too obvious, so change it to Mr Wilfred Wright. You like this, because it is a punning reference to your hero's idea of himself and it patterns nicely. You leave the details about the girl – they fit many people and seem appropriate. Of course, it was a wartime romance, and he advertised in the newspapers. You put your pen down and pause. This seems good, so far. But it is not a story outline. You need time to think about what shape this story will take. You take up your pen again and strike through the first thoughts, writing what follows instead:

Lost Love
Para. 1. Mr Wright remembers the past, as he composes his advertisement.
Para. 2. A few days later, Angela reads the advertisement – her reactions.
Para. 3. Mr Wright collects his mail from the Post Office.
Para. 4. The meeting.
Para. 5. Mr Wright visits the estate agents alone OR,
           Mr Wright visits the estate agents with Angela.

You add several questions to answer:

Did Mr. Wright never marry?
Why did he wait for forty years before looking for Angela?
What does he put in the advertisement?
What has her life been like since the War?
Will she still look beautiful?
What does she think of him?
Does she answer the advertisement?
How does he recognise her?
Does he find her?
What happens in the end?

You have asked yourself a series of questions – those you feel would need to be answered in your story – and then have a rough outline plan of the plot, developing two separate strands, Mr Wright and Angela, and then bringing them together in paragraph four, the meeting. You haven't yet decided which of the two endings to choose – maybe you will give both, leaving it to the reader to decide.

▷ **Writing a draft**   You now feel ready to write a draft of the story, not necessarily worrying too much about correct paragraphing, punctuation or spelling at this stage, though it is best to be as correct as you can, otherwise you will have more work to do later. This is how the story might take shape as a first draft.

Lost Love.

Mr. Wright slowly put his pen back in its case and adjusted his reading glasses on his nose with a sigh. He read over the advertisement he had just written. 'CARTER, Angela. Will Angela Carter, last heard of when working at the Royal Naval Hospital, Dover, get in touch with Mr. Wilfred Wright, with a view to meeting and exchanging old memories. Reply to Box 14.' Before him, on the oak dining-table, was a photograph of a pretty golden-haired girl with an oval face and sparkling eyes. He sighed. 'Ah, Angela. What good times we had in 1940. I wonder where you are now?' Life had been lonely since Mrs. Wright had died.

He shuffled towards the front door, put on his overcoat and scarf, picked up his stick – he had trouble walking far nowadays – and slowly went down the broad gravel drive of Laburnums, and round the corner to the Post Office. …

'Will you leave off pulling that plant to pieces! If I've told you once I've told you a hundred times!' Mrs Brown sank down into a battered armchair, wiping her forehead with the back of a grimy hand. 'Grandchildren are all right,' she thought, 'but not when you have them all day and all the housework to do, too.' She slowly stirred the blackish tea in her cup and lit a cigarette, then glanced at The Daily News.

She turned at once to the horoscope 'The Secret of Your Stars'. 'Aquarius' she read 'Today you will learn something to your advantage. Don't let it slip through your fingers!' Scanning down the page her eye caught what had once been her own name – CARTER, Angela … Will Angela Carter, last heard …' She read on eagerly. This was it – 'Something to your advantage'. It must be one of those young men she had met during the war. Was it the one who had red hair, who was always getting up to practical jokes? Or what about that pale quiet one …? Angela's face broke into an unaccustomed smile as her mind travelled back over the years. Little Jason continued to pull the leaves off the rubber plant one by one.

A week later, on Monday morning, Mr Wright fumed impatiently. It was always busy in the Post Office on Mondays – pensioners came for their money, and shop assistants for cash for the tills. He had come for something else.

'Box 14? Are there any letters for Box 14?' he asked tremulously, when at last he reached the counter. The clerk called across the room.

'Bring those letters for Box 14, will you.' A minute later Mr Wright was handed a large grey Post Office bag, brimming with letters, mostly in pink or mauve envelopes. A strong smell of rose water, eau de cologne and 'Spring Violet' met his nose.

'Oh, good gracious!' he said 'You'll have to deliver them.'

It took a long while to work through the sack, but it was worth the effort. Among the hundreds of letters from Anita, Agnes, Angel-face, 'Your own Petal' and the like, he found what he was looking for: a short letter, written on sky-blue note-paper. It read:

Dear Fred,

How are you? I've often thought of you during all these years. I've still got the red rose you gave me when you left hospital. I pressed it in a book. I'll meet you on Friday, 12th, by the lions in Trafalgar Square

Yours ever,

Angela.

Friday the 12th was one of those days when you know it is going to be wet, as soon as you wake up. Mr Wright had had a long journey to Trafalgar Square, but it would be worth it to see Angela again. He stood damply under a dripping umbrella, by one of the lions among hurrying passers-by, eagerly looking out for a lady with fair hair, blue eyes and an oval face – but there was no-one like that. Maybe he'd picked the wrong lion. There were three more to choose from. He began slowly to walk around the square. Suddenly there was a yell from near him.

'Freddie! Hallo! I'd have known you anywhere!' It was the right voice, but where was Angela? Before he could think further he was clasped by a large, strong stout woman in an old fur coat, dragging a grizzling little boy behind her.

'Oh! Freddie,' she cried 'I've found you at last – after all these years.'

It was raining hard again when the door of Gale and Pearson Ltd. the estate agents swung open and crashed shut. The dripping figure of Mr Wright entered.

'Yes, Sir. Can we help you?' a charming young woman with golden hair and an oval face greeted him.

'Well, yes. I'm looking for a retirement cottage – something small, very small – on a remote island. Something in the Hebrides, perhaps?' Yes, she had something like that. Mr Wright had found what he was looking for – at last.

OR

It was still raining hard when the door of Gale and Pearson Ltd., the estate agents, swung open and crashed shut. A strange couple entered with dripping umbrellas and damp coats, but they looked happy unaware of all that.

'Yes. Can we help you?' a young woman greeted them.

Mrs Brown spoke up:

'Yes, you can, young lady. We're looking for a retirement house – something up-market with a lot of space. Better be near the shops and the schools – I like shopping a lot, and there's the grandchildren to think of. Oh, and with a double garage …' Yes, she had something like that. Angela Carter smiled. She had found what she was looking for – at last.

▷ Improving the draft

You may feel that this story has quite a good shape already. However, wouldn't the opening be more effective if the advertisement came first? You decide that it would and rearrange the first paragraph. You consider following through some of the untied knots left in the plot. For example, it hasn't been established clearly what Angela Carter is looking for. Something can well be added, then, in paragraph two:

'Grandchildren are all right', she thought, but not when you have them all day and all the housework to do, too. Since Mr Brown had died a year or so ago times had been hard. The house that had been big enough for two was bursting at the seams when her five children and all the grandchildren came around to visit. If only she could manage to come into some money …

Then there's the ending. You don't want to choose between the two, so decide to keep both, leaving the story open-ended. You may consider moving the paragraphs around, but the pattern already works quite well and follows your original plan. You decide against changing the sequence of events, but rearrange the first paragraph, so that the story begins with the advertisement, 'CARTER, Angela. Will Angela Carter …, etc.

▷ Editing and correcting the draft

You now go through the draft very carefully, checking for any changes of phrasing you may want to make and correcting any inconsistencies, as well as making sure that spelling and punctuation are correct. You wonder about one of your statements: are there really four lions in Trafalgar Square? You aren't certain, and will have to find out. Even if you are writing fiction, your readers will not accept the situation as realistic if they know that part of your description of a familiar scene is wrong. Also, have you spelled 'Trafalgar' correctly? Yes. 'Acquarius' looks wrong; of course, there isn't a 'c'. Read your story quickly to yourself to see if punctuation seems all right. Do full stops correspond to the main pauses, and the commas to lesser pauses? You give characters' thoughts in the story, as well as direct speech. Have you shown the difference by using single inverted commas for their thoughts and double for speech? You have quoted a letter. How should you set that out? You decide to indent it a few spaces, on either side.

You could work with a friend or in a small group discussing the piece of work, or your teacher or tutor may have made some helpful remarks and corrections. Remember, if that happened, to include the draft work, with any corrections made during the process and information about the help given, with your final version for assessment in the coursework folder.

If your piece of work has been done under supervised (controlled) conditions – and each folder of work has at least one piece of this kind included in it – you would, of course, have had to see to the final correction and presentation by yourself.

▷ Deciding on the type of presentation required

You wonder whether to have a try at printing the story on the word-processor, but decide it would be simpler just to write it out by hand. Your handwriting is quite good when you try, and that is fortunate, since it would certainly detract from the effect of the story if the assessor had to struggle with an illegible scrawl.

The layout presents other problems. How should the advertisement at the beginning be done? You decide to display it – that is, separate it from the rest of the text. And what about the two endings? You could write them side by side in two columns, but decide to make one follow the other.

These matters being settled, you are ready to produce the final copy.

▷ Making the final fair copy

A fair copy is one where all previous alterations and corrections are incorporated. You supply yourself with some clean sheets of paper, and write or type out the story as neatly as you can. The short story would look something like this:

Lost love

'CARTER, Angela. Will Angela Carter, last heard of when working at the Royal Naval Hospital, Dover, get in touch with Mr Wilfred Wright, with a view to meeting and exchanging old memories. Reply to Box 14.'

Mr Wright slowly put his pen back in his case, and adjusted his reading glasses on his nose with a sigh. He read over the advertisement he had just written. Before him on the oak dining-table was a photograph of a pretty golden-haired girl, with an oval face, and sparkling eyes. He sighed. 'Ah, Angela. What good times we had in 1940. I wonder where you are now?' Life had been lonely since Mrs Wright had died.

He shuffled towards the front door, put on his overcoat and scarf, picked up his stick – he had trouble walking far nowadays – and slowly went down the broad gravel drive at 'Laburnums' and round the corner to the post office …

'Will you leave off pulling that plant to pieces! If I've told you once I've told you a hundred times.' Mrs Brown sank down into a battered armchair, wiping her forehead with the back of a grimy hand. 'Grandchildren are all right,' she thought, 'but not when you have them all day and with all the housework to do, too.' Since Mr Brown had died, a year or so ago, times had been hard. The house that had been big enough for two was bursting at the seams when her five children and all the grandchildren came round to visit. If only she could come into some money … She slowly stirred the blackish tea in her cup and lit a cigarette, then glanced at The Daily News. She turned at once to the horoscope: 'The Secret of Your Stars'. 'Aquarius' she read. 'Today you will learn something to your advantage. Don't let it slip through your fingers.' Scanning down the page her eye caught what had once been her own name: CARTER, Angela. Will Angela Carter, last heard …' She read on, eagerly. This was it – 'Something to your advantage'. It must be one of those young men she had met during the war. Was it the one who had red hair, who was always getting up to practical jokes? Or, what about the pale quiet one? Angela's face broke into an unaccustomed smile as her mind travelled back over the years. Little Jason continued to pull the leaves off the rubber plant, one by one …

A week later, on Monday morning Mr Wright fumed impatiently. It was always busy in the post office on Mondays – pensioners came for their money, and shop assistants for cash for the tills. He had come for something else.

(continued)

'Box 14. Are there any letters for Box 14?' he asked tremulously, when at last he reached the counter. The clerk called across the room, 'Bring those letters for Box 14, will you.' A minute later Mr Wright was handed a large grey post office bag, brimming with letters, mostly in pink or mauve envelopes. A strong smell of rose water, eau de cologne, and 'Spring Violet' met his nose.

'Oh, good gracious!' he said 'You'll have to deliver them.'

It took a long while to work through the sack, but it was worth the effort. Among the hundreds of letters from Anita, Agnes, Angel face, 'Your own Petal' and the like, he found what he was looking for: a short letter, written on sky-blue note-paper. It read:

Dear Fred,

How are you? I've often thought of you during all these years. I've still got the red rose you gave me when you left hospital. I pressed it in a book. I'll meet you on Friday 12th, by the lions in Trafalgar Square.

Yours ever,

Angela

Friday 12th was one of those days when you know it is going to be wet, as soon as you wake up. Mr Wright had had a long journey to Trafalgar Square, but it would be worth it – to see Angela again. He stood damply under a dripping umbrella, by one of the lions among hurrying passers-by, eagerly looking for a lady with fair hair, blue eyes, and an oval face – but there was no one like that. Maybe he'd picked the wrong lion? There were three more to choose from. He began slowly to walk around the Square. Suddenly there was a yell below him. 'Freddie, hallo! I'd have known you anywhere!' It was the right voice, but where was Angela? Before he could think further he was clasped by a large, strong, stout woman in an old fur coat, dragging a grizzling little boy behind her. 'Oh Freddie!' she cried. 'I've found you at last – after all these years …'

It was raining hard, again, when the door of Gale and Pearson Ltd, the estate agents, swung open and crashed shut. The dripping figure of Mr Wright entered.

'Yes, Sir. Can we help you?' a charming young woman with golden hair and an oval face greeted him. Mr Wright sat down and smiled.

'Well, yes, I'm looking for a retirement cottage – something small, very small – on a remote island. Something in the Hebrides, perhaps?' Yes, she had something like that. Mr Wright had found what he was looking for at last.

It was still raining hard when the door of Gale and Pearson, the estate agents, swung open and crashed shut. A strange couple entered, with dripping umbrellas and damp coats, but they looked happily unaware of all that.

'Yes, can we help you?' A young woman greeted them. Mrs Brown spoke up: 'Yes, you can, young lady. We're looking for a retirement house; something up-market, on the large side, so that the grandchildren can come and stay and with plenty of space. Better be near the school and the shops – I like shopping a lot, and there's the grandchildren to think of. Oh, and with a double garage …' Yes, she had something like that. Angela Carter smiled: she had found what she was looking for – at last.

You feel rather satisfied with the story, now it is finished. Soon it will be read by your teacher or tutor for assessment, and later it will go into one of your coursework folders. The preliminary notes, plan and draft could be included with it, so that the moderator can look at the whole evolution of the work.

A STEP FURTHER

Always be on the look out for possible material for writing.

Keep a writer's notebook and jot down good ideas or brief references to useful and interesting sources.

SUMMARY

▷ You will have learned the value of first thoughts and how to shape, order and use them.

▷ You will know about drafting, from first draft, through revising and editing to thoughts about presentation and the final fair copy.

Chapter 10

Reading comprehension

GETTING STARTED

Skill in comprehension is an essential part of all examinations in English. First, you have to read instructions about how to fill in your answer book, then read and understand the questions asked in a written examination. This level of reading is for literal meaning, or 'the words on the line', as it has been described. Much of our reading, though, is done 'between the lines', looking for more than one level of meaning, changes of tone, and so on. It can even be important to read 'beyond the lines', by, for example, working out what happened before or after an incident you have just read about, or by considering the moods and motives of some of the people involved. But your search for meaning should always be based on the words on the page; unless they are read with care and thought, problems of understanding will be sure to arise.

The best way to prepare to do well in reading comprehension is to make a habit of reading for information and pleasure as wide a range of texts as you can – novels, newspapers, manuals, reports, autobiographies, and so on. Wide reading should be something to enjoy, especially if you use it to follow and extend your own interests and enthusiasms. It will do far more than help you to build up a vocabulary beyond the average: it will increase your ability to use and understand language in everyday situations, as well as when you are concerned with literature. It is reassuring to remember that you almost certainly have an excellent grasp of ordinary spoken English already. What you need to keep extending is 'book language', in all its varieties.

In the examination you may be reading for a variety of purposes. In the oral examination you may read aloud an unseen or prepared passage. To do this well you obviously have to understand it. You may be asked questions about a passage read silently, or be invited to discuss it with fellow students or an assessor. Coursework will, for most candidates, involve reading a very wide range of material, including at least one literary text. Preparation for reading comprehension in these areas is dealt with in Chapters 6–8 and 11. This chapter is about tests of comprehension of the kind found in *written* terminal examination papers.

LONDON	MEG	NEAB	NICCEA	SEG	WJEC	IGCSE	TOPIC	STUDY	REVISION I	REVISION 2
✓	✓	✓	✓	✓	✓	✓	Close reading: literary			
✓	✓		✓	✓	✓	✓	Close reading: non-literary			
✓	✓	✓		✓			Close reading: pre-released texts			
	✓	✓	✓	✓	✓	✓	Response to theme/s of text			
	✓						Response to language			
✓	✓	✓	✓	✓	✓	✓	Comprehension: twentieth-century texts			
✓	✓			✓			Comprehension: pre-twentieth-century texts			
	✓			✓	✓		Whole works of literature			
✓	✓		✓				Shakespeare: compulsory			

▷ WHAT YOU NEED TO KNOW

Candidates must demonstrate in conversation, discussion and writing that they can

- ▶ read a wide range of texts (including fiction, poetry, non-fiction and drama) accurately and with confidence
- ▶ respond to literature
- ▶ appreciate the characteristics of non-literary and media texts and evaluate the effectiveness of their use
- ▶ appreciate how writers make use of language and how language changes.

(AT2: 1–5)

▷ Reading the material

'Read once quickly; read once steadily; answer relevantly.'

The most important thing to do when tackling any comprehension test in a written paper is, first, to **read the material through quickly** to get an overall idea of what it is about. Some Groups give extra reading time. Candidates are told in general terms what to concentrate on when they read and may make brief notes. When you have read the passage, **read it through again steadily** before looking at the questions. On your second reading, or even third if time allows, try to get involved and interested in some aspects of the material and to become aware of its overall structure and the main idea or topic. When you are satisfied that you have a fair grasp of what the passage is about, look at the questions.

▷ Answering the questions

The second principle, whatever type of response you are asked for, is to **answer relevantly**. One way of ensuring this is to try to answer in your own words, thinking the question through in your mind first, then checking your ideas carefully against the wording of the text, using the line references, if they are given. Even in questions where you are invited to give some sort of imaginative or personal response, be sure to link it to the text. If you feel that you have no idea of an answer, do not despair and do not guess wildly. Go back to the text and look for clues which will help you to work out something that seems likely. Work progressively through the questions, as they will follow the development of the passage: it is more difficult to go back to a question later, because you will have to remind yourself in detail of what has gone before.

Whatever the form of the text, questions will cover both its literal meaning and that between and beyond the lines. In passages by most of the Groups, the questions get harder as you go on, and move from the literal, by gradual stages, to more indirect levels of meaning, and often to 'open-ended' personal response questions. As well as showing your understanding of setting and immediate situation you will be asked about some of the following aspects of the passage:

- ▶ organization
- ▶ pace of the narrative
- ▶ details of an argument
- ▶ author's or narrator's points of view
- ▶ characters' point of view
- ▶ style.

Some or all of these affect how you respond as a reader and examples of all of them will be considered in the following sections of the chapter.

▷ Types of comprehension tests

There are *two* kinds of comprehension tests:

- ▶ those which have questions based on close reading of the text requiring a written answer from the candidate, in his or her own words
  and
- ▶ those which ask candidates to develop an idea from the text creatively, either exploring meaning or reflecting on it from personal experience.

Your answer to the first type should be as compact and correct as possible, unless it is a personal response 'open-ended' question, where there is more scope for your own thoughts and feelings.

With the second type, try to relate your answer to the text loosely, but so that your thinking can be seen to have definite connections with the text.

Reading comprehension is tested by compulsory written papers in all Groups.

You will be asked to:

▶ show that you can understand information and opinion
▶ select material relevant to whatever you are asked to do
▶ show that you can understand straightforward (and some subtle) meanings
▶ recognize different uses of language for different occasions
▶ comment on a writer's aims and intentions.

Coursework showing response to your reading – literary and non-literary – is offered by all Groups, and will be discussed in Chapter 11.

▶ **EXAMINATION QUESTIONS**

In this section it is suggested that you

▶ read each passage with its questions
▶ try to tackle it yourself
▶ look at the general notes on each passage in the Outline Answers below.

The **simplest comprehension test** is a single prose passage, with a list of questions for you to answer in your own words. In the GCSE examinations some questions will require an answer based directly on the language of the passage, and others will require a more personal or imaginative response. Sometimes the passage is literary, as in Questions 1 and 2 following. Most groups also set non-literary passages. Questions 3 and 4 are of this type.

Another form of question consists of two or more passages, connected in theme but varied in style or approach. They may be from any kind of writing (narrative, descriptive, personal, factual, informative) and in a variety of forms (diary or novel extracts, letters, reports, articles, etc.). In your answers you will need to draw on both passages and, to some extent, compare and contrast them. Questions 5, 6 and 7 are of this type.

▶ **Question 1** Reading and Response Higher Tier A–D (Time allowed: 2 hours)
Read the short story below and answer Questions 1a, 1b and Question 2. You should divide your time equally between Question 1 and Question 2.

You are reminded of the importance of clear English and orderly presentation in your answers.

The Trout by Sean O'Faolain

One of the first places Julia always ran to when they arrived in G—— was The Dark Walk. It is a laurel walk, very old; almost gone wild; a lofty midnight tunnel of smooth, sinewy branches. Underfoot the tough brown leaves are never dry enough to crackle: there is always a suggestion of damp and cool trickle.

5   She raced right into it. For the first few yards she always had the memory of the sun behind her, then she felt the dusk closing swiftly down on her so that she screamed with pleasure and raced on to reach the light at the far end; and it was always just a little too long in coming so that she emerged gasping, clasping her hands, laughing, drinking in the sun. When she was filled with the heat and
10   glare she would turn and consider the ordeal again.

    This year she had the extra joy of showing it to her small brother. and of terrifying him as well as herself. And for him the fear lasted longer because his legs were so short and she had gone out at the far end and while he was still screaming and racing.

15 When they had done this many times they came back to the house to tell
everybody that they had done it. He boasted. She mocked. They squabbled.

'Cry babby!'
'You were afraid yourself, so there!'
'I won't take you any more.'
20 'You're a big pig.'
'I hate you.'

Tears were threatening, so somebody said, 'Did you see the well?' She
opened her eyes at that and held up her long lovely neck suspiciously and
decided to be incredulous. She was twelve and at that age little girls are
25 beginning to suspect most stories: they already found out too many, from Santa
Claus to the stork. How could there be a well! In The Dark Walk? That she had
visited year after year? Haughtily she said, 'Nonsense.'

But she went back, pretending to be going somewhere else, and she found a
hole scooped in the rock at the side of the walk, choked with damp leaves. so
30 shrouded by ferns that she uncovered it only after much searching. At the back
of this little cavern there was about a quart of water. In the water she suddenly
perceived a panting trout. She rushed for Stephen and dragged him to see, and
they were both so excited that they were no longer afraid of the darkness as
they hunched down and peered in at the fish panting in his tiny prison, his silver
35 stomach going up and down like an engine.

Nobody knew how the trout got there.

Her mother suggested that a bird had carried the spawn. Her father thought
that in the winter a small streamlet might have carried it down there as a baby,
and it had been safe until the summer came and the water began to dry up. She
40 said, 'I see,' and went back to look again and consider the matter in private. Her
brother remained behind, wanting to hear the whole story of the trout, not really
interested in the actual trout but much interested in the story which his mummy
began to make up for him on the lines of 'So one day Daddy Trout and Mummy
Trout …' When he retailed it to her she said 'Pooh'.

45 It troubled her that the trout was always in the same position: he had no room
to turn. All the time the silver belly went up and down; otherwise he was
motionless. Hunched over him she thought how all the winter, while she was at
school, he had been in there. All the winter, in The Dark Walk, all night, floating
around alone. She drew the leaf of her hat down around her ears and chin and
50 stared. She was still thinking of it as she lay in bed.

It was late June, the longest days of the year. The sun had sat still for a week,
burning up the world. Although it was after ten o'clock it was still bright and still
hot. She lay on her back under a single sheet, with her long legs spread, trying
to keep cool. She could see the D of the moon through the fir tree – they slept
55 on the ground floor. Before they went to bed her mummy had told Stephen the
story of the trout again, and she, in her bed, had resolutely presented her back
to them and read her book. But she had kept one ear cocked.

'And so, in the end, this naughty fish who would not stay at home got bigger
and bigger and bigger; and the water got smaller and smaller …'
60 Passionately she had whirled and cried, 'Mummy, don't make it a horrible old
moral story!' Her mummy had brought in a fairy godmother then, who sent lots
of rain, and filled the well, and a stream poured out and the trout floated away
down to the river below. Staring at the moon she knew that there are not such
things as fairy godmothers and that the trout, down in The Dark Walk, was
65 panting like an engine. She heard somebody unwind a fishing-reel. Would the
beasts fish him out!

She sat up. Stephen was a hot lump of sleep, lazy thing. The Dark Walk would
be full of little scraps of moon. She leaped up and looked out of the window.
Quietly she lifted the ewer of water and climbed out of the window and scuttled

70   along the cool but cruel gravel down to the maw of the tunnel. Her pyjamas
were very short so that when she splashed water it wet her ankles. She peered
into the tunnel. Something alive rustled inside there. She raced in, and up and
down she raced, and flurried, and cried aloud, 'Oh, gosh, I can't find it,' and
then at last she did. Kneeling down in the damp, she put her hand into the slimy
75   hole. When the body lashed they were both mad with fright. But she gripped
him and shoved him into the ewer and raced, with her teeth ground, out to the
other end of the tunnel and down the steep paths to the river's edge.

All the time she could feel him lashing his tail against the side of the ewer.
She was afraid he would jump right out. The gravel cut into her soles until
80   she came to the cool ooze of the river's bank. She poured out, watching until he
plopped. For a second he was visible in the water. She hoped he was not dizzy.
Then all she saw was the glimmer of the moon in the silent-flowing river, the
dark firs, the dim mountains, and the radiant pointed face laughing down at her
out of the empty sky.

85   She scuttled up the hill, in the window, plonked down the ewer, and flew
through the air like a bird into bed. She hugged herself and giggled. Like a river
of joy her holiday spread before her.

In the morning Stephen rushed to her, shouting that 'he' was gone, and
asking 'where' and 'how'. Lifting her nose in the air she said superciliously,
90   'Fairy godmother, I suppose?' and strolled away patting the palms of her hands.

Answer Question 1a, 1b **and** Question 2. You should divide your time equally between
Question 1 and Question 2.

1a   What do you find in the story to suggest that Julia is growing out of childhood and
away from childish things?
and

1b   The writer of the story gives clear descriptions of the place where Julia and her family
are staying on their holiday. Choose two of these descriptions and explain why you
think they are important to the story.
and

2   Freeing the trout is a small incident but it is important in Julia's life. Write about an
incident in your own life which has marked a stage in your growing up.

(London)

▷ **Question 2**   Higher Levels A–D   (Time allowed: ½ hour)
Read the following passage from a short story by the Cuban writer Enriqué Serpa, translated into Modern English, then answer the question which follows it. You should spend
about 30 minutes on this question.

Suddenly a shark had started to swim round his boat. It was a hammer-head, about fifteen feet long, with long broad fins. Instinctively Felipe reached for his harpoon, but he was stopped by the idea that he was not supposed to catch sharks. So he watched the shark, which looked like a dark, flexible tree-trunk. Yes, it was like a tree-trunk, he thought. How much would it be worth? Felipe calculated that any Chinese in Zanja Street would pay at least two dollars for the fins and tail. He felt he should take those two dollars which the sea was offering so generously, to relieve his extreme poverty. Two dollars meant three good meals for his starving children. But then there were the Police and the agents for the Shark Fishing Company to think about.

On the water-front they were always on the lookout for any fisherman bringing in shark fins or tails. And if sometimes they merely confiscated the catch, at others they arrested the fishermen. And after that five dollars fine and they were not even allowed a defence. But two dollars were two dollars, and however hard he worked, it was possible that that day his wife would have nothing to cook. Fishing was always a game of chance and often one's luck did not depend on one's efforts. If only it were possible to make the fish bite! And those fins there, within the reach of his hands. Two dollars.

He made up his mind. Two dollars, for him. What the hell! Quickly, while he was preparing his harpoon, he threw out all the bait he had to keep the fish around. The shark surfaced, showing its stiff dorsal fins, its white under-belly flashing in the sunlight. When it had eaten the bait, it dived slowly, to emerge a few moments later behind the boat.

The harpoon, skilfully cast by Felipe, caught it in the neck and it struggled convulsively, churning up a whirlpool of water with its tail. A few blows with a mallet on the head were enough to quieten it down. Half an hour later its body, without fins or tail, sank, turning on itself to be eaten by its fellows in the depths of the sea.

Behind the mutilated body, like a silent protest, remained a wake of blood.

After tying the fins and the tail with a piece of cord, Felipe rowed towards the coast. He wanted to get ashore as soon as possible, to go early to China Town in search of a buyer. Perhaps with Chan, the owner of the *Canton*, he might strike a bargain. At worst he ought to exchange the fins for food.

And then suddenly fate, dressed in a blue uniform, arrived. Felipe had scarcely tied up his boat when he was startled by a harsh, sarcastic voice: 'This time you can't deny it, I've caught you red-handed.' And as he turned, his heart in a vice, he saw a policeman smiling maliciously and pointing with his fore-finger at the fins and tail. After a moment's silence he added:

"I'll take those."

He bent down to pick them up. But he did not get to touch them because Felipe, jumping forward, grabbed them in his right hand.

"They are mine!" he muttered violently.

For a moment the policeman seemed astonished at meeting such behaviour. But he reacted quickly in an attempt to recover his authority:

"Come on, hand them over or I'll take you and the fins along with me."

Felipe looked at him carefully. He was a small man, skinny and ungainly. His precarious physique was in sharp contrast with his hectoring voice and the stance of a fighting-cock he had assumed. Felipe scowled and felt his arm-muscles contract. And aware of his own strength and of the elasticity of his body, he said to himself:

"This fellow isn't even half a man."

In the meantime, a group of onlookers had collected around him and the policeman.

"Hand them over or you'll be sorry."

"Give them to him," advised a voice, that of an old copper-faced fisherman. And changing his tone:

"Perhaps he can see a doctor with what he gets for them."

Felipe felt the weight of innumerable eyes fixed on him and he imagined the scornful smiles and ironical comments with which the witnesses of the scene would taunt him afterwards. And apart from this, the feeling that he was being made the object of an intolerable injustice goaded him on to disobedience, whatever the consequences may be.

"I'm waiting. Are you going to hand them over or not?"

The bullying voice of the policeman was angry and threatening.

"Neither of us gets them," Felipe said suddenly. And whirling them round his head, he threw the fins into the sea.

Write about what you learn of the different aspects of Felipe in the passage. Give evidence from the extract to show how you came to your conclusion about

(a) his situation
(b) his anxieties
(c) his skills
(d) his attitude to authority.

(NEAB)

▷ **Question 3**   Standard Tier C–G   (Time allowed: 1½ hours)

Answer all the questions in Section A (Reading) and B (Writing). You will be assessed on the quality of presentation in your answers as a whole.

SECTION A: 20 marks

To answer this section you will need to look at the leaflet: Big Pit (Figure 10.1).
  You should spend about 30 minutes on this section.

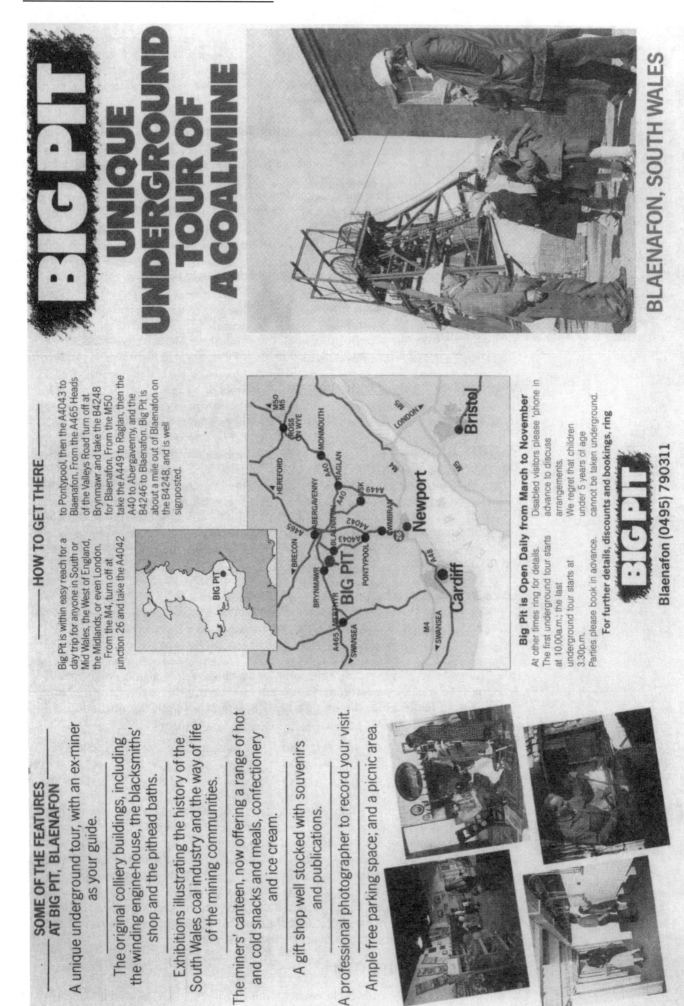

BIG PIT

UNIQUE UNDERGROUND TOUR OF A COALMINE

BLAENAFON, SOUTH WALES

— SOME OF THE FEATURES AT BIG PIT, BLAENAFON —

A unique underground tour, with an ex-miner as your guide.

The original colliery buildings, including the winding engine-house, the blacksmiths' shop and the pithead baths.

Exhibitions illustrating the history of the South Wales coal industry and the way of life of the mining communities.

The miners' canteen, now offering a range of hot and cold snacks and meals, confectionery and ice cream.

A gift shop well stocked with souvenirs and publications.

A professional photographer to record your visit.

Ample free parking space; and a picnic area.

— HOW TO GET THERE —

Big Pit is within easy reach for a day trip for anyone in South or Mid Wales, the West of England, the Midlands, or even London. From the M4, turn off at junction 26 and take the A4042 to Pontypool, then the A4043 to Blaenafon. From the A465 Heads of the Valleys Road turn off at Brynmawr and take the B4248 for Blaenafon. From the M50 take the A449 to Raglan, then the A40 to Abergavenny, and the B4246 to Blaenafon. Big Pit is about a mile out of Blaenafon on the B4248, and is well signposted.

Big Pit is Open Daily from March to November

At other times ring for details. The first underground tour starts at 10.00a.m.; the last underground tour starts at 3.30p.m.

Parties please book in advance.

Disabled visitors please 'phone in advance to discuss arrangements.

We regret that children under 5 years of age cannot be taken underground.

For further details, discounts and bookings, ring

BIG PIT
Blaenafon (0495) 790311

A UNIQUE UNDERGROUND TOUR THROUGH 19TH. CENTURY COAL AND IRONSTONE WORKINGS

Big Pit closed as a working colliery in 1980, exactly 100 years after it first produced coal. In Blaenafon the mining of coal and ironstone on a large scale began in the 1780s and some of these older workings are connected with Big Pit. The pit is now a museum where visitors can go underground and discover how miners have worked and lived over the last 200 years.

The photographs show you something of what you will see – underground roadways, coal-faces, haulage engines, and on the surface the blacksmiths' shop, the baths, and exhibitions.

THE UNDERGROUND TOUR

First you will be kitted out with a safety helmet, cap lamp and 'self-rescuer' just like a working miner. Then you will ride down in the cage to the bottom of the shaft – 294 feet deep. Ex-miners will be your guides and their explanations and anecdotes will bring your trip to life.

The underground tour lasts nearly an hour. During this time you will walk through workings some of which are over a hundred years old. There are many fascinating relics of mining history preserved here, including stables and haulage engines. At the coalface your guides will explain the different methods of extracting coal and the working conditions of the miners.

Although Big Pit no longer produces coal it is still a real mine, so please remember to wear practical shoes and warm clothing.

Layout of Underground Workings

Pithead

Downcast Shaft

Pit Cage

Pit Bottom

Ventilation Doors

Workshops

Welsh Notched Timber

Ventilation Doors

Coal Face

Haulage Engine

Old Ironstone Workings

Stables

Coal Faces

Haulage Engine

Upcast Shaft

Fan House

Look at the leaflet under the heading 'How To Get There'.

A1 (a) What telephone number would you ring to find out more information about a trip to Big Pit?
   (b) At what time of the day does the first underground tour start?
   (c) Who are not allowed to go down Big Pit? Why do you think this is?   (5 marks)

Now look at the section headed 'The Underground Tour'.

A2 What would you see and hear underground on a visit to Big Pit?   (5 marks)

Now look at the leaflet as a whole.

A3 Choose **two** pictures in the leaflet. Say what is in them. Why might these pictures have been chosen to appear in the leaflet?   (5 marks)

A4 How does the leaflet try to attract visitors to Big Pit?   (5 marks)

Think about the information it gives, the pictures shown, the overall layout.

SECTION B: 20 marks
Answer Question B5 and Question B6.
   You should spend about 30 minutes on each question.

B5 Your class has been on a visit to Big Pit. You have been asked by your teacher to write an account of this trip for the school magazine.

Write your article.   (10 marks)

Remember to think about: how the day was planned;
                              the things you saw and heard;
                              whether the trip was a success

B6 Think of a place not too far from your home which people might like to visit. It could be a castle, a farm, a factory, a theme or wildlife park or a zoo. **Now design a leaflet, like the one on Big Pit, which sets out the attractions of this place.**   (10 marks)

You may use pictures and diagrams if you wish but remember to include the important information.

(WJEC)

▷ **Question 4**   Writing Foundation Tier C–G   (Time allowed: 2 hours)
Read the leaflet about recycling (reusing) rubbish (Figure 10.2), and answer the questions which follow. You should spend about two hours on the paper.

1   According to the leaflet, what type of things should be sorted out and recycled?
   (10 marks)
2   Many people feel that too much rubbish is left lying around, both in our towns and countryside. Write an article for a newspaper suggesting ways in which the problems of rubbish could be solved.   (20 marks)
3   You have decided to clear out your room and throw away things you no longer need. Describe your thoughts and feelings as you do this.   (20 marks)

(London)

▷ **Question 5**   Read the following two passages and then answer the questions.   (Time allowed: 40 min.)

From 'If Only They Could Talk' by James Herriot

'If Only They Could Talk' is one of a long series of books describing James Herriot's work as a veterinary surgeon in North Yorkshire in the 1930s.

I stroked the old dog's head as I tried to collect my thoughts. This wasn't going to be easy.
   'Is he going to be ill for long?' the old man asked, and again came the thump, thump of the tail at the sound of the loved voice. 'It's miserable when Bob isn't following me around the house when I'm doing my little jobs.'

WEALTH FROM WASTE

People used to describe Britain as 'an island built on coal, surrounded by fish'. These days, Britain is more like an island built on rubbish, surrounded by pollution. Every year, each household in Britain creates about 1 tonne of rubbish that has to be thrown away. If it *wasn't* taken away, the streets of our towns would be impassable rubbish mountains. But much of our rubbish is not rubbish at all! Most of it could be recycled.

What happens to our rubbish?

Once the dustmen have taken rubbish away, most of it gets dumped in huge landfill sites. Most sites eventually get covered with soil, but they cannot be used to grow crops and they are not strong enough for buildings. Meanwhile, all the rubbish inside them begins to decompose and all kinds of nasty, poisonous things seep down into the soil. Many of them seep into the water supply. Fires on landfill sites are common because of chemical reactions taking place below the surface. Other rubbish is burned in incinerators – but sometimes that releases toxic fumes and leaves poisonous ash behind.

Why recycle?

Recycling makes such perfect sense, it is amazing people are not forced to do it by law! When something is recycled it saves on finding fresh raw materials to make the same item. Most importantly, it cuts down the amount of energy needed to make that item. It takes less heat to make a glass bottle out of broken, recycled glass than it does starting afresh with the raw ingredients. Less heat means using less oil or coal.

How to recycle

The key to successful recycling is sorting. Recycling is more efficient if different types of items are separated into categories – the more, the better. Rubbish

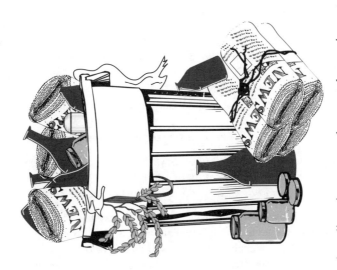

can be split up into paper, glass, metal, organic waste (food, dead flowers, potato peelings, tea leaves, etc.), plastic and things made out of a mixture of items. At the bottle bank, glass can be separated again, into brown, green and clear. By using magnets, metal cans can be separated into steel and aluminium (aluminium will not stick to a magnet).

What can be recycled?

PAPER Paper is made from trees. Each year, everyone in Britain gets through six trees worth of paper. Making new paper harms the environment as the process usually involves chlorine bleach, which pollutes rivers. It's far better to use unbleached, recycled paper. Not only can newspapers be recycled, but also magazines, cardboard, paper bags and envelopes.

GLASS Most high streets now have bottle banks. Remove all tops first, then recycle drinks bottles, jam jars and sauce bottles. *But never recycle bottles that can be reused* like milk bottles. It's more efficient to refill them with milk than to make new bottles. If glass is not reused, it lasts forever, broken and buried in the soil.

ORGANIC MATTER If you have a garden, you need never again throw away vegetable peelings, uneaten or rotten food. Get an old dustbin, drill a few holes in it, and pop off to the fishing shop. Buy some brandlings – worms that will happily munch away on your rubbish. In a few months you will have lovely black compost to put on the garden.

METAL Most cans are made out of steel. As steel is magnetic, you can throw it out and it will be magnetically separated out and recycled at a waste centre. If aluminium cans are not recycled, it is a great waste of the energy it takes to makes them. As they are not magnetic you need to separate them out of your rubbish.

CLOTHES Yes, you can recycle old clothes! Take them along to charity shops like Oxfam. Some will be sold, others will go to the Oxfam Wastesaver Unit in Huddersfield. That is where the thousands of tons sent in by *Blue Peter* viewers in the 1987 Rags Appeal went. Clothes are sorted according to material and returned to textile mills for recycling.

Figure 10.2

'I'm sorry, Mr Dean, but I'm afraid this is something very serious. You see this large swelling. It is caused by an internal growth.'

'You mean … cancer?' the little man said faintly.

'I'm afraid so, and it has progressed too far for anything to be done. I wish there was something I could do to help him, but there isn't.'

The old man looked bewildered and his lips trembled. 'Then he's going to die?'

I swallowed hard. 'We can't really just leave him to die, can we? He's in some distress now, but it will soon be an awful lot worse. Don't you think it would be kindest to put him to sleep? Alter all, he's had a good, long innings.' I always aimed at a brisk matter-of-fact approach, but the old clichés had an empty ring.

The old man was silent. then he said, 'Just a minute,' and slowly and painfully knelt down by the side of the dog. He did not speak, but ran his hand again and again over the grey old muzzle and the ears, while the tail thump, thump, thumped on the floor.

He knelt there a long time while I stood in the cheerless room, my eyes taking in the faded pictures on the walls, the frayed, grimy curtains, the broken-springed arm chair.

At length the old man struggled to his feet and gulped once or twice. Without looking at me, he said huskily, 'All right, will you do it now?'

I filled the syringe and said the things I always said. 'You needn't worry, this is absolutely painless. Just an overdose of an anaesthetic. It is really an easy way out for the old fellow.'

The dog did not move as the needle was inserted, and, as the barbiturate began to flow into the vein, the anxious expression left his face and the muscles began to relax. By the time the injection was finished, the breathing had stopped.

'Is that it?' the old man whispered.

'Yes, that's it.' I said. 'He is out of his pain now.'

The old man stood motionless except for the clasping and unclasping of his hands. When he turned to face me his eyes were bright. 'That's right, we couldn't have let him suffer, and I'm grateful for what you've done. And now, what do I owe you for your services, sir?'

'Oh, that's all right, Mr Dean.' I said quickly. 'It's nothing – nothing at all. I was passing right here – it was no trouble.'

The old man was astonished. 'But you can't do that for nothing.'

From 'Intimate Relations' by Jacqui Durrell

Jacqui Durrell shares with her husband, Gerald Durrell, a love of animals. In the following episode she gives an account of an Emperor Tamarin monkey. This pet is particularly troublesome and has a bad influence on others in their care!

It is lovely having animals living with you, but we feel that, in fairness to them, it is essential that they should have a definite routine. It is also unwise to inflict one's own routine on animals; the best thing is that they should evolve their own. One creature that we did have in the flat who utterly refused to be influenced by us in any way at all, was Whiskers, the Emperor Tamarin. Whiskers is a magnificent creature, being very attractive to look at and getting his name from his enormous white moustache. Gerry had always had a passion for these little monkeys from South America, since the days before the war when he had had a black-headed Marmoset as a pet. They are bird-like in character and fearless, a rule to which Whiskers was no exception.

He arrived in pathetically bad condition (from a dealer, of course) and was obviously suffering from the cage paralysis that often afflicts these South American primates. With the help of our veterinary friend in Bournemouth, we had evolved a perfect answer, but unfortunately, it involved a massive injection of vitamins D and B12. No one liked administering these injections, but unfortunately, if the animals were to be saved, there was no alternative. Poor old Whiskers was given the shot. Unlike others of his species who accepted it philosophically and did not connect the pain with the person who was giving the injection, he immediately turned round, looked at Gerry, and bit him severely on the hand; a warning as to what would happen if he was to try to repeat the operation. Gerry was so amused and taken aback that all he could do was laugh. This pugnacity was characteristic of Whiskers; later he became, for his size (a mere six inches), one of the most ferocious specimens in the zoo. If he adored you, you were fine, but if he did not, he would leap upon your head and try to bite you viciously.

As he was in such a weakened condition when he arrived, it was decided to keep him in the flat for a little while, in order to build up his strength. At this time our Common Marmosets had a youngster who was approximately the same size as Whiskers and so they were brought up as companions. They spent most of their day in a large cage in Gerry's mother's bedroom. She, of course, doted on them. Nothing was too much trouble. She would spend two hours every morning cooking delicacies for them, stewing apples with honey or brown sugar, boiling rice and lentils, making other little tit-bits that she was sure they would like. Of course, this was entirely the wrong treatment for Whiskers and, from being naturally arrogant, he became unbearable. He refused to go into his cage until he wanted to, and he and his friend Popadum tore round poor Mrs. Durrell's bedroom, rioted over the bed, played havoc with her possessions and really completely took her over. They did have their moments of rest when they would sit calmly in her lap, but most of the time they were tearing her knitting out of her hand, hiding her wool, getting in and out of her knitting bag, strewing bits of wool and patterns all over the place – in fact, becoming totally unmanageable.

The questions which follow are based on the two passages you have just read. Answer **ALL** the questions using the information you have gained from reading the passages.

1   What do you learn from these two passages about the feelings and attitudes of the various humans to the animals concerned?   (10 marks)
2   The first passage is mainly sad, the second mainly humorous. Show how these effects are gained in each case.   (10 marks)
3   Jacqui Durell says: 'It is lovely having animals living with you.' How far do these passages prove that it is true and how far do you think they show that it is a matter of opinion?   (10 marks)
4   How does your own experience in dealing with *either* animals *or* people compare with the events in the passages? You may refer to *either* one *or* both of the passages.
                                                                        (10 marks)
                                                                        (SEG)

▷ **Question 6**   Reading – Non-Literary and Media Texts Standard Tier C–G   (Time allowed: 2 hours)

Nightmare Neighbours

A clash with a neighbour can make life hell. And if things turn sour between you and your neighbour, you may not be able to get away from the problem – unless you move house. For this report, we take the disputes which people have most often with neighbours and explain how to deal with each of them.

Noise from next door can drive you mad. It could come from a barking dog or from non-stop all-night parties. If you can't bear it any longer, contact the Environmental Health Department of your local council. You'll need to prove that the noise stops you from enjoying your property or it is making you ill. You will need proof, so keep a diary.

Many house and car alarms seem to go off for no reason at any time of the day or night. If this is a problem you can phone either the police or your local Environmental Health Officer. There is a new law which allows them to turn off a car alarm, and to enter premises to disconnect an alarm which keeps going off.

If your neighbours have the builders in, you may have to put up with drills and cement mixers. There is bound to be some

disturbance; but if you cannot bear the noise, or it is taking place at night, then take them to court to make them stop work. This is called taking out an injunction.

If your neighbour's dog has bitten you or frightens you, you will want to take action. Contact the local dog warden or the police. A court can order that it is muzzled and kept on a lead. If a dog continually enters and fouls your garden the easiest thing to do is to put up a fence!

The parking place right outside your house is not part of your property. You have no legal right to park there.

However, you have a legal right to enter your driveway or garage. Some local councils now operate parking schemes for residents. If your neighbours are always parking so you can't get out, contact the Highways Department of your local council. It is in charge of traffic management.

Call the police if you think your neighbours' parking habits are not legal.

If your neighbour fences off some of your land or starts growing plants in what you think is your garden, then you have a problem. Arguments over land ownership are hard to solve. They can be sorted out in court but this could cost you a lot of time and money. Some disputes are about party walls. These are walls built right on the boundary between homes. You and your neighbour are both responsible for them.

You have to carry out repairs to your side of the wall but you cannot force your neighbours to repair their side.

Many complaints are about building extensions. People who wish to build must have permission. You have 21 days to object. We hope that the information above will help. Good luck!

Neighbours from Hell

I used to think that my little corner of England was quiet and restful – until THEY moved in next door. There are two of them. They are white, woolly and bark all night long. But as I lie awake at night I remind myself that in many ways I am lucky. The neighbours don't hold all-night Karaoke sessions. They do not knock each other about, and at least the dogs do not bite.

According to a recent report, troublesome dogs are the fifth most common cause of argument between neighbours. As a nation we do not love our neighbours. Some of us hate them. We hurl abuse at them, throw water over departing guests and rubbish in their gardens.

Court orders do nothing to improve strained relations.

According to Ken Hume, an estate agent in south London, buyers can be put off if houses nearby have stone cladding or very bright paintwork. But whatever your problems are, don't worry, it could be worse!

Consider the case of John Gladden. He upset his neighbours by making a huge fish out of fibreglass and mounting it on his roof. The council says he should have had

planning permission. That was just the start!

At Christmas he put up an inflatable Santa Claus, and later a huge model of Winston Churchill. He then installed camouflage netting and replicas of military hardware. Hundreds of sightseers poured in and now his neighbours cannot sell their houses.

Most problems with the people next door concern noise. Others arise because neighbours have different lifestyles; a night-shift worker is not likely to be happy living next door to a family with five children.

Estate agents recommend making frequent calls to the area – day and night. Some people have even visited the would-be next-door neighbours to see if they liked them. After all, would someone trying to sell you a house tell the truth? I recently viewed a house which looked promising – until I saw the zoo next door. I decided I could live with the aviary, the rabbits and the cats, but when I spotted the dogs I had my doubts.

"Do the alsatians next door bother you?" I asked. "No," insisted the vendor, "not at all."

"Oh yes they do," piped up their six year old. "They bark all night and keep us awake." Another sale down the drain; another neighbour in the doghouse.

Section A

Attempt **BOTH** tasks.

You should spend about $1\frac{1}{4}$ hours on Section A.

1   Read the report **Nightmare Neighbours**, which deals with the most common problems people have with their neighbours.
    Make a list of these problems and after each item on your list write what advice is given.
    Use your own words as far as possible.   (20 marks)
2   Now read the article **Neighbours from Hell**. Explain how this article not only gives information but tries to interest and entertain us as well.
    You should comment on:
    (a) the caption and headline
    (b) the writer's own experience (she is 'I' in the article)
    (c) the examples of difficult neighbours given in the article
    (d) the writer's choice of words.   (20 marks)

Section B

Attempt **ONE** task only.

3   You should spend about 45 minutes on Section B. Write about 350–450 words.

EITHER

A Weekend of Hell

Imagine that you do not get on with your neighbours, and you keep a diary describing your problems with them.

Write your diary entries for a Saturday and Sunday.

Say what happens, and include your own thoughts and feelings.   (30 marks)

OR

My Home is my Castle

Some people say that it is all right to do whatever you like at home, without thinking of your family or neighbours.

Write the words of a talk you could give to a teenage audience, either agreeing or dis-agreeing with this idea.   (30 marks)

OR

Last Look Round

Describe a time when you moved house, leaving your friends and favourite places behind. You may give a true account or write a story.   (30 marks)

                    (MEG)

▷ **Question 7**   Higher Tier A–D   (Time allowed: ½ hour)
RESPONSE TO UNSEEN TEXTS

Read the following two passages and then answer the questions which follow. You should spend about 30 minutes on this question.

Passage A is part of Psalm 107 in the Bible, in the translation made for King James in 1611. Read the passage carefully in order to be able to answer the question which follows it.

PASSAGE A

23 They that go down to the sea in ships, that do business in great waters;

24 These see the works of the Lord, and his wonders in the deep.

25 For he commandeth, and raiseth the stormy wind, which lifteth up the waves thereof.

26 They mount up to the heaven, they go down again to the depths: their soul is melted because of trouble.

27 They reel to and fro, and stagger like a drunken man, and are at their wits' end.

28 Then they cry unto the Lord in their trouble, and he bringeth them out of their distresses.

29 He maketh the storm a calm, so that the waves thereof are still.

30 Then are they glad because they be quiet; so he bringeth them unto their desired haven.

31 Oh that men would praise the Lord for his goodness, and for his wonderful works to the children of men!

32 Let them exalt him also in the congregation of the people, and praise him in the assembly of the elders.

Passage B is an Anglo-Saxon riddle dating probably from the eighth century and translated at the beginning of the twentieth century into Modern English which tries to give some of the flavour of the original. Read the passage carefully in order to be able to answer the question which follows it.

PASSAGE B

Ship

[The generally accepted solution is ship, which moves on its keel (the 'one foot'), which is braced by beams ('many ribs'), and which has a hole in the deck ('mouth').]

This world is beautiful in various ways, decked with adornments. I saw an artful work go forth, excellent in journeys, grind against the sand, move with a cry; the strange creature had not sight nor hands, shoulders nor arms; the curious thing must move on one foot, go quickly, pass over the plains; it had many ribs; its mouth was in the midst, useful to men; it brings to the people provision in plenty, bears food within it, and each year yields to men a gift of which men, rich and poor, make use. Tell, if thou canst, O sage, wise in words, what the creature is.

(a) What are the 'wonderful works' in Passage A?

(b) What are the different ways in which the ship in Passage B is described as if it were a person?

(c) Using examples from both passages explain how language has changed over time. You might comment on such matters as vocabulary, grammar, meanings, structures and usage.

(NEAB)

Some groups combine Reading and Writing assessment on one paper. Treatment of the combined skills needed for these papers will be considered more fully in Chapters 11, 12, 16 and 18.

▶ **EXAMINATION ANSWERS**

▷ **Question 1**   *Outline answer*

If the passage is a story it is easy to grasp quite a lot about it when you first read it. Look at the questions: you will see that they move from questions about ideas and characters in the story (1a and 1b) to a more personal response, related to an incident in the story. Questions 1a and 1b need a concise statement of detail, and it would be worth making a list of relevant points first, then attempting a quick draft, before writing your final answer. The repetition of the adverb 'always' in the first two paragraphs show that Julia had been visiting the Dark Walk for some years. This year would be different because now she could share it with her young brother, i.e. he now has the experience she had, but presided over by an older sister who can call him 'babby' – all an indication that she is growing out of childhood. Her attitude to childish things is shown when we are told that 'She was twelve and at that age little girls are beginning to suspect most stories'. She dismisses them with disdain: 'Nonsense' and 'Pooh'. Another sign of her growing maturity is a concern for the safety of the trout and her understanding that it is at risk – a fairy godmother won't rescue the fish; it needs a human being to act. She overcomes her fear of the night and the Dark Walk to go herself and carry out the planned rescue. She also is able to keep the secret and joke about the possibility of the rescue being the work of a fairy godmother.

For Question 1b you have to deal with inference by thinking for yourself why these places are important to the story – a step forward in critical reading. You could, perhaps, choose the Dark Walk, and explain that it is a splendid example of a journey through what seems to be a dangerous and frightening place; that Julia feels she has to keep going through it and by doing so learns to control her imaginings. It is of vital importance to the story because that is the place of opportunity for her, later. The best answers would make the point that this is a small example of what we all have to face in life at some time.

In Question 2 you are asked to use your understanding of the story, applying it to an experience in your own life when you felt you had taken a step towards maturity.

▷ **Question 2**   *Outline answer*

The questions all explore aspects of Felipe's character.

(a) This answer is literal comprehension. You simply have to pick out what is his situation. This seems to involve where he is, what he is doing and why he is doing it. Felipe is a fisherman, tempted to kill a shark for its fins and tail for the two dollars price he will get for them, even though he knows it is against the law.

(b) This answer is a continuation of the first, isn't it? He has two sources of anxiety: the need to feed his children and the fear that he might be found out by the police or the agents for the Shark Fishing Company.

(c) His skills are those of his calling – he is very fit and 'aware of his own strength and of the elasticity of his body', and is able to harpoon the shark after it takes his bait. Quote occasionally in your answers, to show that you are drawing ideas from careful reading of the text.

(d) We learn about his attitude to authority towards the end of the passage, after he encounters 'fate, dressed in a blue uniform'. Notice that this is a two-sided affair: the policeman's attitude and behaviour evokes a response in Felipe, doesn't it? Pick out the words and phrases that tell you first about the policeman's attitude: he is 'harsh', 'sarcastic', 'smiling maliciously'; he gives orders: 'Come on, hand them over' and threatens: 'I'll take you and the fins along with me'. He has a 'hectoring' (bullying) voice, and continues being angry and threatening. Now, let's look at Felipe's side of the encounter. He is taken by surprise and reacts instinctively 'They are mine!' He feels he is more of a man in strength and physique than the policeman. Then a crowd gathers, and they also affect Felipe's attitude. He is taunted by what he thinks is their scorn, and by the supposed injustice of the situation. He finally acts in defiance, regardless of 'whatever the consequences may be'.

▷ Question 3   *Outline answer*

A1 (a) *What telephone number would you ring to find out more information about a trip to Big Pit?*

(b) *At what time of the day does the first underground tour start?*

These questions are simply tests of location.

Give one mark for each correct answer.

(c) *Who are not allowed to go down Big Pit? Why do you think this is?*

This question allows for location but also encourages some inference.

Give one mark for the correct answer.
Give an additional 1–2 marks for sensible inferences.   (5 marks)

A2 What would you see and hear underground on a visit to Big Pit?

This tests location, reorganization and some inference.

Give 1–2 marks, according to quality for those who merely locate relevant material in the text.

Give 3–5 marks according to quality for those who reorganize the material with some success.   (5 marks)

A3 *Choose two pictures in the leaflet. Say what is in them. Why might these pictures have been chosen to appear in the leaflet?*

This tests location and inference.

Give 1–2 marks for simple description of picture content.

Give a further 1–3 marks for sensible suggestions or comments on content.   (5 marks)

A4 *How does the leaflet try to attract visitors to Big Pit?*

This tests appreciation of style at a fairly simple level.
Give 1–2 marks for recognition of features.
Give 3–5 marks for comments.   (5 marks)

B5 Account of trip to Big Pit   (10 marks)

Levels 4–5

(Marks 4–7)   These answers are likely to rely very heavily on the Resource Material to produce simple content but with some understanding of the nature of the task.

Level 6

(Marks 8–10)   These answers will show understanding of the nature of the task and some sense of audience. Content will begin to have shape and coherence.

B6 Leaflet on attraction near home   (10 marks)

Levels 4–5

(Marks 4–7)   These answers will show some understanding of the demands of the task and show some awareness of appropriate form and content.

Level 6

(Marks 8–10)   These answers will show understanding of the demands of the task and awareness of appropriate form and content for a particular audience.

▷ **Question 4**   *Student's answer*

This student's answer was written in examination conditions.

---

1   *Metals can be recycled and need to be sorted out because drinking cans are made out of steel and aluminium. You cannot mix steel and aluminium together, so they have to be separated before recycling. It is a good idea to recycle aluminium cans because it takes a lot of energy to make them. Recycling also means that people don't have to find the raw materials to make that particular item. Most importantly, if we recycle everything it means that we don't have to dump large amounts of the waste into landfill sites, which means we can use that land for something more profitable. When we recycle, it takes away any chance of nasty and poisonous germs seeping into the soil or, even worse, getting into the air we breathe, for this is what happens at landfill sites.*

   Rubbish is split up before recycling into different categories – paper, glass, metal, organic waste and plastics.

   Paper is made from trees. This means trees have to be chopped down in their thousands for us to have paper, so to stop us chopping down trees we need to recycle paper, which is a very good idea.

   Glass has to be sorted into different types – brown, clear, green, so it is more effective. It is a good idea when it comes to recycling glass because it cuts down the energy needed to make bottles because it takes less heat to make a bottle out of broken, recycled glass than starting fresh with the raw materials.

2   ***Too Much Rubbish?***

   Have you got too much rubbish on your streets or in your home town? You think it could be dangerous? Want to do something about it? Well, you should, and by reading this article it may be able to help.

   The first thing you have to do is organize a litter pick. Get together with the whole community and walk around the streets and parks (public places) and pick up any litter or rubbish and put it in a bag. Take it to the sorting base where they can unmix it and then send it off to be recycled. Sounds easy enough? You'd have thought someone would already be doing it. Well, they probably aren't so do your bit. Just spend an hour or so picking up rubbish around your street or local park.

   Another way to stop the litter build up is to write to your local council and complain about the mess and how unsafe the rubbish is, and ask what they intend to do about it. You could even ask for or demand road sweepers to do the job.

   Once your community area is clear, you can't stop there. You have to keep going, recycle everything possible from paper to metal, otherwise you may find yourself in the same position again in the future.

   If none of what I have said has worked well, all I can say is move house to a better, cleaner area!

3   *Oh well, today's the day. I'll finally get rid of all that junk in my drawer. I'll start at the top and work my way down.*

   First drawer, those jeans. I remember climbing that big willow tree in the park in them. Paul got stung by a bee that day. He cried all the way to hospital. Nothing else in this drawer to go.

   My school drawer, all my essays come next. Think I'll have one final flick through them before I recycle them. All that work! Mrs Jones got really angry with us when I did this one – that Tony Smith played up. It all brings back happy memories. Those were the days; we had some great moments in school, especially when we were told off by Mrs Lucas, because she couldn't keep a straight face, and burst out laughing which made us all laugh, too, and that made her even more mad. I even laugh now to think of her face.

(continued)

> This is the final drawer – my grandad's war medals and the bit of shrapnel he got stuck in his leg. I wonder if I could bring myself to recycle that metal? This drawer brings back only sad memories of my grandfather who's dead now. Seeing all my old stuff being cleared out is sad, but, as the saying goes 'Take out the old, bring in the new!'

Examiner's comments

1   The candidate covers most of the points made in the article, but this is rather a list, repetitive. It is expressed in appropriate style, with only occasional minor awkwardnesses of expression.

2   Here the candidate has tried to consider presentation. The capitals of the title draw attention and the opening rhetorical question echoes in the reader's mind. Style here is different from that in Question 1 – more like speech, as it suitable for a lively article, but there is a good deal of relevant content here and new ideas, not in the stimulus material, too. The final joke is fun!

3   This is very attractive and readable. The memories are coming bitter-sweet and attached to particular articles. Recycling is mentioned when he/she wonders wistfully about melting down the shrapnel which belonged to his/her grandfather. Style is chatty but the essay is written in sentences. It is well paragraphed – each drawer has a new section of the writing.

Overall, the candidate has made a really good effort here; this is a paper on the C/D borderline.

▷ Question 5   *Tutor's answer*

This answer is by no means the only one possible, but it indicates a way of tackling it that will cover the chief requirements of a typical mark scheme. It is likely that marks would be awarded for picking out information from the passage and, to some extent, responding to implied meanings.

Question 1

The people whose feelings and attitudes to animals are shown in the two passages are James Herriot, a veterinary surgeon; Mrs Jacqui Durrell, an animal lover; her husband, Gerry; his elderly mother; and Mr Dean, an old man who owns a dog. In general terms, the feelings and attitudes of the people concerned depend on the way that they come into contact with animals. James Herriot takes a professional attitude and has expert knowledge. We know this by what he says, e.g. his diagnosis: 'You see this large swelling. It is caused by an internal growth'; 'it [the cancer] has progressed too far for anything to be done ...' His attitude to treatment is realistic. Bob is to him a patient, not a pet. It is his job to advise action, however painful his advice may be, and he recommends that 'it would be kindest to put him to sleep'. His behaviour throughout is also considerate: he strokes the dog's head and allows time for a final leave-taking of master and dog. He speaks reassuringly as he injects the fatal dose and his refusal to take payment shows that he has a deeper compassion than mere professional kindness.

In contrast, Mr Dean sees Bob as a pet and much loved companion. He responds with strong feeling. He speaks 'faintly' and looks 'bewildered'; his lips tremble and he falls silent and avoids the vet's glance. He is near to tears. Most readers of this passage will identify with him and share some of his grief.

Jacqui Durrell is more like James Herriot – animals come and go in her life: Whiskers is one of a number of animals to share her home. She, too, knows how to treat them professionally. She has an affectionate, amused view of Whiskers and his antics: 'Poor old Whiskers was given the shot.' (Compare how differently the expression 'the old fellow' in the first passage affects the reader.) Gerry's mother, however, like Mr Dean, has such a passion for animals that she treats them too tolerantly, allowing them to become totally 'unmanageable'. There is a contrast between her and Mr Dean: his attitude is shown with approval, but the reader is made to feel that she is misguided: 'of course, this was entirely the wrong treatment.'

Question 2

The passages are contrasted in mood. The first is mainly sad. The writer achieves this effect by the use of affectionate terms – 'the old dog's head', 'Bob', 'the old fellow', 'the loved voice', and in the way the bond between master and dog is shown to be threatened. The dog is helpless and at the mercy of the humans and, ironically, they must, as an act of kindness, kill it. The pathos of the old man is established in the description of his behaviour throughout, especially the strong feeling he shows. This pathos is increased by the stark and cheerless account of his environment. We see things through the eyes of the narrator, James Herriot, and share his compassionate mood as it grows; for example, he finds it difficult to open the discussion, and he speaks briskly but feels 'the old clichés had an empty ring'. The details of the final caress by the old man are sensitively observed and the contrast of the room, 'faded', 'cheerless', 'frayed', 'grimy', anticipate the bleakness the old man will feel when Bob has gone.

A great deal of the humour of the second passage results from the lively behaviour of the animals, and of Whiskers in particular. His name is comic as it reminds us of 'his enormous white moustache'. The reader is invited to share Gerry's amusement when he is bitten for his act of kindness, which is not appreciated. (Compare here the passive, and therefore pathetic, behaviour of Bob in a similar situation.) His size, 'a mere six inches', makes his ferocity and aggression seem funny. The list of his antics with Popadum, resembling those of very naughty children running riot, amuses, and the doting response of Gerry's mother, because it is so inappropriate, is humorous too. Looking closely at this part of the passage we are struck by the vitality of the language, full of exuberant action in such verbs as 'tore', 'rioted', and in the participles 'tearing', 'strewing'.

Question 3

Evidence from the passages to support this statement can be found. Mr Dean definitely expresses his appreciation of Bob's companionship when he remarks: 'It's miserable when Bob isn't following me around the house when I'm doing my little jobs.' Man and dog have been together for a long time and Bob returns his master's regard by thumping his tail 'at the sound of the loved voice'. The reader is in no doubt at all, as the many references already given in this answer illustrate, that Mr Dean finds the thought of separation from his dog very painful. The positive side of this emotion is the love he feels, but it is clear, too, that having animals living with you is not always a 'lovely' thing. In the second passage we are told that 'Gerry had a passion' for animals and the couple usually had several living with them in their home, and that Gerry's mother indulged them like children, even allowing them to rest in her lap. This shows the pleasure of living with them. On the other hand, it is possible to form a very different opinion from the passage. The creatures are demanding and probably costly (the need for a vet's advice, for instance); they impose a routine upon the household, and readily create havoc and do quite a lot of damage. Finally, they are not always grateful for the attention of humans, and may reward them with a bite!

Question 4

(Here you are asked for your personal opinion, so your answer will inevitably be different from mine, and everyone else's, to some extent.)

In the first passage a pet owner has noticed that his dog is ill. When the vet is called in he confirms that the dog has a terminal complaint and should be 'put to sleep'. The owner agrees, but is heart-broken. This made me remember an occasion when I was given a puppy as a Christmas present, fulfilling a wish that I had had for a very long time. It was tiny, beautiful and helpless. The house was full of people and activity because it was Christmas and the puppy scrambled about, amusing everyone with its antics. Suddenly it crawled, whimpering under a sofa: it was clearly hurt. When the vet came (after a long delay in which we helplessly watched the puppy suffering) he said that its back was seriously damaged and it would die in agony if he did not painlessly end its life. It was a terrible moment: the contrast between the special happiness of the gift on Christmas Day and the unexpected tragedy was almost too much to bear. I have never forgotten it.

On the other hand, being dominated by your pet is humiliating and annoying. In the second passage, Gerry's mother goes to endless trouble to prepare delicacies for the marmosets, and allows them to share her bedroom and even sit on her lap, but they begin to presume on her good nature and become 'unmanageable', 'rioting' and behaving mischievously, to the disapproval of the other adults in the household. I was similarly repaid for my care and doting affection for a stray cat. He quickly changed from a skinny, timid creature, hiding in the corner of the kitchen, to a huge over-fed monster, imposing his will on everyone. He demanded entry to all parts of the house, behaving in a very unpredictable fashion, and if he was thwarted, retaliated by tearing paper off the walls, among other things. Like the Durrells, I learned that it may not be wise to let the animal establish its own routine.

▷ **Question 6**   *Outline answers*

This question is likely to appeal to most candidates in content, though there is rather a lot of reading involved. First, notice the balance of marks: 40 for Section A, 30 for Section B. You should make sure that you spend a fair amount of time on each section of the paper, and probably a bit longer on Section A.

Question 1

You are asked to write *in a list* and *in your own words*. Beware of copying phrases for your list directly from the passages. First, jot down your list in rough, then rearrange the points in the most logical order. After that, think how you will introduce the list and finally, write the whole answer as a fair copy.

According to the article **Nightmare Neighbours**, the following are the problems mentioned as most frequent, alongside the suggested remedies:

Problem	Remedy
noise of animals **noise** of parties	collect evidence and inform the local Environmental Health Officer
noise of house and/or car alarms	inform the Environmental Health Officer
noise from building work on a neighbour's house	get an injunction to limit the noise disturbance to reasonable hours
aggressive **pets** who harm or frighten you	tell the police or dog warden
troublesome **pets** who invade your garden	erect a fence
parking across your driveway or garage entry	tell the Highways Department of the local council or the police. NB You have no right to the road space immediately outside your house!
disputes about **boundaries** and party walls or fences	take the neighbour to court – but this is expensive
overgrowing shrubs or trees	prune them to the boundary but do not take any fruit
extensions to next door buildings	object in writing to the council, ensure that planning permission has been sought, and canvas local support for your point of view.

This list is organized logically:

    problems of **noise**
    problems of **pets**
    problems of **parking**
    problems of **boundaries and buildings**

There are other ways of grouping the points, though:

    problems of **pets** (noise/aggression/invasion)
    problems of **buildings** (noise/extension)
    problems of **boundaries** (fences/gardens)

Think of the best order for your list.

Question 2a

As you are not given any direction about presentation, write in paragraphs here.

The caption sets up warning bells in the head; it catches the reader's attention to make him or her want to read on, doesn't it?

Question 2b

At first, the reader may think that the writer of the article may live next door to a noisy neighbour, but then you learn that this is not so; actually, she describes her own experience as trivial in comparison with that of some others, but it serves to show that every one of us may face this problem at some time or another. She is then able to give examples of more extreme cases, such as Mr Gladden, and even generalize about the British attitude to neighbours. 'As a nation,' she says, 'we do not love our neighbours. Some of us hate them ...'. (It is a good idea to support your points with snippet quotations, as in the last sentence).

Question 2c

The examples given in the article of difficult neighbours are amusing because they are so extreme: extroverts who decorate their properties garishly, the eccentric John Gladden, who draws crowds to stare at the strange additions to his property, the 'menagerie' keepers. They are not too extreme to believe in, though. They certainly illustrate provocation and the desperate attempts of despairing neighbours to conceal the true facts, as they seek to sell up and move: 'No ... not at all ...', only to be shown up by their more candid infant: 'Oh yes, they do ...'!

Question 2d

The writer chooses words and phrases to contrast peace such as 'quiet', 'restful' with those suggesting disturbance, 'bark all night', 'all-night Karaoke sessions', or irritation, 'troublesome', and excessive or extreme behaviour, such as 'huge fish', 'huge model of Winston Churchill', etc. She writes in a relaxed style, with some cliché, which would make most readers feel comfortably at home with the article: 'knock each other about', 'strained relations', 'military hardware', 'down the drain', 'in the doghouse' – this last has a punning reference to the pets just mentioned, amusingly.

Question 3

You should set your work out with subheadings. Do not write in jottings, though, as you have been asked to write in complete sentences.

A Weekend of Hell

<u>Saturday, 31 May, 1997</u>

As this is the first really sunny day, this year, I thought I'd spend it in the garden, but guess what: the Nortons decided to do the same. They had their lunch on the patio – at least that's what they call the strip of concrete by their back door. It seemed to be a lunch for under-fives – about twenty of them – and it went on from 12.00, until their parents came for the children at gone five. There was non-stop shouting, shrieking, crying, and fighting all afternoon. Chrissie Norton – that little red-headed fiend – climbed up in their apple tree and repeated everything we were doing at the top of her voice: 'They're eating egg sandwiches'; 'they haven't got ice-cream'; 'there's an ugly old woman over there who looks like a witch'. Just as it went quiet, my nose caught a whiff of acrid smoke. You've guessed – they had lit a bonfire, at five o'clock on the first lovely warm evening of the year. I went in and shut all the windows.

<u>Sunday, 1 June 1997</u>

Today the Nortons had a row with the Wests over cutting the privet hedge. They said it was shading their garden. Mr West told Mr Norton to leave it alone and stormed into his bungalow, red-faced, yelling: 'I'll see you in court!' Happy days ... It's church this evening. I hope the vicar doesn't preach from the text: 'Love thy neighbour'.

▷ **Question 7   *Outline answer***

Here you are asked to consider each passage in turn. In your answer, do not be content with one or two points: a careful search will find several. This question requires close reading of the passage.

(a) The 'wonderful works' in Passage A are the wonders of the sea, part of God's power in calling up storm winds and great waves, which terrify and threaten the lives of sailors. It also praises his power to calm the storm and bring men safely to shore.

(b) You may have noticed how vividly the riddle is expressed. Part of this effect is personification, that is, giving the inanimate thing described human characteristics. Look again closely, and then make a note of these human features. I have listed: 'journeys', 'grind against the sand', 'cry', 'strange creature had not sight nor hands, shoulders nor arms', the thing 'must move on one foot'; 'it had many ribs'; 'its mouth was in the midst'. That's quite a lot, isn't it?

(c) This question is more difficult. Here you need to look at the different aspects of the writing and compare them with Modern English. You could take each feature in turn, e.g. vocabulary. In Passage A (the seventeenth-century English text) there are unfamiliar words: 'the deep' (for 'the depths of the sea'); 'reel' (for 'walk unsteadily'); 'haven' (for 'place of safety'); 'assembly' (gathering – rather like a school assembly!). Though written in Modern English, Passage B has phrases with an archaic tone, e.g. 'artful work' (we would say now 'well-made by a craftsman'); 'go forth' (for set out) and so on. You probably noticed the endings to the verbs in Passage A 'lifteth' and 'bringeth' – English used to be conjugated. By close examination you can pick out many changes, and perhaps add that, as English is not a dead language, it is changing constantly, even today.

A STEP FURTHER

Even in the busy time when you are preparing for your examinations, it is important that you keep on reading widely and, as you read, 'interrogate the text', that is, be fully involved as reader, thinking about the content and questioning it. Notice also how different writers have styles to suit different purposes. This is the best way to prepare for reading comprehension tests.

SUMMARY

▷ You will have found information about a range of reading skills, including close reading, to prepare you for the different types of comprehension tests you are likely to meet.

▷ The different types of tests are literary and non-literary comprehension, responding to passages with a common theme, and responding to the language and style of a passage.

▷ You will know that you must be prepared to respond to pre-twentieth-century texts, including Shakespeare, as well as twentieth-century texts; some of these texts should be whole works of literature.

From reading to writing

▷ **GETTING STARTED**

There are many ways in which you can use your reading by writing a response which shows creativity in your coursework. This chapter is about exploring and developing what you read: ideas, themes, aspects, can be taken further, giving you the opportunity to be imaginative or creative, rather than to study in detail the exact meaning of what is read.

The following is a list of some of the types of writing you might do, stimulated by reading of different kinds:

▷ Suppose you have read two short stories on the same theme, but different in style. Discuss what makes them different and how they compare to any experiences you have had of this kind.

▷ Read a play and imagine you are one of the characters. Write about what you think of events with hindsight, looking back some years later. Take a story you know and like and consider producing it on television. Which episodes would you want to choose to make the greatest impression on an audience? What would you need to leave out? Would you want to add extra characters or incidents? What difficulties do you think you might meet as a producer?

▷ After reading a novel, write a review of it, to encourage someone else to read and enjoy it.

You can write on some of these topics immediately, using your own thoughts and feelings. For others, you might need to get more information – do some research. There are ideas for writing in most of what you read, if you are looking out for them.

TOPIC	STUDY	REVISION 1	REVISION 2
Writing down your first response			
Using a flow chart			
Asking yourself questions			
Going from first to final draft			

▷ **WHAT YOU NEED TO KNOW**

The kinds of writing already discussed in this chapter vary a good deal. For all of them, though, you need to bear certain things in mind. First, you should find something in what you read that will really make you want to write and sustain a response. Then, your first enthusiasm and interest should carry over into the writing you do. Next, take time to think about what you have read: let ideas develop in your mind. When you are ready to start writing, work out some possible approaches on paper. Your writing will probably be more successful if you work through one or more drafts before coming to the final version. Some practical ways of going about writing from your reading are dealt with below.

'Ideas for writing about your reading'

▷ **Writing down your first response**

To help you prepare to write there are a number of useful skills you can acquire. Capturing your **first response** on paper can be very useful when you come to write. If you make a few notes, you can read them to refresh your memory, but they must be notes that will bring the first experience of reading back to life for you.

Remember to

▶ keep notes short – you don't want to paraphrase the book
▶ use your own words
▶ keep your notes well spaced, so that you can make additions later.

▷ **Using a flow chart**

Some people prefer to make a **flow chart**. By doing this they can keep their options open, and let their ideas flow for a longer period before they become set into a fixed form. Figure 11.1 is a flow chart made by a student preparing to write after reading Harper Lee's *To Kill a Mocking Bird*. He wanted to write about prejudice in the story and began by putting his ideas down quickly as they came to him.

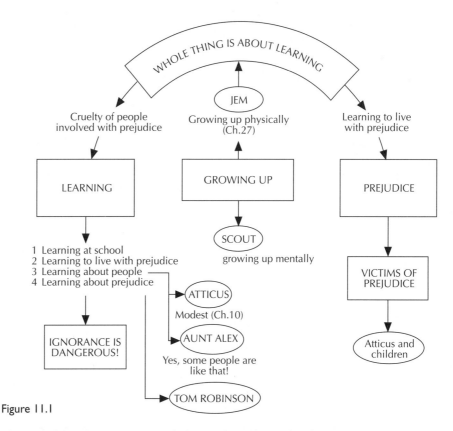

Figure 11.1

If you make a chart, it is a good idea to discuss it with a friend, or make one as a group.

▷ **Asking yourself questions**

You may sometimes be given a definite writing assignment based on a book or extracts, but at other times be in an 'open' situation where you decide what you write. To get started, then, it may be helpful to **ask yourself questions** which interest you, e.g. in the example above, the student may well have asked himself: 'Which characters show prejudice in this novel?' He may have gone on from there to his flow chart and a plan, and so reached the point of writing a first draft.

▷ **Going from first to final draft**

Drafting a piece of coursework is another important skill to acquire. You write a first version, or **draft** as it is called, following your notes, flow chart or plan, and then you read it through and make alterations, improving the arrangement and wording, the spelling and punctuation. Here are two examples of how the piece of work on Prejudice grew from first to final draft.

This was the first draft the student wrote:

GROWING UP

'A first draft'

1   This book is basically about a childhood which vanishes. It involves learning and prejudice both subjects having strong links with each other. It involves Jem and Scout Finch, who are brought up into a world of prejudice, racial and otherwise. They have a lot to learn, for ignorance is dangerous.

2   They are growing up amongst blacks. They feel slightly uncomfortable, I think, but Scout at least shows no real sign of prejudice. There is a lot of difference between the two races, which can be seen when the children visit Calpurnia's Church in Chapter twelve, when the author says 'Negroes worshipped in it on Sundays and white men gambled in it on weekdays', and before the trial of Tom Robinson when Jem said 'around here once you have a drop of Negro blood, that makes you all black'.

3   They also have to learn about prejudice and people. Scout is prejudiced against the Ewells, because of the way in which they made them lose the court case. They are prejudiced against Mrs Duboise, because they do not know her well enough to form any real conclusive view of her, until she is dead. They have to learn about people like Aunt Alexandria, who plays quite an important part in her growing up, although they do not realise it. They have to learn to control their prejudices, like the one against Boo Radley, where it is not until the end of the book that they form any reasonable conclusion on Boo Radley.

4   There are a very wide range of characters in the book, several of which Scout is unreasonably prejudiced against at first, like Boo Radley, Mrs Duboise and Tom Robinson. However, she does not know her father very well. She thinks of him as rather senile, and a bit cracked, taking on the court case, which she is not very enthusiastic about. She is not experienced enough with people to know her father very well. She does not perceive his modesty, and will not let anyone know too much about him.. She is immensely pleased in Chapter ten when Atticus shoots the mad dog with incredible accuracy. Her view of a father is 'someone to boast about in school' because, as Scout herself says after the incident: 'Ain't everybody's daddy the deadest shot in Maycomb County!'

5   The children are victims of prejudice, which is imposed by Atticus defending Tom Robinson. He is branded a traitor in his elder circles, which penetrates even Scout's social life and she is called names; for example, when her cousin Francis says that Atticus is 'ruinin' the family' by being 'nothin' but a nigger-lover'. This is another 'fact of life', and he intentionally did this in Maycomb County, and an example of the cruelty of the people in those days of the depression, when men have to hate someone, so they hate those of another race. Prejudice is essentially a preconceived idea of someone without any solid evidence. It can be between sexes, classes (esp. England) religion, race, appearance and politics. As I have already said, the main victims of prejudice in this book are: Mrs Duboise, Atticus, Scout and Jem Finch, the Ewells, who bring back their own prejudice, and Tom Robinson.

6   The two children are not growing up in exactly the same way; Scout is growing mentally more than anything, and Jem, who is thirteen, is growing more physically. Dill, Scout's 'future fiancé', is a very important topic in Scout's maturity, because he impresses on her a more ladylike manner, which shows that she has grown up from her tomboy days in first grade, when she was always fighting and doing the wrong thing. Dill is becoming more masculine towards the end of the book, when he runs away from his 'new' father to join Scout, which is a very fanciful but interesting story. He had matured into a young gentleman since they had first met him, and had helped Scout mature in the same way. However she is still pleasantly, maybe even helpfully, innocent, which is shown when she and Jem walk into the circle of men surrounding her father, and asks Mr Cunningham about his entailment, and tells him how his son does at school. If she was four years older, she would never have done that thing, but in her innocent questions she was uncovering something very important about her character. She, one eight-year-old child, could bring a whole crowd of grown men to their senses. 'Hmp, maybe we need a police force of children ...' said Atticus.

7   One of the major parts in the story was played by Tom Robinson. When the truth is discovered about him (even though it is to no avail in a court of law), Scout realises the error in having preconceived ideas about black people. As she has lived all her life among blacks, she knows them, and should not feel prejudiced towards them. However, there is still a childish misconception in her mind, and a secret dislike for Negroes after what she had been through. But Tom Robinson was different. He seems nice, innocent of the disgusting crime

which he is accused of having done, and he tries to make the people like him, although knows that he cannot succeed because he is black. He is honest, and when asked whether he could have raped Mayella, says yes. He is also a very strong man, and he wanted to escape very much. This gives Scout a very different view of him, and of the whole subject of prejudice.

This was the final version:

GROWING UP in To Kill a Mockingbird

This book is basically about a childhood which vanishes. It involves learning and prejudice, both of which are strongly connected. It is about Jem and Scout Finch, and Atticus, their father. The children are brought up in a strongly prejudiced world, both racially and otherwise, on which subject they have a lot to learn, because ignorance is dangerous.

They are growing up amongst Negroes, who they have lived with all their lives. They seem unintentionally prejudiced towards them, but it is not a strong feeling of dislike, as towards other characters in the book. There is a great deal of difference between the two races, which is evident when the children visit First Purchase Church with Calpurnia, 'where Negroes worshipped on Sundays, and white men gambled on weekdays'. It is also obvious before Tom Robinson's trial when Jem says 'around here, once you have a drop of Negro blood, that makes you all black'.

They also have to learn about prejudice and people. Scout is prejudiced against the Ewell family, partly because of the way in which they inhabit the Maycomb rubbish tip, and partly because of the way that their lies affected the court case, and helped to convict Tom Robinson. She is also prejudiced against Mrs Duboise, and the way in which she speaks and acts towards the children, but she does not know her well enough and does not have enough experience with people to form any conclusive view of her, until she is dead. She teaches them a lesson not to retaliate without thinking. They have to learn about people like Aunt Alexandra, and to control their prejudices, like those against Boo Radley, because it is not until the end of the book that they form any reasonable judgement on him.

The children are victims of prejudice, imposed by Atticus defending Tom Robinson. He is branded a traitor by his friends and family, and this means that the children are called names, e.g. when their cousin Francis says to Scout that her father is 'ruinin' the family' by being 'nothin' but a nigger-lover'. This aspect is important because it means that the children can learn what it is like to be victimised, and it is a fact of life which Atticus is very eager for them to learn. In fact, it is reasonable to suggest that he took up the court case for one reason that the children could learn this very important fact. The story is set during the Depression; times were hard and men had to hate someone, so they picked people of another race. Prejudice is essentially a preconceived idea of someone without any solid evidence. It can be between sexes, classes (especially in England) religions, races, appearances and politics. As I have already stated, the main victims of prejudice in this book are: Mrs Duboise, Atticus, Scout and Jem Finch, the Ewells (who seem to bring back their own prejudice), and Tom Robinson.

The two children are not growing up in exactly the same way; Scout is growing mentally more than anything, and Jem is reaching puberty, and growing more physically. Dill, Scout's 'future fiancé', is a very important aspect of Scout's maturation and helps to change her from a tomboy in first grade, when she was forever fighting and doing the wrong thing, to a more ladylike girl aged ten. Dill himself is becoming more masculine towards the end of the book, when he runs away from his 'new' father to join Scout (a very fanciful but interesting story). He has matured into a young gentleman since they had first met him. Scout, however, is still innocent of the reasoning of men, which is exemplified when she walks straight into the circle of men outside the county jail to be next to her father, and asks Mr Cunningham, who meant business, and not to be played up by eight-year-old girls, about his entailment, and tells him how his son Walter is getting on in school. If she was four years older, she would never have done this, but in her questions she was uncovering something very important about her character, and the character of any child at that age; the innocent, purposeful attitude of the girl, and the don't-take-no-for-an-answer personality. If she, one eight-year-old child, could bring a crowd of grown men to their senses, then as Atticus says, 'Maybe we need a police force of children!'

There is a very wide range of characters in this book, some of which Scout is prejudiced against at first. There is her father, whom she does not seem to know very well. She thinks of him as being rather senile at times, and maybe even a bit crazy, taking on the court case in the way that he does.

She does not have enough experience to perceive his modesty, his strange methods, like making Jem go and apologise to Mrs Duboise, knowing full well that he might have had his head blown off, his experience in life, and his being a good father. His modesty, not letting anyone know about his talents, is

(continued)

'A final version'

> *important. She is very pleased in Chapter ten when Atticus shoots the mad dog with incredible accuracy, because, as Scout herself says, 'Ain't everybody's daddy the deadest shot in Maycomb Country!'*
>
> *One of the most important parts of the story is played by Tom Robinson when the truth is discovered about him (even though it was to no avail in a court of law), Scout realises the error in having preconceived ideas about anybody. As she has lived all her life among blacks, she knows them, and should not feel prejudiced in any way towards them. However, there is still a childish misconception in her mind, and a secret dislike for negroes. But Tom is different. He seems nice, innocent, incapable of the disgusting crime which he is alleged to have committed, and he tries to make the white people like him, but knows that he cannot succeed because he is black. He is honest in Scout's mind, and strong, and all these factors combine to give Scout a very different view of prejudice.*
>
> *A similar example is that of Boo Radley, Scout simply bases her evidence that he is mad on tales told to her by the neighbours. But it really seems that he is a bit mad and childish, but he needs someone to exhort him. Scout knows so little about him, that it is not until the very end of 'To Kill a Mockingbird' that she realises that she had given Boo nothing in return for his kindness, and she deeply regrets it. Boo Radley played another very important part, even more than Tom Robinson, in giving Scout a final opinion on the folly of prejudice.*

Notice how several changes have been made – e.g. the original fourth paragraph moved to later in the piece – until the boy was satisfied with his version.

► EXAMINATION QUESTIONS

All Groups will require candidates to show examples of their written response to a variety of reading materials. **NEAB** (Syllabus B), **MEG** and **SEG** require coursework of the kind considered in this chapter, and **NEAB** (Syllabus A) has similar questions in its written paper (see an example below). You may find you have several pieces of coursework of the right sort to choose from for your examination folder; try to choose a piece or pieces which show that you can:

▶ fully understand what you read
▶ clearly convey your thoughts and feelings about it
▶ select what is relevant
▶ organize your writing effectively.

Here is a question typical of the kind you might choose to write on.

▷ Question 1

Choose a story you like and write a review of it, so that someone of your own age would know whether he or she would be likely to enjoy it.

Try to think how you would attempt this assignment before going on to the Outline Answers below. Choose a story and make some notes, or a flow chart, ready for a first attempt at a draft.

The next question represents the type of reading-into-writing opportunities to be found in written papers.

▷ Question 2

Writing: Higher Tier A–D   **(Time allowed: 2 hours)**
In this question a passage and a comprehension exercise, using more closed questions, will already have been attempted by candidates. Read the two extracts carefully, then answer the questions that follow.

SECTION A

Read the following extracts and then answer **ALL** *the questions which follow.*

Passage 1

Going to the shore on the first morning of the holiday, the young English boy stopped at a turning of the path and looked down at a wild and rocky bay, and then over to the crowded beach he knew so well from other years. His mother walked on in front of him carrying a bright-striped bag in one hand. Her other arm, swinging loose, was very white in the sun. The boy watched that white, naked arm, and turned his eyes, which had a frown behind them, towards the bay and back again to his mother. When she felt he was not with her, she swung round. 'Oh, there you are, Jerry!' she said. She looked impatient, then smiled. 'Why, darling, would you rather not

10   come with me? Would you rather…' She frowned, worrying over what amusements he might secretly be longing for which she had been too busy or too careless to imagine. He was very familiar with that anxious, apologetic smile. His concern sent him running after her. And yet, as he ran, he looked back over his shoulder at the wild bay; and all morning as he played on the safe beach, he was thinking of it.

Next morning, when it was time for the routine of swimming and sunbathing, his mother said: 'Are you tired of the usual beach, Jerry? Would you like to go somewhere else?'

'Oh, no!' he said quickly, smiling at her, feeling guilty that he was neglecting

20   her. Yet, walking down the path with her, he blurted out, 'I'd like to go and have a look at those rocks down there.'

She gave the idea her attention. It was a wild-looking place, and there was no-one there, but she said: 'Of course, Jerry. When you've had enough, come to the big beach. Or just go straight back to the villa, if you like.' She walked away, that bare arm, now slightly reddened from yesterday's sun, swinging. And he almost ran after her again, feeling it unbearable that she should go by herself, but he did not.

She was thinking: 'Of course he's old enough to be safe without me. Have I been keeping him too close? He mustn't feel he ought to be with me. I must

30   be careful.'

He was an only child, eleven years old. She was a widow. She was determined to be neither possessive nor lacking in devotion. She went worrying off to her beach.

As for Jerry, once he saw that his mother had gained her beach, he began the steep descent to the bay. From where he was, high up among red-brown rocks, it was a scoop of moving bluish green fringed with white. As he went lower, he saw that it spread among small promontories and inlets of rough, sharp rock, and the crisping, lapping surface showed stains of purple of darker blue. Finally, as he ran sliding and scraping down the last few yards,

40   he saw an edge of white surf, and the shallow, luminous movement of water over white sand, and, beyond that, a solid heavy blue.

He ran straight into the water and began swimming. He was a good swimmer. He went out fast over the gleaming sand, over a middle region where rocks lay like discoloured monsters under the surface, and then he was in the real sea – a warm sea where irregular cold currents from the deep water shocked his limbs.

When he was so far out that he could look back not only on the little bay but past the promontory that was between it and the big beach, he floated on the surface and looked for his mother. There she was, a speck of yellow under

50   an umbrella that looked like a slice of orange peel. He swam back to shore, relieved at being sure she was there, but all at once very lonely.

(Adapted from *Through the Tunnel* by Doris Lessing)

In the following extract the narrator tells us how he prepared to move from his junior school to the secondary grammar school which was some distance from his home. He also tells us how he felt about the change.

Passage 2

All this was during a time which seemed carefree and radiant when I looked back afterwards in such longing, from the middle of my misery. I was still at my first school when I had the bicycle. Then I sat for a scholarship to go to a secondary school. We were given clean squares of pink blotting-paper and pens of unpainted wood with bright nibs which had never dipped in the ink. I sat with a big space around me, tense with fear and importance, trying to breathe properly.

My father had to fill in a long questionnaire asking if he would be prepared to pay for my uniform and books, and I think it was more than he could manage.
10   Everything for that place had extra shillings on it. There were anxious discussions which I was not supposed to hear.

In the summer holidays my mother took me to buy a new cap and tie, and the badge of Memorial Road School for my jacket. The colours were purple and grey, and the badge was just a large 'M' in a purple frame. After that we went to the bus station and set out to find the school itself.

I remember us getting off the bus and twisting through several streets in a quiet district where everything was strange, going over some black dirt near a small park where there was a sand-pit for playing in, climbing slowly most of the time.

Suddenly at the top of the road all I could see was a line of railings made from
20   metal tubes, like scaffolding. There was only sky behind it, and I cried out: 'It's like the seaside!' I knew it was impossible for a promenade and the sea to be up there, but I started pulling my mother along, making her walk faster, till we reached the top.

It was a large piece of flat common, dropping gently, with no buildings until a low factory began, behind a line of poplars that seemed a long way off. To the right and left there were houses and streets, but I looked straight out, as I would have done at the edge of the sea. 'That's where Uncle Jim works,' my mother said. She pointed at the unreal factory, glinting innocently behind the far-off trees.

We had come a little out of our way. An old man directed us back downhill to our
30   right, and soon we stood in front of a grim, high building that reminded me of the city hospital. It was so large, so forbidding, that I could not imagine myself going there. Because it conveyed nothing I was quite brave, standing beside my mother staring across the queer blankness of the tarmac playground at the dead school with its rows of blind windows. There were three more weeks of holiday before I had to face the first day. My mother murmured: 'You'll be all right,' and the words, or perhaps the anxiety that had crept into her voice, gave me a twinge of uneasiness. I was not really worried until then. I tried to pretend she had spoken without thinking, for something to say, and was not comforting me.

We found our bus stop and went home. It was Friday, which meant fish-cakes
40   and home-made chips for tea, with moist new bread. I always looked forward to Fridays.

When the first Monday was still a week away a little fear came into me. Instead of dying it grew stronger, until by the Sunday it was a dread. The next day I would have to go, there was no escape, no way out, and in my despair I felt I should never trust my parents again. They had betrayed me, trapped me in some terrible sly way. I did not stop to think that I would have had to leave my old school in any case, because I was too old to stay there. I only knew I was being wrenched out of a place where I was rooted and happy, though I had never realised it before.

50   Somehow I managed to get up next day, eat some breakfast and then put on the blazer and cap with their hateful badges. But as my mother held open the back

gate and I wheeled my bicycle through dumbly, I saw by her face that she understood.

'Never mind, you'll soon be home,' she said hopelessly. 'The first day's always the worst.'

(Adapted from *Native Ground* by Philip Callow)

Answer **ALL** *the questions.*

Questions on the first passage

1 Look at lines 1–15. How do you think Jerry regarded his mother and his relationship with her?
2 In your own words, write down the thoughts and feelings of Jerry's mother, which are suggested by lines 16–33.
3 (a) Describe in your own words the main features of the 'wild bay'.
   (b) Using quotation and/or reference, explain what you think Jerry's reaction was to swimming in the 'wild bay' separated from his mother.

Questions on the second passage

4 Look at lines 1–7. What were the boy's feelings at the thought of leaving his junior school?
5 Look at lines 29–38. How does the writer suggest that the boy disliked the appearance of his new school?
6 In your own words, explain what you understand by the following:
   (a) 'There were anxious discussions which I was not supposed to hear' (lines 10–11).
   (b) 'The next day I would have to go, there was no escape, no way out, and in my despair I felt I should never trust my parents again' (lines 43–45).
   (c) 'I only knew I was being wrenched out of a place where I was rooted and happy' (lines 47–48).
7 By referring to the passage, describe the impression you get of the home life of the boy and his relations with his parents.

SECTION B

Choose **ONE** *of the following, and write 350–600 words.*
Credit will be given for your ability to describe scenes, people, thoughts and feelings and for your choice of words.

1 Write about the return of Jerry and his mother to their villa that evening. You may, if you wish, write as if you are **either** Jerry **or** his mother or you may write a play script.
2 With reference to the second passage, describe the boy's first day at his new school in such a way as to bring out his feeling about what happens to him.
3 Write an account of a visit to the seaside you made with your parents. You may write in any way you like but you might like to try writing about a time when you were younger and particularly enjoyed new challenges such as swimming, climbing on the rocks, or going out in a boat; **or** you might like to write around the idea of being lost, or cut off by the tide. The account can be real or imaginary.
4 The second extract is all about the fears and worries that build up in people when they have to face something new and unknown, like going to a new school, or having an operation; even going to the dentist, or to a party if you do not know many people.
   Write about something **you** worried about a lot. If you like, you can include both what you felt **before** the event, and what it was really like when it happened.

(MEG)

▷ EXAMINATION ANSWERS

▷ **Question 1**   *Outline answer*

There are as many answers as there are books to review and readers to respond. Even so a good book review has to keep a balance between saying something true about the book's contents – enough to interest but not so much that the reader feels there is no need to go on to the book itself – and offering a fresh and individual response. The main problem with the first requirement is the temptation that some reviewers have to summarize the plot at great length, losing the mood and vitality of the original work and boring the reader. One way round this is to choose one or two key incidents that will attract or intrigue, and offer them as tasters. You might begin with a striking quotation, highlighting one of these incidents. Again, avoid listing characters with just a sentence of description. Think of ways of saying something about them that will arouse interest, leaving the reader wishing to find out more. Your own response is an equally important part of a review. It can be negative, but there is a chance that you will write a less successful review of a book you dislike (if you are trying to be fair) than of one you really enjoy. Additional details worth including are comments on other books of a similar type that you would recommend, or other books by the same author. Finally, a bright review cover, with a picture or design that sums up for you something important about the book as well as showing clearly the author and title, is a good idea.

Student's answer

Here is a student's answer to Question 1 above. The book reviewed is *It's My Life* by Robert Leeson.

A Book Review
Book It's My Life

Author Robert Leeson

It's My Life is about a fifteen-year-old girl called Janice who has a lot of trouble to take care of when her mother leaves her father, her brother and her. The reason for this, no one knew. Janice had a lot of trouble also because she had been asked out and wasn't sure of what to say. She told the boy that she would go out with him and they made a date. When Janice came home she couldn't go because her father said that Friday was his night out and that she would have to stay home and look after her brother. Janice got annoyed and didn't turn up which annoyed her very much.

Janice went to try and get a job but the interviewer recognised Janice as Janice's mother used to work there, and told her that he would contact her. Janice had to go to another interview to see if she could get a job. The interviewer told Janice that he told her that her mother left on a train (he didn't know where) because she couldn't take the strain any longer.

You could tell that Janice's mother was up to something when Janice came home and found the kitchen stored up with food. (Valerie stored up the kitchen with food to last her husband, son and daughter for a while.)

I didn't really have a favourite character as I didn't enjoy the book much. I found the book boring and hard to concentrate on because I don't really read books like this. The type of book I like reading is The Pedestrian by Ray Bradbury. They are interesting. I also like adventures, horror and romantic books. The best I like are short stories as I can finish them in one go.

Examiner's comments
The writer has chosen a book that she has read right through and to which she has a definite response, even though it is not one of approval. She has given the title and author clearly at the start. Then she has written three paragraphs giving an account of the story, but the best of these is the third, where an incident is retold, conveying the actual feel of the book. She has given her opinion of the quality of the book in the fourth paragraph. It is rather a pity that she did not really enjoy it: she would almost certainly have had more to say if she had liked it. She concentrates instead on other, similar books she knows about. Overall the result is a little unbalanced; ideally, more space should have been given to evaluation. However, despite the errors, this is a readable review, with sufficient detail to make a reader want to go on to the book itself.

▷ **Question 2**   *Outline answer*

Here are outline answers to the questions set on the two passages in Section A.

Passage 1

1   There is clearly some anxiety about his mother, indicated by his frown, and the concern which sent him running to her. He was familiar with her gestures and ways, and felt more secure when he was with her.

2   Using your own words, you can touch on her concern to give Jerry some independence from herself, yet her worry that he be safe and well. She wanted him to know he was loved, yet not to overdo it so that he felt her too possessive.

3   (a) The bay was surrounded by high, red-brown rocks. There were bits of sharp rock here and there, some peeping above the water line, with white surf at the waters edge. Beneath the water was white sand and further out, as the water became deeper, the colour became a deeper blue.

For three marks only some of these points need be mentioned, using your own way of expression.

(b) Clearly there is an element of excitement and pleasure, indicated by how he ran straight into the water and the speed with which he swam out from the shore. There was still a concern for his mother's welfare, indicated by his looking for her even as he was floating on the surface of the water. This concern is reinforced by the words 'relieved at being sure she was there'. He also felt lonely at being separated from her.

Passage 2

4   His feelings included a sense of importance at having the opportunity to take a scholarship to go to the grammar school. There was also fear, perhaps of the exam itself and of the thought of going to a new and unfamiliar environment, should he pass. He was very happy at his original school, as indicated by the first sentence.

5   The use of the words 'grim', and the likening of the school to a 'city hospital', indicate that the boy disliked the appearance of the new school. This is followed by other words and expressions which suggest dislike, 'forbidding', 'blankness of the tarmac playground', 'dead school', 'blind windows', etc.

6   (a) The parents were discussing the cost of sending their son to the expensive new school, and were clearly worried as to whether they could afford it. However they did not wish their son to be aware of these financial problems, but somehow he had overheard them.

(b) The next day was the Monday, the first day at his new school. It was certain that Monday would come, no matter how much he wished it would not, so there was no escape from his dread of going to the new school. He was extremely cross with his parents; he saw it as their fault that he had to leave the happy, familiar primary school and go to the unknown school that had looked so forbidding on his first visit to it.

(c) He couldn't understand the educational system and why children had to change schools at certain ages. What he *did* know was that he was being forced to leave a school in which he had been happy and contented, and at which he had become familiar with all its ways.

7   There are many possibilities here. Remember to *use* the passage as evidence for the points you make about the home life of the boy and his relations with his parents.

Section B

In Section B you are invited to write on one topic only. You will see that the four topics are of two kinds: those (1 and 2) which are directly related to the passage read, and those (3 and 4) where you are quite free to respond imaginatively in an individual way.

If you find personal writing difficult, probably one of the first two questions would be the better choice, as you have the material in the passage to give you a start. Even if you enjoy personal writing, the passages will help, if you choose 3 or 4, because your mind will be filled with thoughts of taking up a challenge, struggling to achieve something new or facing a worrying, new experience. Notice that suggestions are made here to help you think along relevant lines from the start.

A STEP FURTHER

Look out for reviews of books and plays that you know in the press or magazines that you read. Think about the differences between the book and the film or television version. Each of these shows how a screen-writer and director interprets an original text.

SUMMARY

▷   You have been given information about writing based on your reading and how to make use of your first responses as reader.

▷   Planning devices, such as a flow chart, are discussed and also asking questions to get the most out of the texts you read.

▷   There was more information on drafting, planning and editing your work.

Chapter
12

Summary

▷ **GETTING STARTED**

Writing a summary typically involves the following steps: reading through the material or listening to gather information, selecting important points that you want to bring out, writing those down in a suitable order, making a draft and writing a final, corrected version. In their written papers GCSE Boards will not usually ask candidates simply to write a summary, but nearly all will set questions and coursework exercises that require some form of task based on printed material for a particular purpose being put in order and then summarized, e.g. an extract from a guidebook, a diary, two contrasting eye-witness accounts of the same situation, or extracts from a newspaper article. You may be given information in statistical form occasionally.

The **National Criteria** state that in English candidates must be given opportunities to show that they can

▶ understand and convey information
▶ understand, order and present facts, ideas and opinions
▶ evaluate information in reading material and in other media, and select what is relevant to specific purposes
▶ show a sense of audience and an awareness of style in both formal and informal situations.

LONDON	MEG	NEAB	NICCEA	SEG	WJEC	IGCSE	TOPIC	STUDY	REVISION I	REVISION 2
✓	✓	✓	✓	✓	✓	✓	Understanding and conveying information			
			✓		✓		Organizing and presenting facts			
✓	✓	✓	✓	✓	✓	✓	Evaluating information from texts			
					✓		Evaluating information from media			
	✓	✓	✓	✓	✓		Selecting and presenting information			
		✓			✓		Distinguishing between fact and opinion			
✓	✓	✓	✓	✓	✓	✓	Showing a sense of audience in conveying information			

▷ **WHAT YOU NEED TO KNOW**

There are several very important things to get right in order to produce a good summary – that is, one that reflects correctly the facts and opinions in the material you are given, and which can be easily followed by the readers for whom it is intended.

'Bear your readers in mind.'

There are a number of **questions** to ask yourself at the outset:

▶ Who do I have in mind as the readers (sometimes called the 'audience') of this piece of writing?
▶ What sort of style will they respond to most readily?
▶ Which are the key ideas/opinions that I *have* to include?
▶ Which are the minor ideas/opinions that I *could* include?
▶ How long should I make it?
▶ How should I set the work out: in short paragraphs, columns, as a letter, etc.?

If you are given any instructions, read them carefully and think about the way you need to shape and present your summary, from the start.

▷ Writing in an appropriate style

You may have to choose between a fairly formal style in Standard English, if you are writing a report or article, or a more relaxed style to suit, say, members of a youth club or readers of a local paper. In the second case, remember that this could include a wide range of readers, so keep your style generally 'reader friendly', without using slang or writing inaccurately. Good communication is directed *to* someone, so if you want your work to be readable by a particular group you need to find a style to suit them. It may help to try to imagine a typical member of the group you are addressing, and write for that person.

▷ Selecting the key ideas

'Go for key ideas'

At first sight this may seem to be a matter of individual choice but, if you think about it, there are always certain key points which need to be brought out when considering any issue. These points may have details or minor arguments associated with them, of course, and opinions may differ as to how important the points might be. Sometimes you will have to think hard about what to leave out, but the effort should be made, since too many details produce a cluttered effect and make it hard for the readers to take in what you really want them to notice.

▷ Organizing the key ideas

How you do this depends on the material you are working with and the directions given. If you are asked to write from one point of view only, keep to that. If you are asked to write a balanced account, give each side about the same amount of space. Sometimes it is good to begin with the key ideas, to think them through so that you can state them clearly, then to write a series of short paragraphs expanding them. Alternatively, you might be able to put your details and minor points into linked sentences, then finish strongly with the key ideas. Another possibility is to contrast key ideas as you go, taking in the details. There are many ways of arranging material and none is necessarily the right one. Whatever you choose, remember to explore all relevant aspects of the topic as clearly as possible. In the following section you will find some techniques to help you to do this.

▷ Length

'How long is a summary?'

How long is a summary? This is rather like saying 'How long is a piece of string?' The answer is 'As long as it needs to be'. But remember that if you are actually told what the work is to be – e.g. that it is to be a fact sheet, a letter, a pamphlet – you should be realistic and not write something which is obviously much too short or too long. If you are given a word limit, write **that number** of words or **fewer than the number of words asked. Exceeding word limits usually results in a penalty.**

▷ Presentation

Finally, and very important, you need to consider presentation. Most pieces of summary and directed writing need a heading of some kind. It may be a banner headline:

GOOD OLD DAYS RECALLED BY RISLEY SENIOR CITIZENS

or a catchy title

Guide Through the Jobs Jungle

– whatever it is, it should sum up the main topic in a few words.

Probably a piece of continuous writing in three or four paragraphs is the most usual form of presentation, but you may need to consider arrangement and layout features if, for instance, you are writing an article for a newspaper, a brochure or a pamphlet. Letters, of course, also have a special layout and varieties of style, depending on the degree of formality involved.

> ## USEFUL PRACTICAL APPROACHES

There are a number of useful techniques to help you with summarizing and directed writing. Suppose for a piece of coursework you decide to write a short guidebook to your town to attract visitors of your own age. You could first look up the official guidebook and gather some facts from it, selecting those that seem likely to be worth including. Next, these could be arranged in a form that would allow you to see at a glance the possible arrangements for your own guide. There are several ways of doing this:

Key ideas

You list key words or phrases in the most suitable order, e.g.

YOUNG RISLEY

Places to stay; Food; Sights; Sports; Fashion; After dark.

A flow chart

You put down key headings and associated details in a series of circles, then link the circles by arrows. You can experiment with various links and cross-connections, as shown in Figure 12.1.

Figure 12.1

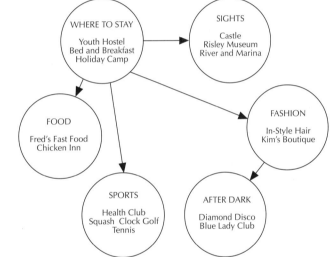

A topic tree

You draw a tree-like structure, where each 'branch' is a main idea and each 'twig' a minor point, as shown in Figure 12.2.

Figure 12.2

'Why not try a topic tree?'

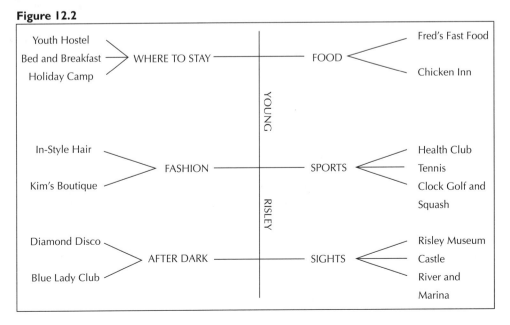

Key questions

You list a series of questions you hope to find answers to, e.g.

YOUNG RISLEY

1   Where can visitors stay?
2   Where can visitors eat out?
3   Which sights of the town will appeal?
4   What sports are there?
5   What is on at night?

▷ EXAMINATION QUESTIONS AND COURSEWORK TOPICS

Let us start with a selection of the kinds of questions you might find in a written paper.

▷ **Question 1**   The following extracts from letters to a newspaper discuss some proposed revised regulations governing laboratory experiments on animals. Using only the ideas contained in these letters, (a) write a short editorial in *two* paragraphs, one pointing out the limitations of the old regulations and another showing the advantages of the new proposals. The editorial should be approximately 200 words in length. (b) Write a pamphlet for Animal Rights on the theme of laboratory experiments.

You should spend about $\frac{3}{4}$ hour on each question.

Dear Sir,

I think that the general public is not fully aware of the shocking way that many animals are treated by people using them in experiments. Do they know, for example, that anyone can get a licence for so-called 'scientific experiments', as long as they work in a laboratory? People apparently don't even have to say what the experiment is for. True, they are supposed to operate in suitable premises but who is checking up? There are only fifteen inspectors to cover the whole country. That may have been all right when there were only a few hundred experiments a year, but last year there were more than three million.

Animals can be obtained from more or less anywhere. No questions are asked. Some say it's a highly organised business collecting unwanted animals, strays, even the pet from your front lawn, for use in laboratories. There may well be a need for science to make use of animals to some extent to further knowledge, but it is high time that people thought of the rights of animals as well as their uses.

Dear Sir,

I have never written to you before but the letter I read last week about animal experiments made me sad. To think how these animals suffer. I've been told that over eighty per cent of experiments on live animals are done without anaesthetics. Then, when the scientists have found out what they want, the animals are killed.

Surely there must be other ways of getting this information. Why must animals always be used? Someone should put a stop to all this cruel treatment. I thought we were supposed to be a nation of animal lovers!

Sir,

As a local councillor closely connected with the working party on the use and abuse of animals in laboratory experiments I should like to draw the attention of your readers to some of the ideas put forward for revising the regulations.

It is proposed that only properly qualified people should be granted a licence and only after details of the purpose and design of the experiments have been considered, and it has been made clear that no alternative to animals could do as well. These licences would be issued to individuals rather than to institutions. The use of strays would be stopped altogether. All animals used for research should come from properly registered agencies.

At the moment there are penalties for performing experiments without a licence – six months in prison, or a fine of up to £2000. We should like to see this increased to up two years in prison or an unlimited fine. We also want more inspectors, so that they could oversee what is going on – not just put their heads around the door of a laboratory.

Scientific enquiry depends on a continuing supply of animals, but as a humane society we must do our best to control conditions and limit animal suffering.

Over one point the committee seems in some doubt: they recommended that the 'degree of pain an animal suffers should be balanced against the value of the experiment'. Is that really an improvement over the old practice of uncontrolled pain while the experiment lasts?'

Here are some questions for summary and directed writing. Questions 2 and 3 should each take ¾ hour, and would carry 15 per cent of the overall mark.

▷ **Question 2**   Reading and Writing Standard Tier C–G   (Time allowed: ¾ hour)
The following letter appeared in the *Belfast Telegraph*. Read it, and using the correct letter format write a letter to the Editor, *Belfast Telegraph*, Belfast BT1 1EB, giving your response to the points raised.

Thugs run the streets

I am writing to inform you of events which occurred in Belfast City Centre on Saturday last. I hope that by bringing these matters to public attention something will be done to ensure that they do not occur again.

I brought my four-year-old daughter with me into town to do some shopping. As soon as we got off the bus we became aware of crowds of young people, both girls and boys of about 16 years old standing around corners and in the doorways of some shops. It was clear that some were in gangs of one kind or another by their dress, hairstyles and general behaviour. I was shocked when suddenly they began to run at each other; my daughter was knocked to the ground and, naturally, became very frightened by this stampede. She became quite hysterical and I had to call a policeman to assist us in getting back on to the bus.

This situation cannot be allowed to continue. Decent people cannot come into town while these thugs run the streets. The authorities will have to do something to keep young people off the streets. It is clear that young people of today lack common sense, maturity and consideration for others. Young people of my generation did not behave like this, possibly because their parents had control over them. If parents cannot control their children then it is up to the Government, the City Council and the Police. As a rate payer I demand that something should be done.

(Mrs) Joan White

▷ **Question 3**   Reading and Writing Standard Tier C–G   (Time allowed: ¾ hour)
The following are statements made by witnesses to a road accident, which occurred near a bus stop, in which a schoolgirl was knocked down by a car. Put yourself in the place of a police officer who has to write a factual report on what happened and who was responsible. Base the report on your interpretation of the information given by the witnesses.

A Mr John Black, aged 27 – Passer-by

The kid had no chance. The car came speeding up the inside lane, he was just trying to avoid the queue in the other lane. Next thing I knew was that the girl was lying across the bonnet of the Escort. You should have heard the screech of brakes.

B Mr Peter White, aged 41 – Motorist

I was in the outside lane in the line of traffic. The lights were red for traffic travelling straight on along Main Street but the green filter light was on for traffic turning left up Station Road. The red Ford Escort was coming up the inside lane signalling to turn left when I saw the brake lights on and heard the screech.

C Mr Jim Brown, aged 38 – Bus Driver

Those kids are the same every day. I'm surprised this has not happened before now. They are always running around, chasing each other. I was coming behind the car and I had to brake too. I was doing about 15 m.p.h. so I suppose the Escort was doing the same. He was signalling to go up Station Road. I didn't see the wee girl but there was a crowd of kids at the shop.

D Susan Gray, aged 15 – Schoolgirl

It was about 4.15 pm and I was waiting for the bus as usual. Sharon wanted to buy sweets at the shop on the other side of the road. She looked around before stepping out. The red Escort AZB 392 just came from nowhere. The driver was sneaking up the inside lane because there was a line of cars waiting at the lights. I think it was shock more than anything but she went in the ambulance which I called. I wonder who is going to tell Mrs Green?

(adapted from **NICCEA**)

▶ **Question 4**   Reading and Writing Higher Tier A–D   (Time allowed: 1½ hours)
Read the following newspaper article and then answer both (a) **and** (b).

SCHOOL BUS STOPPED AS PUPILS GO ON RAMPAGE

Police were called last night to Park Road, Midtown, when a school bus travelling from Midtown High School was halted by the driver after a fight among the pupils.

According to the driver, Mr Len Jones, the trouble began with children squirting cans of lemonade at each other, and throwing paper and chewing gum from the bus windows. A fight then broke out between two groups of pupils. Mr Jones claimed that he was unable to concentrate on driving the bus because of the disturbance and distraction behind him. He said that pupils had been warned previously about bad behaviour on school buses.

A police spokeswoman stated that as a result of a 999 call a Panda car went to Park Road and ten children were taken off the bus and left to walk home. In view of the potential danger to other traffic, the driver had been right to refuse to continue.

The head teacher of Midtown High School, Mrs C. Wall, has promised an immediate investigation and has said that the pupils will be severely punished.

Now answer (a) AND (b), basing your answers on the information given in the newspaper article.

(a) Write Mr Jones's report to the Bus Company Traffic Superintendent explaining what happened on the bus.
(b) Write a letter from Mrs Wall to be sent to the parents of all pupils who travel on the school buses explaining what happened and making it clear that misbehaviour on the buses will be severely dealt with.

(adapted from **NEAB**)

▶ **Question 5**   Foundation Tier C–G   (Time allowed: ½ hour)
Read the following extract, and then answer the question below it.

Mrs Webb

Mrs Webb is elderly. Here she describes her life.

I was brought up in the country, in a cottage on a farm. My father was the cowman, and next door lived the horseman. I always loved the countryside. I remember the woods near us, a carpet of bluebells in the spring; and in the autumn there was blackberrying and mushrooming.

I left school when I was twelve and I had to go into service. I went to a young couple who were farmers, and I had to live in. It was about fifteen miles from home and it seemed to me the back of beyond. It was a big, rambling place, and I was the only help they had. I got one and threepence a week. They weren't bad to me, but they used to go out a lot and I'd be in the place on my own. I was literally terrified.

I helped the mistress make butter, and sometimes I used to milk the cows as well. Anyway, I didn't last long. I got so lonely. I went to a butcher's wife near Wellingborough. She was a terror. There was another maid there, and fortunately we got on well together. We could laugh and cover up for each other if we did anything wrong. We slept in an attic, and we had to be up at six o'clock in the morning.

I had fifteen places in twelve years, and only at one of them was I treated like a human being.

They didn't think of us as people like themselves. We were different. Occasionally my father and brother used to come and see me, and I felt really unhappy when they left. I wanted to say 'Take me away with you', but of course they couldn't. You had to work; your parents couldn't afford to keep you.

I've been married twice. I met my first husband when he was home on leave from the Great War. We were married in Lowick church. It's a beautiful place, a lantern tower and some glass hundreds of years old. Anyway, he was gassed and he had dysentery, and he was never really well after that. A lot of the time he couldn't work at all. In the end, I got a cottage in the country, near where I was brought up. I thought, 'Get him into the fresh air. He'll be better there.' I thought he might be able to do a bit of agricultural work, but he couldn't. We moved in the February, and he died in the August.

Ten years ago I went on a holiday for the elderly, and that's where I met my second husband. We had seven years of real happiness. I don't know, do you think you have to pay for the happiness you have? Do you think you have to give it back in sorrow? But beneath it all there's always been this feeling of being different. I've no children for one thing, and that makes a difference.

Your local librarian is compiling a booklet of short articles by young people who have interviewed elderly citizens in the community. You have interviewed Mrs Webb.

Write your article. Make clear what you found interesting in the things she said.   (SEG)

▷ **Question 6**   Higher Tier A–D   (Time allowed: 40 min.)

Some people were opposed to the building of a fixed Channel link. Here are some notes made by an opponent of the scheme who was worried about the effects that it would have on the environment. Study them carefully and then write **ONE** of the following.

Bridges – would destroy view of cliffs
('last remaining stretch of unprotected coast exhibiting natural erosion'
- Nature Conservancy Council 1985)

Rare species on chalk land   Waste from tunnel would be
  – spider orchid   dumped on shore. Visual aspects?
  – 4 rare moths as well   Danger to fish?
could be wiped out?

'Euroroute' starts in   Where would construction
Farthingloe Valley   sites go? Rail lines, new
– completely unspoilt and   roads. Kent crowded anyway!
beautiful

Villages as well   Newington and Peene

                                           Noise dirt and traffic (ugh!)

KENT (encyclopedia entry)

Large county in S E England. Often called 'Gateway to England' because nearest county to France. Dover and Folkestone are main ports for ferry services. Tourist resorts like Whitstable and Margate still very popular. Industries – cement and paper making (newsprint for London papers is still produced here). Still called 'Garden of England' as well for apple and cherry growing in rural areas. Also famous for hops, used in beer-making, and oysters near Whitstable.

Write **ONE** of the following:

    EITHER

(a) A letter to the Editor of the *Dover Gazette* opposing the scheme on environmental grounds.

    OR

(b) A leaflet to be issued by *Friends of the Earth* to households in the area, putting these points to local people.
OR

(c) A speech to be made at a public inquiry to discuss the proposals.
OR

(d) A reply to these arguments suggesting that there are other points to be considered in favour of a fixed link. You can write this as **either** a speech **or** a letter to the newspaper.

(**MEG**)

▷ **Question 7** Using local gazetteers and guidebooks prepare a leaflet for teenage visitors, pointing out the things of interest about your village or town.

▷ **Question 8** Write 'a guide to an interview' for young people applying for a first job.

▷ **Question 9** Using a tour brochure for far-away holidays, write (a) an advertisement for holidays in India, based mainly on information in the brochure, (b) a letter to a friend and (c) a short letter of appreciation to the tour operator for a good holiday.

▷ **EXAMINATION ANSWERS**

▷ **Question 1** *Outline answer*

(a) Make two lists, one giving the limitations of the old regulations and the other the advantages of the proposed new regulations, and try to place the points on them in a logical order. Then draft the editorial. Compare your version with those in the 'Tutor's Answers' below.

(b) For the pamphlet, choose facts carefully, and sort them out with bold display techniques (as described in Chapter 5).

Tutor's answer

(a) Here are two lists of points that could serve as the basis of a summary. Check them against your own:

Limitations of the old regulations
1 The old regulations are out of date because the number of experiments has increased vastly.
2 Licences have been issued to unqualified applicants, without enquiring about the purposes of the experiments.
3 There are not enough inspectors to cover premises throughout the country regularly.
4 Licences allow experiments without anaesthetic, which leads to suffering.
5 No enquiries are made about the source of animals used for experiments.
6 It is permissible for animals to suffer until the main point of the experiment has been gained.
7 Penalties for unlicensed experiments are only six months in prison as a maximum or a fine of up to £2000. This is too little.

Advantages of the proposed new regulations
1 Provision will be made for many more experiments.
2 Only properly qualified persons will be eligible for a licence.
3 The purpose and design of experiments will be carefully considered.
4 Animals must be obtained only from registered agencies.

5 Uncontrolled pain will not in general be permitted.

6 The committee may refuse permission for use of some animals, especially cats, dogs and horses.

7 Penalties for unlicensed experiments will be increased: up to two years in prison or an unlimited fine. This will be a more realistic deterrent.

An appropriate editorial might read as follows:

ANIMAL RIGHTS IN THE LABORATORY

Few issues have brought such a large post-bag from readers as this one. Certainly the old regulations no longer reflect a world where experiments on animals have increased vastly. Inspectors have always had a limited role, and there aren't enough of them to monitor the work done or to ensure that experimenters are properly licensed and controlled. The issue of licences needs investigating; the maximum penalty of six months in prison or a fine of £2000 just does not deter. No questions are asked about the source of animals used and over eighty per cent are experimented on without anaesthetic. The pain suffered is disregarded, until the main results of the work have been established.

By the revision now proposed, most of these abuses would stop. Only those qualified would be licensed, and only after the purpose and design of the experiment had been approved, the onus being on the applicants to justify their need to use animals. Penalties for unlicensed experiments would be increased – up to two years in prison, or a large fine. Animals would be supplied only from registered places.

One problem would remain: the need to balance outcomes of research against the pain inflicted. Many would say that we still haven't got that right.

(b) A pamphlet is shown in Figure 12.3.

MASSIVE KILLING BY WICKAM

80,000 Animals die every year at the Wickham Research Laboratory in vain. The notion that results from animal tests can be directly applied to humans has been proved false, time and time again:

*Aspirin causes birth defects in cats but not in humans.

*Penicillin is toxic to guinea pigs and hamsters.

*Morphine sedates people but excites cats.

*Benzene causes cancer in rats but not in humans.

There are many alternatives to animal experimentation, either for cosmetics or drugs. Some of these methods, such as population and clinical studies, have been used successfully for years and some methods have been developed recently with advances in scanning and computer technology.

A great deal of research can be conducted in test tubes using human tissue cultures which have proved to be an extremely effective means of developing drugs and producing vaccines.

Unfortunately, research to develop non animal testing methods is seriously underfunded. To try and soothe this problem, a group called BUAV (British Union for the Abolition of Vivisection) is calling for a Government-funded strategy to promote the use and development of humane research methods.

Animal testing causes needless pain and suffering to thousands of animals each day. It is of little or no value and can, in fact, produce dangerously misleading results. Relying on animal testing drains time and resources away from the use and development of more valuable research methods. Human and superior research alternatives do exist. For more information call BUAV 0171-700 4888.

Figure 12.3

▷ **Question 2** *Outline answer*

You are asked to write a response to a letter from the correspondence columns of the *Belfast Telegraph*. The writer has adverse views about some sixteen year olds and it is likely that you will react strongly against them. There is no reason why your letter should not offer an equally determined defence but, rather than allow yourself to get carried away, recognize that the writer has been genuinely upset by her experience and make some positive efforts to reassure her. In addition, you must answer the points raised in the letter, and not be tempted to put in a lot of material of your own. The main charges to be answered are as follows: the liking for young people to go around in crowds, to wait about aimlessly; to dress the same and to behave in an excited and unruly way. These are based on direct observation by the writer. She also alleges that young people are 'thugs', who lack common sense, maturity and consideration for others and are not like their parents' generation when young, probably because of a lack of discipline in their homes. The writer urges strong intervention by the authorities – e.g. the Government, the City Council and the Police – to maintain order.

Remember to write in an appropriate style – that of a responsible teenager, addressing the public, and with an appropriate layout, i.e. formal, for a letter to an editor of a leading newspaper.

▷ Question 3   *Outline answer*

Here the point of view is that of a police officer gathering information from eye-witnesses. The officer has to decide which pieces of information are substantiated, and therefore can be considered to be 'facts', and which are opinion. This may be quite a difficult thing to do. The facts may be no more than the following: the girl's name, the time of the accident, the details of the car involved, the place of the accident, the state of the lights at the junction and anything about the driver's behaviour that observers agree on.

A report presents balanced arguments, backed up by evidence, and should be written in a formal style – Standard English.

▷ Question 4   *Outline answer*

Here you are asked to write a report and a letter, based on the same piece of material – a newspaper article about the behaviour of school children on a bus. As in Question 3, the report will need to be a careful statement of fact, with sensible arguments which are supported by evidence. The Bus Company Traffic Superintendent will probably want to follow up this report and will need sound evidence to work on. The facts are few: the driver stopped the bus in Park Road, Midtown, and a police car, responding to a 999 call, arrived at the scene and ten children were taken off the bus. The driver also alleges that school children have been warned before about bad behaviour on the bus and that, on this occasion, there was fighting and other unruly behaviour by the children. Those statements are not proven, and would need to be closely investigated. The report should be written in a formal style, in Standard English and be correctly sequenced.

The letter from the head teacher is likely to treat the same information rather differently. She is addressing parents and her purpose is to prevent any future disturbance on the school bus by impressing on them the importance of their children behaving in a disciplined fashion. She may well highlight those aspects of the situation that will suit her purpose, e.g. the alleged fighting, squirting cans of lemonade, paper throwing from the bus windows, etc. Her tone will be serious and her style fairly formal, but, as she seeks the parents' cooperation, the letter may be semi-formal in layout.

Dear Mr and Mrs ....

....

....

....

....

Yours sincerely,

(Signed)

▷ Question 5   *Outline answer*

The extract is monologue – a transcript (probably edited, as it is rather too fluent and non-hesitant for speech). Your task is to turn this into a report in a style suitable for young people who will read your article, bringing out points of interest in Mrs Webb's account. You have no word limit, but time is short, so you should aim to write no more than 200 words or so. First, make a list of points that you want to include, maybe covering Mrs Webb's country childhood, her years as a servant, her marriage, her husband's ill-health and death, finally her second marriage. Draft the points probably in that order, as she is telling her life story, then read through what you have written for suitability of style, paragraphing and correctness of expression. Remember that 5 per cent of the marks will be for these skills. Don't forget to give your work a suitable title – something to distinguish your article from the rest, and make the reader want to know more, e.g. *Mrs Webb: the Cost of Happiness*.

▷ Question 6 *Outline answer*

Using a page of notes made by the opponent of the building of a fixed Channel link, you have the choice of kinds of writing: a letter, a leaflet, a speech or a considered statement in favour.

Again, it is best to start by listing the key points to be made, either for or against, depending on the question you choose. How you proceed depends on the topic on which you are working. If it is (a), then you need points opposing, in a formal letter, in Standard English, with appropriate layout. If you choose (b) you must consider especially the readers of your piece of writing (local people) and its form (a leaflet). Your style should be lively (though correct) and fluent. You should put points for both sides of the case in a way that draws attention. This demands an eye~catching layout, with banner or subheadings. You could consider numbering points for and against. If you choose (c) you should offer the same balance of material, but remember that oral communication works rather differently from the written word. In your speech think of the audience you would be addressing – the general public. As part of your style find some ways of drawing them in, of persuading them to your point of view. (As more will be said about speech writing in Chapter 15, you may find it helpful to refer to that chapter now.) Question (d) requires the same approaches as either (a) or (c), but notice that it has to be in favour of a fixed link.

▷ Question 7 *Outline answer*

To begin here find a guidebook (better, find two) on your area. Then make a flow chart or topic tree of the key points, adding minor details next, to be included in your leaflet. Try writing it out in draft, and aim at producing three or four paragraphs.

▷ Question 8 *Outline answer*

List some key areas and then rewrite your list in what seems the most helpful order.

You might begin by suggesting a letter confirming attendance; then stress the importance of suitable dress and arriving on time. Your audience will be young people seeking advice, so keep your tone lively and choose a style that is likely to appeal to them. You could consider some presentation aspects, too, suitable for a leaflet.

Student's answer

Here are the preparations made by a student for a summary – a guide to an interview.

Summary and Directed Writing

ROUGH

Note points   A Guide to an Interview   150 words

1   Careful not to be criticized for being slow and unenthusiastic.
2   First impressions very important. Appearance and manner of movement. Personality.

3   Bold with views of your own/news etc. Warm, friendly and outgoing.
4   Like people that take an interest in the real world and can keep up discussion on current affairs.
5   Independence, don't ask too keenly about hours and salary.
6   Seem keen and enthusiastic. Don't be monosyllabic.
7   Be punctual.
8   Keep a clear head, use initiative.

Examiner's comments

The writer has decided on eight main ideas. They do not seem to be in any particular order, e.g. 'first impressions' comes second and 'be punctual' seventh. Points (1) and (6) are more or less the same, in reverse. He has chosen a title, which is a good idea.

A better summary might have resulted if he had gone through a second planning stage and reorganized the sequence of his points: (7), (2), (6) and (1), then (8), (3), (5) and (4) would make a more logical order.

Here is his final version:

> First impressions are very important in an interview, both of appearance and manner of movement. Be careful not to be criticized for being slow and unenthusiastic. Personality is also very important, so be bold and stick to your views. Young people with views of their own are particularly admired. Also be warm, friendly and outgoing. Most employers like people who take an interest in the real world, so make sure you're able to keep up an intellectual and interesting discussion of current affairs and news.
>
> Do not seem too keen about knowing your possible hours and salary – remember they're interviewing you, and not vice versa. Independence is also very much admired; seem keen and enthusiastic, answer questions properly and don't be monosyllabic. Make sure you turn up punctually with no feeble excuses. Keep a clear head, use your initiative and Good Luck!

You will see that he has rearranged the points as follows: (2), (1), (3), (4), (5), (6), (7) and (8), which makes quite a good summary, except for the repetition of the ideas mentioned above, in points (1) and (6). That could have been weeded out at the planning stage. Notice that the tone of the guide is appropriate – there are quite a few commands: 'Be careful …!', 'Don't seem too keen!'; but also a friendly tone: 'Good Luck!' It ends well.

▷ Question 9   Outline answer

Ask yourself some key questions: 'What would I enjoy on the holiday described in the brochure?'; 'What are the basic amenities on offer?'; 'What about the price?'; and so on. List them, and jot down an answer to each, using details from the brochure. You now have the basis for your advertisement and letters. Think how the tone and style of the letter to your friend will differ from that to the travel company. Write the letter to your friend first. How will you begin and end it? Will there be an address and a date? You have quite a range of choice here. Now turn to the second letter and think about its form. Keep it short, and begin and end it suitably.

Student's answer

> **(a)**   **Holiday Brochure**
>   **'Intersun'**
>
> Having problems? Need a break? Then come and see any of our Intersun travel agents. We've any place to suit any one in India. And the unbeatable prices:
>
>   Bombay £480
>   Delhi £575
>   Madras £520
>
> These are just some of the cities from which you can choose. You may choose Bombay then we can arrange for you to see some of India's famous film stars.

(continued)

The beaches are golden from the everlasting sun which beats down on sun bathers. You can pick the right spot for you to sun bathe.

The food is just fabulous. There's no time for any particular food. You can eat anytime. Apart from Indian food you can have any other food that pleases you.

Rush now before it's too late!

*   *   *

(b)

Five Star Hotel
51 Central St
Bombay
Fri 22nd Nov.

Dear Sonia,

Hi, how are you? I am sorry I couldn't write sooner. I've been really busy enjoying myself with Saqib. I didn't think that £480 would be so cheap for all this. There's guided tours, good food, air-conditioned bedrooms, bathrooms. The view from our window is just beautiful. We've taken some photos for you to see.

The beach is just five minutes away; the best time to go there is in the evening sunset. We made some friends at the beach yesterday. They also came for a holiday from London.

Tomorrow we're going to the Indian Film Industry; I've heard a lot about that. I am looking forward to going there and so is Saqib. You know how he is with acting, plays, films etc.

We've only been here a week and we've got three more weeks; I wish it was longer. It's so nice to get away for a while. You should do that and I'd advise you to go to Intersun travel agents – they are the best. Hope to see you soon.

Love,

J

P.S. I've written the address. If you wish to write, then please do, and let me know what you want from here.

*   *   *

(c)

40 Court Gdns
London SW1
Tues 17th Dec.

Intersun Ltd
142 Union Rd
London W1
Dear Manager/ess,

Thanks to your wonderful travel agency 'Intersun' my boyfriend and I had the best time of our lives. We both visited Bombay for four weeks. Everything was just perfect the way you described it. It was just like a dream land. We didn't want to come back. I hope to go back there again. Thanks again.

Yours sincerely

(Miss J C)

PS. Your surprise hotel in Bombay was excellent.

Examiner's comments

The student has included four key ideas, so that her advertisement is clear and uncluttered. She includes those in the letter to her friend. This has a casual tone: 'Hi, how are you?' and 'Love, J', but it is correctly expressed. In contrast, the letter to the tour operator is friendly, but more formal. It has few details, but one main idea: to express thanks for a wonderful holiday. All three pieces are readable and clear – successful communication, in short!

▶ A STEP FURTHER

This chapter is quite closely related to others – Chapters 8, 11 and 16.

You probably use summarizing skills frequently in your general work, but further practice is always useful. Try out some of the ideas here when you are making your own notes. If you are reading a play, novel or short story, take a scene or incident, and try to write about it from the point of view of one character.

'Train yourself to summarize'

Compare news items in different newspapers, and try writing your own version. Look at advertisements, prospectuses and brochures, and select points of interest from a particular angle. In these ways you can train yourself to read accurately and write clearly and concisely – the basic requirements for good summarizing.

SUMMARY

▷ You will have read about how to gather information, sequence it, make a draft and correct it.

▷ You were reminded of the National Criteria, that you should be able to understand and convey information and order and present facts, ideas and opinions, evaluate from a variety of media and pick out what is relevant for particular purposes, re-presenting this in a style suitable for a given audience.

▷ Useful planning techniques such as key ideas, a flow chart, a topic tree and key questions were outlined.

▷ You will have found advice on choosing the best style, how to pick out key ideas and organize them.

▷ There was advice on keeping to word limits, considering layout and presentation.

Writing narrative

▷ ## GETTING STARTED

It has been suggested that narrative is a 'primary act of mind'; that is, we all shape our experiences in life into a narrative form. How do you tell people in the evening what your day has been like? You cannot include everything that has happened, every feeling you experienced, every thought you had. Nor do you spend time thinking out the best way to recount your experiences. No, you simply narrate selectively, highlighting what was most important to you, in roughly chronological order: this is basic narrative. Quite often, when telling about what has happened, you have to present yourself acting against someone, or acted against. When doing this, if you think about it, you are likely to show the qualities in yourself that you want others to admire, and if you came out of the experience badly, use humour to lessen your humiliation. Suppose you had been picked on by a school bully or superior and had been too afraid to stand up for yourself? Aren't you more likely to cast yourself in a heroic role than admit to your cowardice? If so, then you are not only narrating events, but also introducing an element of imagination. This is similar to telling a story.

That is not to suggest that composing narrative comes naturally, and is easy. You will have many opportunities to write narrative on various subjects for coursework and will probably be set a question of this sort if you take a written paper. What follows in this chapter is advice on how to go about writing effective narrative.

LONDON	MEG	NEAB	NICCEA	SEG	WJEC	IGCSE	TOPIC	STUDY	REVISION 1	REVISION 2
✓	✓	✓	✓	✓	✓	✓	Third person narrative			
✓	✓	✓	✓	✓	✓	✓	First person fiction narrative			
✓	✓	✓		✓			Narrative from one viewpoint			
✓	✓	✓	✓	✓	✓	✓	Figurative narrative			
✓	✓	✓	✓	✓	✓	✓	Fantasy and science fiction narrative			

as coursework

▷ ## WHAT YOU NEED TO KNOW

Candidates must demonstrate in their writing that they can:

▷ make use of different forms of writing (including stories, scripts, letters, newspaper articles and reviews) to suit a range of purposes and contexts

▷ plan, organize and paragraph using appropriate punctuation

▷ choose a vocabulary which is suited to its purpose and audience and use correct grammar and Standard English where appropriate

▷ correct, edit and revise their own writing

▷ show an awareness of how language is used in writing.

(AT3: 1–5)

A successful narrative is likely to be satisfactory as regards

'Five points to remember
when telling a story'

▷ relevance

▷ selection of incidents

▷ point of view

▶ structure

▶ style.

Consider each in turn.

▷ **Relevance**   Whether you are writing on a theme chosen by yourself entirely or answering a question in a written paper, it is important to focus clearly on the chief area of concern for your narrative, and keep to it. Only move away to a parallel set of happenings or ideas, or flash back or predict forwards if by doing so you will make the central theme clearer or increase its power. When we are narrating our everyday experience, as mentioned above, most of us do so automatically, and those who do not are soon labelled as speakers who offer a 'rigmarole' or 'go all around the houses to get to the point'. These commonly used phrases indicate how impatient listeners can become when forced to listen to the rambling account of others' experiences. Certainly, when many pupils write a story they depart from the directness and pointedness of many of their real-life accounts. It is a mistake, for instance, deliberately to decide to be extremely original. What you intend as striking and refreshing may seem to the reader perverse or even obscure. One pupil chose the title 'Day Trippers' and wrote about a disco with this name; another devoted several pages to events about a cruiser named 'The Catch' in a story of that title.

A more usual form of irrelevance is when the writer has an opening or closing sentence or two relating to the title, and then continues with something quite different. 'Day Trippers' might begin with a group of friends setting off for a day by the sea and, by the second paragraph, finding that they had become caught up with a gang of criminals in a car chase. 'The Catch' could easily tell the story of a family holiday: sightseeing, shopping, sunbathing, visiting museums, cafés, sampling the nightlife – and then, in the final paragraph, going on a fishing trip on which father lands a salmon.

There is one way of departing from the obvious meaning of the title but still writing relevantly. Many titles can be considered in two ways, both literally and figuratively. In the example of 'The Catch' a pupil wrote an excellent short story about a fishing boat called 'The Catch', taken out by two young boys for a first attempt at the sport. Starting with the boys pushing off from the shore, with their hearts full of excitement and their heads of grand dreams of the three-pounder they hope to hook, the story proceeds through the calm of waiting, the slow hours dragging by and the false alarms. and culminates in the dramatic moment when there is a sharp tug at the line. Feverishly, one boy winds in, his rod bending and line taut under the weight. With a jerk which topples him backwards into the boat, he swings his prize catch clear of the water: it is an old bicycle tyre! As the writer pointed out in his final reflections – there was a catch to the day's sport in 'The Catch', and the boys laughed at the deluding name of the boat as they rowed home.

▷ **Selection of incidents**   Suppose you are writing a story called 'The Catch' and have decided to combine a literal and figurative treatment, as described above. After a few moments thought many ideas will clamour for attention.

First, you have to choose your main focus, your **theme**. Let the story be, as an example, about a tense moment when a lowly member of the cricket eleven tries to make a catch which would dismiss the opposing team's best batsman – and drops it! Second, you need to decide which **events** to discard and which to keep. Obviously, the moment of the catch is essential. Will you work up to it slowly, building suspense, or start dramatically with it, and let the rest of the story go back to the earlier hopes and fears of the would-be catcher? These are just two possible arrangements among many. Certainly, the story has to give some kind of context to the significant moment. But that is all. It is not even necessary to give the feelings of the fielder when he drops the ball: as a strong anti-climax it would make a fitting end to a story – but more of that below. Now you must try to give your story **effective shape**. Will you write about all the events of the morning, from when the fielder got up, had his breakfast, put on his whites? Probably not. On the other hand, if he did all these things in a daze, dreaming of future glory on the field, anticipating saving his team from defeat, all this could be included, because it would make the moment of dropping the catch

'Being literal and being figurative'

such a let-down for the hero. Will you give an account of every ball and run in the match? Of course not: you will choose parts of the match which will help the main focus.

Choice depends very much on the individual writer. No two treatments will be the same. The important thing is to think about how the events you select help your theme to have maximum impact on, and interest for, the reader.

▷ Point of view

Who tells the story? Often stories are told from the point of view of the so-called 'omniscient' author; that is, one who knows everything and chooses what to tell and what to withhold. Often, again, the point of view offered is that of a character in the narrative, possibly speaking in the first person. Some students find this hard to maintain. They become so involved in what they are writing that they switch from the name of the character to the personal pronoun, and back again. Beware of this elementary mistake. Henry James, the novelist, liked to have the story told by a wise friend of the main character, who would be likely to know a great deal about the situation but also was close to the hero or heroine. In the story about 'The Catch' outlined above, for instance, it would make a good deal of difference whether the chief point of view was that of the star batsman, or the hopeful fielder. Try experimenting with different angles in the narrative: it can have quite dramatically different effects. Some stories are even deliberately told from two contrasting points of view – a 'two-sides-of the-truth' approach, where the reader is left to decide which is preferable, or whether both are equally acceptable.

▷ Structure

'Begin and end well.'

What has already been said implies a number of important things about structure. Learn to make the most of your material by organizing it effectively. You may prefer to do a brief outline **plan**, or have a plan in your head. Five minutes' thinking before you write can make a lot of difference. Also, **beginnings** and **endings** are very important: you need to catch the reader's attention at once, and hold it, perhaps through developing events to a climax, to make the reader want to read on. Try to include some unexpected turns in the action, or some variety of narrative approach, so that your story is not a level, even piece of writing, unless that is an effect you really want to achieve. Finally, find some way of resolving the situation in a satisfying or challenging way, perhaps leaving the reader guessing. This sort of story is called 'open ended'. Readers form their own idea of how matters end, using the clues you have given.

An essential part of your organization will be **paragraphing**. Paragraph logically, as phases of the narrative evolve, not just every ten lines or so. If you paragraph logically you can control the pace and growth of your narrative. Practice in plotting a narrative is worth the effort. After deciding on a beginning and concluding idea, break the body of your story into, say, four or five paragraphs (remember, economy is essential if you are given a work limit), each with a **key idea** for development.

For example, a possible plan for the cricketing story entitled 'The Catch' might look like this:

▷ **Opening paragraph:** The moment of the catch; hero feels weak at the knees as he sees the ball falling towards him from a great height. The crowd goes quiet, in anticipation.
▷ **Body of the story:** The morning of the event; excited preparations; good luck wishes of friends and relatives hardly heeded by hero in dreamy state of mind.
▷ **In the pavilion before the match:** Hero notices photographs on the wall of old teams going back many years; dreams of personal glory as he walks eagerly out onto the field.
▷ **Concluding paragraph:** The ball is nearly on him. He cups his hands. The ball goes into them and then out again! He has DROPPED IT!

▷ Style

Good style has been described as 'mind style', because it reflects individuality. Even so, there are several ways of making narration more interesting by varying your approach. Stretches of dialogue can carry the story forward sometimes, and a descriptive passage may help to set the scene. Characters' reflections on what is happening often give depth to the events of the story, and so on. Try to show plenty of variety and don't be afraid to experiment.

EXAMINATION QUESTIONS

Here are five suggested questions.

Question 1   Write a story about a hunt.   (WJEC)

Question 2   Hijack!   (MEG)

Question 3   War Games.   (London)

Question 4   Write a story about someone who is or was bullied at school. You should write from the point of view of **either** the victim **or** the bully, as he or she looks back at the event.

(London)

Question 5   Write a story about a relationship that went wrong.

EXAMINATION ANSWERS

Question 1   *Student's answer*

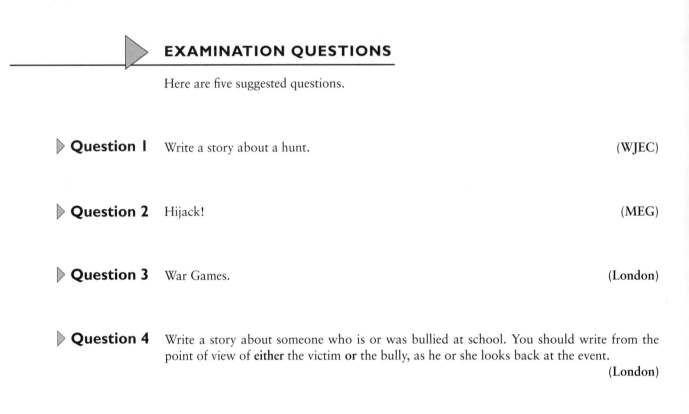

Tiger Hunt

The scent of humans fell upon his nose. He scampered from the shallow pool he lay in. He ran like a paper being pulled in a hurricane. The men kept track of him flashing past at the speed of light. The hunters kept chasing him.

The tiger was terrified now, but there seemed to be no escape, as he ran along the plains the black stripes on his coat kept showing up, like bands of darkness.

The poacher took his aim but – disappointedly – missed.

The tiger trampled through the long grass. He desperately ran on. The hunter raised his gun, tightly pulled the trigger and sadly, and very sadly the tiger stopped running. He stopped panting. He stopped breathing. He was no longer terrified. He rested in peace: a gun shot wound, as big as an apple, lay deep in him.

The poachers retired. Another skin to sell, more money and another innocent tiger slaughtered by men illegally and viciously.

Examiner's comments

'Tiger Hunt' is a most economically written short story. What it leaves out in detail is made up for in pace and dramatic suspense. Notice the direct opening. Here is a group of verbs which move on the action. See how many more good words and phrases are used: 'scampered', 'kept track', 'flashing past'. Sparsely written though this is, the writer has included some figurative expressions: 'flashing past at the speed of light' is rather a well-worn comparison, but the idea of a paper in a hurricane is original and interesting. The short paragraphs have the effect of moving attention quickly from the tiger to the hunter, and back again. The death of the tiger is described almost in slow motion. Notice how the very short sentences produce this result, and also the repetition of 'stopped', and the drawing out of the phrase 'and sadly, and very sadly', which also has a powerful emotional appeal. The final paragraph stresses the cruelty of the attack, the grotesque satisfaction of the poachers and the pathos of the victim. The words 'by men illegally and viciously' stir our conscience, and widen the issue.

▷ Question 2   *Student's answer*

Essay Plan

Para 1:   Despite unsuperstitious, Mondays always bad – boring, then various things happening – generally bad.

Para 2:   Sunday night contemplating this Monday, thinking it might be a better day/uneasy feeling about it/going away.

Para 3:   Monday morning – bitterly cold, etc. Describe the journey to airport, action there.

Para 4:   Getting on plane – Describe activities, etc.

Para 5:   The hijack – Describe fear and confusion. Describe what happens – Intercom announcing time on Monday.

Para 6:   The hijackers are won over, we manage to get off the plane. As we do we hear an announcement at the airport – Tuesday morning.

First consider the pupil's outline plan above. Paragraph 1 anticipates Monday. Paragraph 2 concerns Sunday evening, but also anticipates Monday. Paragraphs 3–5 concern events on Monday. Paragraph 6 has action taking place on Tuesday morning. Overall, some forty-eight hours is the planned time sequence, and it is economically handled in the narrative plan.

The second thing to notice is that there is a theme related to the time-sequencing, i.e. that Mondays are always dull days and at first the Monday of the hijack ran true to form. Ending with the announcement that it was Tuesday morning is a good idea, then, suggesting double relief: both the hijack and Monday are over!

The third thing worth mentioning is that the plan gives a few necessary details of happenings: journey to the airport; the weather (when it is considered important to mention it); the chief character's feelings – early depression, then confusion and fear and relief when the hijack is over; the idea of two announcements, etc. This plan promises a well-organized story. Now read the story itself, noticing how closely the writer kept to the plan, and considering how successful a piece of narrative you think it is.

Hijack

Mondays had always been bad for me and considering I'm a very unsuperstitious person, that probably sounds rather hypocritical yet something always did seem to go wrong on a Monday, rather than any other day. I was born on a Monday. I broke a leg on a Monday and my grandfather died on a Monday and there were many more disasters as well!

I was sitting by the open fire in our living room on a Sunday night, thinking about this and wondering if it really was mere coincidence. It was in the middle of January and we were going skiing tomorrow and I wondered if anything would go wrong. We got up very early the next morning, as our plane was leaving at seven a.m. London was going through a very cold spell and the roads were covered in ice and snow, so the traffic was hideous. When we finally arrived at the airport it was still bitterly cold and we were all feeling very annoyed, and our tempers certainly didn't improve when we discovered that our plane had a two hour delay.

Eventually we were allowed on board and as the 'fasten your seat belt and no smoking' light went on, a surge of relief swept through us … we were finally on our way. A few minutes after take off we were served breakfast.

Suddenly two men stood up at the front of the plane, holding guns. I'm not quite sure how it happened. I don't think anyone was. Many people didn't seem to realise what was happening and the people who did were in a blind panic; several women fainted and the rest were screaming or trying to clamber to the back of the plane. The rest, like me, were obviously still not able to fully take in the awfulness of the situation. The hijackers started to shout and threatened to shoot and gradually the noise subsided. The

(continued)

---

plane it seemed had been ordered to land as planned in Austria which it did. As we came into the airport we could see guards all around yet they didn't approach us. The plane was completely silent now and everybody sat waiting.

As the hours went by the tension mounted. Some attempts were made by the police to talk to the hijackers but to no avail. By this time one shot had been fired but luckily no-one had been hurt. The electricity suddenly went off too and so we had no lights or heat. As it began to go dark the hijackers were evidently getting more and more nervous. For some reason I didn't feel scared – just numb. I suppose it was shock. In the distance I heard the intercom at the main airport announce that it was 9.30 p.m. on Monday night. It was rather ironic, I thought to myself, how this happened on a Monday. Several hours later a spot-light was put on us. This must have been the last straw for the hijackers who leapt up and started shouting 'Everybody off! Get off! Everybody off!' There was a hysterical plunge for the door and when I got out into the fresh air I heard the airport intercom again, this time announcing that it was one o'clock on Tuesday morning. Thank God, Monday was over!

Examiner's comments

In some respects 'Hijack' works well as a story – the opening offers a definite point of view and strong sense of anticipation: 'Mondays had always been bad for me and considering I'm a very unsuperstitious person, that probably sounds rather hypocritical yet something always did seem to go wrong on a Monday, rather than any other day.' The rest of the paragraph enlarges our awareness of the first person narrator's wry sense of humour, too!

Notice how suspense is gradually built up, from the narrator's thoughts on the Sunday evening as he reflects by the open fire: 'I wondered if anything would go wrong.' Things aren't very comfortable on the Monday morning: 'the traffic was hideous'; 'it was still bitterly cold'; everyone is ill-tempered when they hear about the two hour delay to the flight. All these preliminaries help to confirm our suspicion that this Monday will be as bad as the narrator feared it might be. There is one short paragraph, lulling our fears, but in the next the disastrous climax is reached: 'Suddenly two men stood up at the front of the plane, holding guns.' The final sentence of this action-packed paragraph indicates an uneasy calm, just as frightening as the frantic activity it follows: 'The plane was completely silent by now and everybody sat waiting.'

Next, with excellent economy the writer copes with time passing and anxiety in one sentence: 'As the hours went by the tension mounted.' Then, unfortunately, paragraphing breaks down. The 'I hate Mondays' theme, though, is picked up again, echoing the first paragraph: 'It was rather ironic, I thought to myself, how this had happened on a Monday.' The eruption of action in the finale, when the hijackers 'leap up' and shout 'Everybody off! Get off! Everybody off!' and the passengers all make 'a hysterical plunge' for the door, is dramatic and exciting. The escape into fresh air would make a suitable conclusion, but the writer neatly ends his story by reminding us that 'it was one o'clock on Tuesday morning. Thank God, Monday was over!'

There are some errors here – weak indication of where new paragraphing begins, sparse use of commas and some slips of expression, but overall this is a good short story.

▷ Question 3 *Student's answer*

Here is a candidate's answer, written in examination conditions.

War Games

Nikita was playing in the amusement aracade. He was playing with the war games. That was to be the cause of the catastrophe. Nikita was only twelve then. … Twenty-five years later, Nikita was elected as the Minister of Arms and Nuclear development in Russia.

Bradley, the rowdy thirteen year old, lived on the outskirts of Washington. He was sitting in a deckchair, playing war games. … Twenty-five years later, Bradley was elected as Minister of Arms and Nuclear development in America.

*The war had begun between Russia and America, and there was no one to stop it. The cause was unknown, but the **concequence** was apparent. Two people in the world were to blame for this **upheavel**, namely Nikita Skoblowsky and Bradley Northcut. They would have to stop it.*

(continued)

> *To Nikita and Bradley, this whole thing was a game … a war game – the kind they used to play when they were kids. That was back in the twentieth century … now it was the year two thousand and twenty, and things had changed. American troops had fired endlessly with **aluminum lazers**. However, their fire was only returned by the equally well-**equiped** Russians. The fields were **fledged with dead, blood-ridden** corpses. Both American and Russians were **entwined within** each other … that is, when they were dead. The firing could not be heard, because the **lazers** had silencers on them. The troops were so used to their way of life, and had not even thought of ending the war.*
>
> *Nikita was sitting in his living room, watching the television screen, and premeditating his next move. He had a choice of two buttons to press, one was a green one and the other a red one. If he pressed the green one, it would signify his surrender. If he pressed the red one, he would activate an atomic bomb that would send the entire universe up in flames!*
>
> *Bradley lay on a bunkbed, gazing at the remote control in his hands. On it were two keys, a green one and a red one. If he pressed the green one, it would signify his surrender. If he pressed the red one, he would activate an atomic bomb that would send the entire universe up in flames! Bradley lay on a sunbed, gazing at the remote control in his hands. On it were two keys, a green one and a red one. If he turned the green one, Nikita would presume he had surrendered. If he turned the red one, his atomic bomb, which was lodged beneath the sea, disguised as a submarine, would **errupt**. That would destroy the world.*
>
> *Everyone in the world was tense. They were all imagining their fates if Nikita and Bradley refused to surrender to each other. Meanwhile, the American and Russian soldiers **continuied** killing each other. They had to die one day, so what difference did it make, if they died now?*
>
> *'If Nikita presses his green button, and Bradley turns his green key, we'll all live in peace. However, if Nikita presses his red button and Bradley turns his red key, then …!' thought the world.*
>
> *Simultaneously, Nikita pressed his red button, and Bradley turned his red key. … After all, to them, it was just a war game.*

Examiner's comments

This is a neat idea: war is seen as a game – a metaphor or figure of speech. After all, wars and games have quite a few common features: opposing sides, competitiveness, team spirit, national fervour, skill, strategies, etc. – the comparison has been made before. The candidate sustains this idea throughout the piece, as an extended image, repeating it in the final sentence 'after all, to them it was just a war game'. The piece is economical and patterned: one sentence balances the corresponding sentence throughout. It is accurately expressed, for the most part. There are a few examples of words misused – 'the fields were fledged (filled?) with blood-ridden (bloodied?) corpses'; 'entwined within (with?) each other' – and several spelling errors – the words in bold should be consequence, upheaval, aluminium, lasers, equipped, erupt, continued. When reread, the piece appeared to be simple, rather superficial – not really exploring the ideas of war and games very deeply or fully, though it is elegantly constructed. In that respect it is rather above-average writing.

▷ **Question 4** *Student's answer*

This was a coursework story, written by a boy.

> *Waiting on the platform for his morning train, something familiar about the back of a fellow commuter caught Jack Grigg's attention. … There he stands, Basher Bradley, the notorious, belligerent fifth-former who is held in awe by all.*
>
> *'Ah!' a chronic spasm electrified Jack's back as the picture of Basher inflicting pain crystallized in his mind, and memories of the past came flooding back to him.*
>
> *Basher was of medium height and well-built. His ears were thin and unfleshy, resembling antennae, and he had large protuberant eyes, that seemed to have some sort of scanning device.*
>
> *Basher classed himself as the know-all and be-all of the school. Whether in high spirits, he would take a younger boy to the nearby river, and fill his pants with squelchy, sloshy mud. Then to 'top it all up', as he used to say complacently, he'd thump on the boy's backside and look at him with his face full of glee.*

(continued)

One day, Jack was at the school dance when he was notified that he was dancing with one of Basher's train of girl friends. He immediately stopped dancing and for the rest of the evening tried to keep a low profile. However, Basher's scanning devices did not desert him. Thinking he had been successful in evading Basher, Jack got on his new bicycle. Just as he was about to cycle off, he was grabbed by the collar and pulled off by two hands which felt like snake's skin that had been sandpapered. Thinking he was going to be subjected to another torment of beating, he began to beg. Basher took pity on his body but said that he would have to pay. He placed the bicycle over the railway track and made Jack watch its limbs go flying as the train severed through it.

For six months Basher ruled the school and put both teachers and pupils at risk. It was rumoured that Basher had left to join the army. It took the rest of the boys a while to burst into ecstasies because they were apprehensive about his return. Jack prayed and relished the thought that Basher would not come back, but praying was just a useless strategy. There was a little voice in the back of his mind, saying 'Basher will return; he will always return, in some form or other.'

Basher's impact on Jack was too great to be able to be erased and, even after many years, the mere thought of him still sent a shiver down his back. Thanks to Basher, Jack would always remain the frail, timid, skinny little boy he once was.

Examiner's comments

The writer could have chosen one of several approaches for this piece of writing: he could have written about it as personal experience, or tried a shorter descriptive portrait of the bully with more incidents – either could have worked well. Instead, he chose a single episode as the core of his narrative and placed a 'frame' around it. The episode is from the school days of Jack Grigg. The advantage of recalling it when Jack is older is that the episode takes on far greater significance. The reader is invited to see its shaping influence on the character of Basher Bradley's young victim.

The narrative opens very well. Two time sequences are established in the first of the sentences: a commuter catches sight of what seems to be a familiar back among the thronging fellow-passengers and is painfully reminded of the past. Notice how the present tense is used, though, for the introducing of Basher, to give him greater impact. Basher, in his bullying prime, is skilfully described and then the writer goes on to the episode which Jack's memory most strongly recalls. This is told in 'flashback', and the emotional involvement here is low-key, the tone cool, because it happened a long time ago. Think for a moment how differently you would feel about a similar incident which had just happened to you.

The conclusion of the story reminds me of the opening: there 'a chronic spasm electrified Jack's back' at the thought of Basher in action, and we read again of 'a shiver down his back'. Altogether this is a well-constructed and very effective piece of narrative writing.

▷ **Question 5**   *Student's answer*

Here is a coursework short story on the set theme of a relationship that went wrong.

After the Ball

The ball from the previous night had been all that Cindy had imagined it would be, and much more. She became a beautiful princess for one short night and danced with the prince of her dreams until nearly 12.00. As Cindy sat crouched inside the fireplace, her thoughts kept drifting back to the prince and their time together. Her knuckles nearly bleeding from scrubbing the bricks and now stinging from the ammonia in the water, she worked unconsciously, while her mind was somewhere far away.

Cindy's thoughts were interrupted by a knock at the front door. As she rose from the ashes to see who was calling, the prince stood in front of her, holding the slipper she had worn the night before. She slowly slipped the shoe onto her foot as her envious stepsisters watched in anticipation. To their dismay and to Cindy's delight, the slipper was a perfect fit. Cindy had less than a moment to collect her thoughts before the prince swept her off her feet and carried her to the awaiting horse-drawn carriage. They rode directly to the coast where they were married and then celebrated on a sunny beach for nearly a month.

After a joyous honeymoon, Cindy and her prince went home to a castle of their own. Cindy was excited to make a comfortable place for her and her new husband, and as soon as they arrived, she began to make

(continued)

the place her own. She slaved long into the night and even though her prince was calling to her, she continued to work until the morning. Their second day at home was similar to the first. Cindy cleaned all fifty rooms herself and washed the kitchen floor three times. She did twelve loads of laundry, too. Once again, she did not retire until the prince had long been asleep.

On the third day the prince hired a full staff of servants to cook and clean and wait on both Cindy and himself, hand and foot. Cindy tried to spend the morning relaxing with her husband but by noon she had relieved the servants on duty and taken over their responsibilities herself.

Week after week Cindy kept up the same schedule, only her obsessive behaviour was getting much worse. The prince grew tired of his wife and was forced to find the companionship he had been longing for outside his home. Cindy was so busy cleaning she barely noticed her husband's absence. Her only request of him was that he would remove his shoes outside and place his dirty clothes in the bin, so that she could wash them.

After months of the prince pleading with Cindy to seek help, he felt he had no other option than to leave her. The prince felt neglected and abandoned and wanted to begin a new life. On a Sunday afternoon he packed a few of his belongings and went to tell Cindy that he had had enough. He looked all over the place for her. She was nowhere to be found, so he left, without saying goodbye. Cindy was crouched in the fireplace cleaning away the dirt, and never even heard her prince leave.

Examiner's comments

This is a very successful reworking of the Cinderella story. The events are familiar to the reader and we are given only the barest narrative, so the writer directs attention to what is different. This story does not have a happy ending. The ending leaves us wondering, too. Is this a story about someone who is emotionally disturbed? Is it about the likelihood of a mismatch between lovers going wrong, because in the end they will revert to their own way of life, whatever the change in their circumstances? However you read it, this use of an old folk tale makes very compelling reading.

▷ A STEP FURTHER

A great deal may be learned from being alert to the narrative techniques of others, especially writers you admire. Remember to notice effective openings and conclusions, twists of plot, aspects of character development, and so on. Remember, too, that few writers, even great ones, are wildly original: they have learned a great deal of their craft from reading other writers, and often name authors who have influenced them in their work, so there is no reason why you shouldn't take some tips from other writers, too. Study especially collections of short stories. There are many collections that you will enjoy and from which you can learn a great deal.

SUMMARY

▷   Narrative was discussed as an essential part of human psychology and communication.

▷   The distinction between narrative and story was outlined, and such features of both as the selection of incident, taking up a point of view, shaping events, and choosing an appropriate style.

▷   National Curriculum requirements that you should be able to use a variety of styles to suit various purposes were discussed.

Chapter 14

Writing dialogue

GETTING STARTED

Writing dialogue is something that you may be given an opportunity to do in a written paper for some of the GCSE Boards, and it is certainly well worth attempting dialogue if you are submitting coursework. In the imaginative writing section of **WJEC** papers, some questions will require writing of a particular form, but others may leave candidates free to choose their approach; here then may be an opportunity for writing dialogue, or a short play. The coursework guidelines of the same Board say 'one of the two pieces of imaginative writing may be either poetry or a drama script', and **London** says similarly that coursework 'may include dialogue and verse'. The **NEAB** syllabus for GCSE offers candidates opportunities 'to recount real and imagined experience in any appropriate form such as narrative, description or drama.'

	LONDON	MEG	NEAB	NICCEA	SEG	WJEC	IGCSE	TOPIC		STUDY	REVISION 1	REVISION 2
as coursework	✓	✓	✓	✓	✓	✓	✓	Direct speech in narrative				
	✓	✓	✓	✓	✓	✓	✓	Dialogue in a play				
	✓				✓	✓		Television dialogue				
	✓	✓	✓	✓	✓	✓	✓	Indirect speech in narrative				
as coursework	✓				✓	✓		Story-board planning				

WHAT YOU NEED TO KNOW

▷ **Dialogue and spontaneous talk**

The first thing to remember is that **dialogue is not simply spoken English that has been written down**. Compare the following lists of some of the features of **dialogue** and **spontaneous talk**.

Dialogue

'Dialogue isn't just written down talk'

▷ selected to make a dramatic point
▷ often in complete sentences
▷ less often ungrammatical
▷ vocabulary is more controlled by dramatic situation
▷ moods to be conveyed indicated by stage directions or by including adverbs, e.g. 'Goodbye!' [*wistfully*]
▷ lacks non-verbal features.

Spontaneous talk

▷ loosely structured and often rambling – repeating itself or missing out information that is known or shared
▷ not in complete sentences
▷ often ungrammatical
▷ has a wide vocabulary range which can include slang, technical terms and formal words
▷ depends on stress, pace, pitch and volume to convey mood

▶ depends on contact with a listener – uses non-verbal features, e.g. gesture and facial expression.

Some kinds of talk, e.g. a radio sports commentary, having a telephone conversation or making a formal speech to the school assembly, are perhaps midway between spontaneous talk and dialogue. Check each against the lists above and think how each poses special problems for the speakers in terms of the situation they are in. Take a radio commentary, for example, where listeners depend on the speaker for full details of the scene. There may well be a considerable range of types of people listening, so any commentary must be widely intelligible in choice of language, as well as lively and accurate. Contrast talking on the telephone: you cannot see how your listener is responding and the listener cannot see you waving your hands or frowning. What do you do to your speech to compensate for this? You may have written out a speech to be given at assembly, but how are you to keep a live audience's attention in the way you deliver it?

▶ **Dialogue and direct and indirect speech**

A second point to remember is that **dialogue in a play is not the same as a stretch of direct speech in a story**. (It is, incidentally, often a good idea to include snatches of talk in your personal writing – it adds liveliness and a touch of realism.) These two kinds of written speech will be rather different, though, and if you use indirect speech in a story, that will differ again.
Compare the following:

▶ JANE [*sadly*]:   It's bad news, I'm afraid. I won't be allowed to come.
JOHN [*angrily*]:   Oh, that's not fair!

▶ Jane came into the room slowly and sadly. She paused before she said 'It's bad news, I'm afraid. I won't be allowed to come.'
John shouted out 'Oh, that's not fair!'

▶ Jane came into the room slowly and sadly. She paused before she said that she was afraid it was bad news. She wouldn't be allowed to come. John replied angrily that it was not fair.

The three examples differ in effect.
The first – **dialogue** – has most impact: it is vivid and seems to be happening now. On the stage, or in a television play, you would hear the tone of voice and the extra volume of John's angry retort, and see the expressions and gestures of both speakers.

'Can you tell the difference between dialogue, and direct and indirect speech?'

The second – **direct speech** – happened in the past. The only hints that you are given as to the mood of the speakers are the occasional adverbs 'slowly and sadly', or verbs such as 'shouted'.
The third – **indirect speech** – has an even more distanced effect. The speech is in the past and is reported. We lack a sense of either speaker being immediately present and responding personally to the situation.
In order to convey these degrees of immediacy, each type of speech has to be presented differently, in terms of punctuation and layout. How to do this will be discussed below.

▶ **USEFUL PRACTICAL APPROACHES**

▶ **Identifying dialogue**

Compare the following extracts: one is a stretch of dialogue from a play and the other is a transcript of an actual conversation. Can you tell which is which?

GUS   I saw the Villa get beat in a cup tie once. Who was it against now? White shirts. It was one-all at half-time. I'll never forget it. Their opponents won by a penalty. Talk about drama. Yes, it was a disputed penalty. Disputed. They got beat two-one, anyway, because of it. You were there yourself.
BEN   Not me.
GUS   Yes, you were there. Don't you remember that disputed penalty?
BEN   No.
GUS   He went down just inside the area. Then they said he was just acting. I didn't think the other bloke touched him myself. But the referee had the ball on the spot.

BEN   Didn't touch him! What are you talking about? He laid him out flat!

GUS   Not the Villa. The Villa don't play that sort of game.

BEN   Get out of it.

MARY   Hello ... hasn't it turned cold!

SALLY   Um ... it's freezing.

MARY   I'm ...

SALLY   You're making sausage rolls. Having a party?

MARY   No-o.

SALLY   [*laughs*].

MARY   No, they're for our tea.

SALLY   Um ... they look very, very more-ish!

MARY   Get off! [*laughter*] Get away! You ... you ... [*laughter*].

SALLY   Lena come home, then?

MARY   Yeah.

SALLY   How long's she staying, 'cos I ...?

MARY   Don't know. Let's hope it's a bit longer than last time!

It's quite difficult to tell which is which, isn't it? The first extract is from a play by Harold Pinter called *The Dumb Waiter*, whereas the second extract was written down from a recording of two women talking. Go back to the checklist of features of spontaneous talk and dialogue and you will probably agree that the first is really much more orderly than the second, even though the speakers are conversing casually. The second has 'Ums', and false starts of a kind that could be very confusing in writing, whereas the first has clearly defined utterances – often complete sentences. The vocabulary in the second could range very widely, as the chat continues, but in the first it is very much concentrated on the matter in hand. We cannot easily gauge the changes of mood in either extract, because we cannot see and hear the speakers. Nevertheless, features and facial expression, as well as stress. changes of pace, pitch and volume, would be very important aspects of the second extract, and would be added by the actors in the first. So dialogue, however informal, is usually more orderly and clearer than normal speech, and each speaker usually responds directly to what the last has said.

▷ **Writing dialogue**

Dialogue is easy to write because it is simple to punctuate, if you follow a system of presentation such as that shown above, i.e. write the names of the speakers on the left, followed by a colon, and end each remark with a full stop. Put any brief directions, e.g. about the speaker's mood, in brackets, before the colon. Avoid long narrative stretches between dialogue. If you must have stage directions, keep these as short as possible, and preferably put them at the beginning of the scene.

'Why not try a story board?'

Scripts for television drama require a rather special approach. One device worth knowing about is a **story board**. Here, you break down the action into a series of shots, maybe some long shots (for scenes at a distance), middle-distance for shots not so far away, a few panning shots (where the camera sweeps around the scene) and occasional close-ups. Next, you draw a series of strip pictures, indicating below each which shot it is and the dialogue you want to use to match it.

Figure 14.1 shows the start of a story board for the play entitled *Excuses* – see Question 1 below. This helps to keep to the point and achieve an effective dramatic pace and overall tight structure. It is well worth trying – even in the planning stage of any piece of drama.

Figure 14.1

Middle-distance shot – sets scene.	*Close-up of Clare – looks worried.*	*Middle-distance shot – close to school gates.*	*Middle-distance shot – at the disco.*

C: Hi, Sam.
S: Watcha! Have you finished with the stuff you borrowed?
C: No, not quite.

S: What's wrong?
C: Oh, nothing. Just thinking about something.
S: What are you thinking about? You look as if you've done something really bad.
C: Not really.
S: Anyway, when are you going to bring 'em?
C: Soon.
S: How soon?
C: Say in a week's time?
S: All right.

C: Going to the disco tonight? It's going to be really good.
S: Yeah, I'm going, but guess who's taking me?
C: Who?
S: Clinton.
C: You mean Clinton Jones?

S: Oh, Clinton. This is great!
CJ: I can see that you're enjoying yourself.
S: Yeah. Oh there's Clare.

▷ **EXAMINATION QUESTIONS**

Here is a selection of the types of questions that will give you opportunities for writing dialogue.

▷ **Question 1**   Write a short play entitled *Excuses*.

▷ **Question 2**   Write a short dramatic scene about a memorable incident at school or college.

▷ **Question 3**   Write an episode as a continuation of a television drama series that you enjoy watching.

▷ **Question 4**   Write an exciting episode from a story involving conversational exchange.

▷ **EXAMINATION ANSWERS**

▷ **Question 1**   *Student's answer*

Excuses

CLARE   *Hi, Sam.*
SAM   *Watcha! Have you finished with the stuff you borrowed?*
CLARE   *No, not quite. [Pause]*
SAM   *What's wrong?*

(continued)

CLARE	Oh, nothing. Just thinking about something.
SAM	What are you thinking about? You look as if you've done something really bad.
CLARE	Not really.
SAM	Anyway, when are you going to bring 'em?
CLARE	Soon.
SAM	How soon?
CLARE	Say in a week's time?
SAM	All right.

[A week goes by]

CLARE	Going to the disco tonight? It's going to be really good.
SAM	Yeah, I'm going, but guess who's taking me?
CLARE	Who?
SAM	Clinton.
CLARE	You mean Clinton Jones?
SAM	Yeah him.
CLARE	Boy, he's gorgeous.
SAM	Yes, Clare.
CLARE	What you going to wear then?
SAM	Well, I'm going to wear my short white skirt with my white Wham-style jacket top. I was going to wear my black leather jacket with them but you've got it and two weeks have gone.
CLARE	Yeah, I know and I thought I might wear it to the disco tonight.
SAM	You thought, you might wear it. What about me? It's my jacket, you know. Oh forget it.
CLARE	See you tonight then?
SAM	Yeah.

[The disco]

SAM	Oh, Clinton. This is great!
CLINT	I can see that you're enjoying yourself.
SAM	Yeah. Oh, there's Clare.
CLARE	Watcha Sam.
SAM	Hi, Clare. I thought you said you were going to wear the leather jacket.
CLARE	I changed my mind.
SAM	You changed your mind. I could have worn that rotten jacket.
CLARE	All right don't get so heated!
SAM	Clare, if you've done something to the jacket let alone the LPs and the bicycle I'll kill you
CLARE	Keep your flippin' voice down, the music's not so loud you know.
SAM	Clare, I want to know what you've done with my things.
CLARE	All right let's go in the toilets.
SAM	And don't try to sweet-talk me.
CLARE	Sam, just listen, will you. I was going to Julie's house on your bicycle with some of the LPs in the bag I had on my shoulder and, of course, I was wearing your jacket. Anyway, as I got to the gate I parked the bike behind the brick wall but I forget to chain and padlock it. Anyhow, Julie opened the door and we went up to her room but then your jacket got caught on one of the hooks on Julie's door and tore half of the arm off and there was no way I could mend that. After playing the records I was about to go when Julie's brother Michael came in, jumping on the records and smashed them to bits. I came running down to take the bike and that was gone. Sam, I nearly went through Julie's window! I thought I'd keep giving excuses while I thought of a way to buy them back, without you knowing …
SAM	Oh my God, Clare, you're right. You're going to buy them back. What am I going to tell me mum?
CLARE	Sam, please don't be angry with me …
SAM	Don't be angry, you must be crazy. Just buy back my things and don't ever ask me for anything again. Never!

Examiner's comments

This has been quite well laid out: notice the brief setting of the scene and the notes, to indicate music playing. The characters interact through the dialogue, which is appropriately casual, and some slang is used as tempers rise. Clare's long speech at the end is getting dangerously like a stretch of narrative, though, isn't it?

▷ **Question 2**   *Student's answer*

This short play is called *The Governors' Meeting*, and concerns the investigation of an incident between a pupil and teacher.

The Governors' Meeting

This play is set in the office of the head mistress, Mrs Catherine Williams. Five people are attending this meeting: Mrs Margaret Keating (the mother of the pupil being discussed), John Andrews (best friend of Ken Samuels, the teacher who was attacked), Walter Richmond (friend of Margaret Keating's husband) and Elizabeth Walker (Chairperson of School Governors).

WALKER   *Would you like to come in, ladies and gentlemen?*

   [They all go into the room.]

WILLIAMS   *Take a seat, please.*

[They all sit around a large table.]

WALKER   *First I must say thank you for attending this meeting. Now, we are all here to discuss the incident involving Jennifer Keating and Mr Ken Samuels, the Humanities teacher. I have made out five copies of the report. Would you all please take one.*

[They all take one and read them.]

KEATING   *This isn't fair at all! This is not what happened! He's lying! This report is all lies!*

WILLIAMS   *Calm down, Mrs Keating. Perhaps you would like to give your account of the incident.*

KEATING   *Well, Jennifer was talking quietly to a class mate when she was told to shut up in the most rude way. Anyway she refused because of the way he spoke to her. She was then asked to leave the room and she refused still. So he took her by the arm and pulled her out of the chair to lead her out of the classroom and she pulled away and he fell over and hit the floor. That's what happened. No big deal! You see, Mr Samuels should be sacked for dragging my daughter about, not my daughter expelled for just defending herself.*

WILLIAMS   *Well, Mrs Keating, if that's the case, then it makes no difference. You see, she still refused to do as she was asked, so she still would be punished.*

KEATING   *Yes, but why should she do anything anyone tells her to do? I'm her mother, I tell her what to do, no-one else!*

WALKER   *Mrs Keating, you are not being very co-operative at all! While Jennifer is in school she is under our authority and we have every right to tell her when she is in the wrong.*

ANDREWS   *Mrs Keating, imagine if you can, that you are looking after a friend's daughter. Now this little girl happened to be helping herself to your dinner for the night. Tell me, Mrs Keating, would you think that you have no right to tell this little girl what is wrong to do and what is right to do or would you tell her that it is wrong to take something not belonging to her, and take it away?*

KEATING   *I'd kill the little cow if she pinched my dinner!*

ANDREWS   *Well, there you are, so what makes you think that only you can tell people what to do and nobody else is permitted to, especially with your daughter?*

KEATING   *Yes, all right, I was being a bit stupid, wasn't I? But that's still no reason to expel my daughter.*

WILLIAMS   *Well, Mrs Keating, we will decide that at the end of this meeting.*

WALKER   *Let's get on with the meeting shall we? Now, going by Mr Samuel's report, Jennifer was talking and chewing gum when the rules clearly say that chewing gum is strictly forbidden. So that's one rule broken. Another is, one way or another, Jennifer Keating did actually assault Mr Ken Samuels.*

RICHMOND   *Yes, but only because he assaulted her!*

WILLIAMS   *Ah, but Jennifer gave him reason to.*

RICHMOND   *I see. If it was the other way round then Jennifer would probably still get the blame.*

WALKER   *Mr Richmond. It doesn't matter what you would like to think, the truth is she did assault Mr Samuels so there are no ifs and buts about it.*

RICHMOND   *Yes, O.K. I'm sorry.*

(continued)

WALKER	Now, another broken rule was swearing, and swearing is also strictly forbidden and we will not have our pupils abusing the teachers no matter what!
WILLIAMS	Well I'm sorry but the only possible thing we can do is to suspend Jennifer for a little longer, in order to be fair to both sides. It is not a serious enough case for Jennifer to be expelled. Mr Samuels was hurt but it wasn't intended that way. So I have decided that she should be given a clear warning and told not to do it again. If she can abide by these rules then I am willing to have her carry on at this school. Is everyone agreed?
KEATING	Yes, that sounds fair to me. I'm sure she won't do it again.
WALKER	Well, we shall have Jennifer back in two weeks from today.

[Everyone mumbles, some with relief and some with disagreement. They all get up and leave the room.]

Examiner's comments

Notice how economically the scene has been set and the characters introduced. Further directions are given in brackets between speakers, and the scene ends with a final brief direction. The dialogue is realistic, lively, involving give and take, but keeping to the point and furthering the development of the dramatic incident. There is some casual speech ('Yes, O.K I'm sorry') when it is appropriate, but the Chairperson of the Governors, in contrast, always speaks with a degree of formality. Altogether, this is a successful scene.

▷ **Question 3**   *Student's answer*

This example concerns two brief incidents from an imagined continuation of the television series *EastEnders*.

EastEnders

[Hannah and Tony are re-wed and living happily in the house, done up nicely.]

TONY	Hannah, I just want you to know that I'll do my best to make things work out ... for us.
HANNAH	Tony it will work out, it must. I don't want it to go wrong again, especially with the children.
TONY	I know. By the way did I tell you Kelvin took his exams again? He passed some of them, but he had a little problem in ...
HANNAH	... Maths?
TONY	Yes.

[They both laugh.]

EastEnders

[In the laundry Caroline drops a box of soap powder just as Kelvin and Ian walk in.]

KELVIN	Oh let me 'elp you!
CAROLINE	Thanks.
KELVIN	Grm ... You new around 'ere or you just poppin' in for a quick wash?
CAROLINE	No, I just moved in, in the council flats just around the corner. Near the doctor's place.
KELVIN	You mean Dr Legg? I see.
CAROLINE	I got to go now, my room-mate will be wondering where I got to.
KELVIN	Who's she then?
CAROLINE	No. HE. He's my boyfriend. You see we got engaged just before we moved here.
KELVIN	Boyfriend! Engaged! Oh no!!
CAROLINE	What's wrong – did I say something wrong or something?
KELVIN	No. Here's your powder. I gotta get out of 'ere. Come on Ian!

[They leave quickly.]

Examiner's comments

Television soap operas consist of many short episodes and the writer has caught the spirit of a quickly changing set. Stage directions are kept to a minimum and the dialogue is very realistic. Both scenes are very economically constructed, and begin and end effectively.

▷ **Question 4**   *Student's answer*

This story's merit depends on the use of conversational exchanges throughout.

The Hunt

Before he knew it, it was four in the morning. He'd been at the table all night. His marker now ran at fifteen thousand. A little less than an hour ago, he had been winning, but since that, nothing. He placed his bet, red seven. In fact, he staked his life – he thought he just about had the roulette game cracked.

He was called into Mr Jarmain's office at five thirty. He felt tired and depressed. Mr Jarmain spoke evenly.

'Mr O'Brien. I'm sorry, but I've got to call in your marker.'

'Why?' asked O'Brien. 'You know I'm good for it.'

Mr Jarmain looked at him seriously. He couldn't believe that two years ago this young man had been one of the country's most **sort** after writers.

'Mr O'Brien, you know the rules of the house. You have a credit limit and it's up. We can't allow people to run up a debt that exceeds fifteen thousand.'

'Mr Jarmain, I'm waiting for an answer on my latest piece. I should know tomorrow. All I'm asking for is another ten.'

'I can't – you know that.'

O'Brien was pale. He didn't have that much money but he wanted one last shot.

'Remember, you have five days in which to clear your marker. … And one more thing, Mr O'Brien.'

'Yes?'

'Don't let me have to come looking for you.'

Mr Jarmain pointed to the door with his hand. O'Brien knew the meeting was over …

Four days had passed since he had walked out of Mr Jarmain's office. He still didn't have any money. He had called on people he thought of as friends. They had said they couldn't possibly lay their hands on that type of money at short notice.

Walking back to his flat, O'Brien was suddenly aware of a car parked outside the building's entrance. One of Mr Jarmain's **hevies** had seen him approach and he climbed out of the car.

'Mr Jarmain wants to see you,' he said.

'Is it important?' asked O'Brien.

'Don't be smart with me. Just get in the car – and quick.'

He still had one day in which to pay the money, so why did Mr Jarmain want to see him so urgently?

As he stood outside Jarmain's office, O'Brien could hear little **snipits** of a telephone conversation. Then the door opened.

'Mr Jarmain will see you now.'

Silently, Joshua walked in.

'Ah, there you are Mr O'Brien. I was **begining** to wonder if I would be seeing you again.'

'I've still got one day left, and I am a little short,' replied O'Brien.

Mr Jarmain had no time for excuses. He knew very well O'Brien had been ringing everyone in town for a loan.

It was Mr Jarmain who broke the silence.

'You have twenty-four hours to get my money – understand?'

O'Brien nodded, and was led from the room …

O'Brien picked up the phone, then put it down. Reluctantly, he picked up the phone again and called his ex-wife. He explained the situation. He knew she wouldn't refuse because their daughter needed a father – even if it was an unsuccessful one. She agreed to make up the money – he asked for a little more than he owed – altogether it was seventeen thousand in the case.

O'Brien entered Mr Jarmain's office with a good feeling. He knew Jarmain was a card man himself. He placed the case on the table, and opened it. Mr Jarmain stared in disbelief.

'There's seventeen thousand there. How about one last gamble?' said O'Brien.

'What's the stakes?'

O'Brien knew he had him.

(continued)

> *'Double or quit.'*
>
> *'You know I'm a card man, Mr O'Brien, so what's this about?'*
>
> *'It's simple,' he said. 'Just shuffle the pack and take a card – one each.'*
>
> *O'Brien walked down the street towards the car. In his hand he still had the case. The money was still his – and more besides. It felt good.*

Examiner's comments

This is a slick story, a pastiche of a particular type of narrative. Though it has considerable qualities of organization and economy of expression, notice how much the use of conversation adds to the dramatic effect. As well as normal direct speech, e.g.

'Mr Jarmain wants to see you,' he said.

'Is it important?' asked O'Brien.

this candidate makes good use of exchanges much closer to dialogue. By dropping the reporting clauses 'he said', 'he replied', etc. he can achieve a much more immediate and fast-moving effect:

'… And one more thing, Mr O'Brien.'

'Yes?'

'Don't let me have to come looking for you.'

In this last example, the exchange has added menace, from the impersonal way it is presented, hasn't it? (Note the spelling errors: sought/ heavies/ snippets/ beginning.)

Dropping the reporting clauses is known as **free direct speech**. Why not try it when appropriate in your own writing?

A STEP FURTHER

As you read plays, or watch them in the theatre or on television, be alert to the skills of the dramatist, and try some of them out for yourself.

The importance of a clear presentation or layout, of realism in dialogue and a good shape to a scene have already been discussed.

You could go on to study how characters are established and react to one another in plays that you read, and notice that most plays have a fairly limited number of characters. It can be confusing for the audience if too many people are introduced too quickly.

You may pay particular attention, also, to how scenes begin, end and often reach some point of climax. If your play moves along at a very steady pace all the time, perhaps it would be written better as a story. Experiment with the same situation in two kinds of writing, e.g. *The Governors' Meeting* could also have been written successfully as a report, and *Excuses* as a short story.

SUMMARY

▷   The difference between spontaneous talk and shaped dialogue was established.

▷   You were shown how to set out dialogue, direct and indirect speech.

▷   Script-writing and story-board techniques were mentioned.

▷   There were examples of using dialogue in narrative as direct and free direct speech.

Chapter 15

Persuasive writing

▷ GETTING STARTED

Some kinds of speech and writing are deliberately presented from one point of view, e.g. political or debating speeches. Others try to offer a balanced treatment, giving equal weight to the views of either side. Sometimes, if you feel very strongly about an issue, this can be a hard thing to do.

This chapter to some extent follows on from Chapters 8 and 12. When you research and write up a topic, you may wish to persuade the reader to agree with your point of view. Similarly, when you write a summary, you may be asked to present it so as to influence a certain kind of reader. **WJEC** Coursework options require two pieces of work 'employing argument or expressing opinion', and most of the Groups require or suggest some coursework of this sort.

LONDON	MEG	NEAB	NICCEA	SEG	WJEC	IGCSE	TOPIC	STUDY	REVISION 1	REVISION 2
✓	✓	✓	✓	✓	✓	✓	Structuring argument			
			✓				Logical reasoning			
✓	✓	✓		✓	✓		Expressing opinions			
✓			✓			✓	Persuasive writing			
✓							Considering both sides of an issue			

▷ WHAT YOU NEED TO KNOW

▷ Get your facts right

'It can be hard to take a balanced view'

The most important first step is to **get your facts right**. Opinions are more likely to carry weight if your arguments are well informed. Your own views, however sincerely held, will carry little conviction with readers if they can easily demolish what you are saying on the basis of better information.

Getting your facts right involves knowing about both sides of an issue, and this has the advantage of helping you to put yourself in the place of those you wish to persuade, or present your case to. If you can see all round your subject, you will be able to defend, as well as attack; you will also be able to challenge your audience about what you think may be their misheld opinions as well as to urge what you wish on your own account. When writing, as well as when talking, it is best not to let your emotions get the better of you. Clarity of thought and argument is usually more persuasive than strong feeling, however sincere.

▷ Plan your argument

It is a good idea to **plan your argument** so as to make it as effective as possible. A simple plan for a piece of persuasive writing can be made by outlining the sections to be covered, as in the following example.

1 A strong, or challenging opening.
2 A series of headings, following the stages of the argument:
    (a) 'This discussion is about …'
    (b) 'Some people consider that …'
    (c) 'But others consider that …'
    (d) 'You yourself may feel that both …'

(e) 'However, I would hope to convince you that ...'

(f) 'In conclusion ...'

3   Make your own conclusion memorable, reassuring, even a battlecry – whatever seems appropriate.

▷ **Be clear**   Once you have gathered material from which to make a case, and are planning the stages of the argument, try to **be absolutely clear**, avoiding giving any impression that you are in a state of confusion. Try to be simple and forcible, and do not introduce a mass of unnecessary detail.

▷ **Be telling – and compelling**   You will want to hold your readers' or listeners' attention, so **be telling – and compelling**. Avoid dealing entirely in general statements. Try to **enliven** what you say or write with a few well-chosen examples, or an anecdote, e.g. something humorous or dramatic. Most people find that some variety of this kind makes a general argument much easier to follow. A direct appeal is better than an indirect, so avoid using the impersonal 'one'; 'you' is preferable.

▷ **USEFUL PRACTICAL APPROACHES**

There are some devices of persuasive writing that have been familiar from the time of the Greek civilization and have often been used since. Of course, persuasive writers and speakers can distort the truth, leaving out vital information and becoming, in short, propagandist. Even so, there are some devices of style in persuasive writing that you could well employ, such as the following:

▷ **Exaggeration**   To overstate your case grossly is self-defeating, as the audience will become suspicious. To go amusingly beyond the facts may, however, help to persuade:

> For every house they have built, we shall build five hundred!

An opponent's position can be mocked and undermined by exaggeration:

> We know that those against us never have any difficulty whatsoever in making ends meet.

▷ **Figurative language**   It is best to be sparing with imagery in argument. However, an appropriate extended image can be very telling because it carries the argument forward in a memorable way:

> Here in England we have a proud heritage. Remember, only a few, a brave band, fought at Agincourt; only a few fought the Battle of Britain. Once again we turn to only a few, as brave and as determined as those noble ancestors to fight and conquer.

▷ **Persuader words**   'Certainly', 'surely', 'definitely', 'it goes without saying' – words and phrases such as those give your readers or listeners the feeling that they *must* agree with you, or be unreasonable!

▷ **Repetition**   Remember, especially when delivering a speech, that things said once are easily forgotten. Effective persuasion consists of making a point, sometimes several times in different ways:

They always speak of their generosity to the community. Was it generous of them to close the Community Hall? Was it generous to stop the project to build more low-cost housing for local people? No, friends, we have a different understanding of 'generosity'.

▷ **Rhetorical questions**   These appear to be addressed to all members of the audience, but do not require an answer. They can give an audience a sense of being involved all together.

> Will you stand by and let this happen? Will you?

The reader or listener is not supposed to look up and say 'No, we won't!', but rather to accept the writer's or speaker's position. This is a device of style which should be used sparingly; too much will tip over into parody and sound ridiculous.

▷ EXAMINATION QUESTIONS

Here are some questions which give an opportunity for persuasive and argumentative writing. Try an outline plan for one or two before reading the comments in the following section.

▷ **Question 1**   Write about the advantages and disadvantages of co-education.

▷ **Question 2**   'The teenager of today is more responsible and more involved in the fate of the world than teenagers of earlier years.' Discuss this proposition.

▷ **Question 3**   The motor car: a blessing or a curse?

▷ **Question 4**   How far do you think individuality should be expressed through appearance?

▷ **Question 5**   Which arguments would you put forward in favour of a national curriculum for primary schools?

▷ **Question 6**   Plan a speech outlining what you consider should be recognized as pupils' rights.

▷ **Question 7**   Write a speech as community representative in favour of restricting the traffic flow through the main streets of your town or village.

▷ **Question 8**   'Good fences make good neighbours'. Write the words of a speech to be given to a teenage audience in which you set out to persuade them to agree with this point of view.

▷ **EXAMINATION ANSWERS**

▷ **Question 1**   *Student's answer*

The advantages and disadvantages of co-education

The question of whether co-education is such a good idea is constantly being asked by many people.

The most important issue that parents would first want to be reassured on if their children were to be sent to a mixed school would be the effect that co-education would have on their son's or daughter's studies.

Members of the teaching profession are often just as worried about the effects that a mixed class would have on the general discipline. Boys, when mixed with girls in class, tend to go in for more answering back than usual and even the best of teachers could sometimes lose control. Girls, on the other hand, tend to be quieter and take a less active part.

The effects that co-education would have on the general standard of work would depend largely on the boy or girl concerned. Assuming that the teacher kept control, then some boys and girls would probably find the competition fiercer, and to keep face, would be likely to work harder – resulting in a general raising of standards. On the other hand, boys and girls with less will-power would be easily distracted from their lessons and might be better off in separate schools.

Many boys and girls often feel awkward when in the company of members of the opposite sex, either from natural shyness or from self-consciousness. For them, compulsory company is very helpful for they do not have to make the move to meet other friends but see them and get to know them every day, and may even be encouraged to take part in school activities, such as plays and operas, with them.

From these few points, it may be seen that the choice between co-education and separate education is a difficult one and that it is not possible to say if one is definitely better than the other.

Examiner's comments

This answer is well planned and well balanced throughout. It starts with arguments rather against the idea of co-education: parents' concern about standards; the possible adverse effects on boys and on girls; and teachers' worries. The two following paragraphs consider both sides of the case, however: sometimes teachers do lose control; sometimes standards will fall, but, on the other hand, they may be raised in the face of stronger competition, etc. There may be awkwardness for boys and girls at first, but greater familiarity should be beneficial. The final paragraph is a good example of moderation. What is needed in addition are some examples or anecdotes to make one or two of these well-argued points really vivid and memorable. In general, though, this is a competent piece of work.

▷ **Question 2**   *Student's answer*

The teenager of today is more responsible and more involved in the fate of the world than teenagers of earlier years.

I think this statement is true, mainly because the problems are much greater than they were years ago. Also the problems that arose years ago were not publicized and widespread as they are now. The teenagers of today have realized that things like the atom bomb will be a major problem when they become older, as well as the storage of nuclear waste. They should have a say in the matter as it is they who will have to solve the problem in years to come.

Adults go on about the Ban-the-Bomb enthusiasts and say they're just layabouts who think they are big if they support it. In my opinion a minority are, but the majority are sincere in their wishes. The older generation don't realize that the younger generation do take an interest in politics and the future of the world.

Earlier teenagers were aware of the problems of their time but didn't do anything about it. They are probably too scared of the authorities to hold demonstrations and protest marches. The teenagers of today are definitely more involved in the fate of the world, and a lot of them are certainly as responsible as the older generation. All generations, though, have good and bad in them.

Another problem that has made teenagers more responsible is unemployment. They have to consider what sort of future there is for themselves and their children.

Examiner's comments

The use of the first person pronoun throughout this essay has the effect of catching the reader's attention: here apparently is someone telling you what he or she actually thinks. There are phrases throughout which express strong support for teenagers and, equally important, an awareness of bias against them – that they are considered by some to be boastful 'layabouts' if they take up a cause they believe in. In general the reader is involved, and carried along by the individual 'voice' of this piece of writing. Organization, though, could have been better: the final paragraph, for example, would have fitted in well after the second paragraph, before the discussion is broadened to what adults today think, or what teenagers in the past were like. The sentence 'All generations, though, have good and bad in them', would have made a rather appropriate ending if it had been placed last.

▷ **Question 3**   *Student's answer*

Here is a student's outline plan for this question. Read this first, before going on to read the essay itself.

'Try a few devices of style.'

Plan
Need for cars
1   *Form of transport*
2   *Gives you more time*
3   *Can be used for work or leisure*
Expensive
1   *A luxury*
2   *Tax; insurance*
3   *Petrol; maintenance*
4   *Status symbol – Rolls, Jaguar*
5   *Car clubs – restoring cars*
6   *Types of cars – sports, saloons*
Pollution
1   *Fumes – wildlife*
2   *Noise*
3   *Motorway – build through countryside*
Conclusion
1   *Essential to many people*
2   *Keep industry going*
3   *Need for balance between nature and the car*

Examiner's comments

The plan is simple but clear. The writer thinks of the arguments under four headings: Need for cars; Expensive; Pollution; and Conclusion. Section one is obviously arguing for the motor car and three is obviously against, and so is section two at the beginning, although it is hard to tell whether points (4) to (6) are for or against. The Conclusion begins by supporting the motor car and ends with a balanced argument. This seems a promising outline plan for an essay which considers both sides of the argument.

The Motor Car: a Blessing or a Curse?
The first motor car was invented one hundred years ago by a Mr Daimler, who was duly helped by Mr Benz. At the time the invention was seen to be something of a folly and was merely felt to be a play thing for the wealthy. Today the story is different; the motor car has become for many people an essential form of transport, which gives comfort and pleasure. In remote areas of the country where buses are infrequent and trains do not run, the car transports people to work and after work provides the transport for leisure outings.

(continued)

Cars are very expensive to buy, not though as costly as they were before mass production came into being; they come in many forms from sports cars to beach buggies. The sports car enthusiasts often spend countless time and money on their machines; chrome plated engines are just a small luxury for these car lovers. Wives and girlfriends have to take the back seat when it comes to a choice between the annual classic car show or the holiday in Spain. I for one feel this is taking the love of the car just a little too far, but I can see the reason they enjoy their cars so much. Nothing can diminish the thrill and feeling of automatic superiority when behind the wheel of a true aristocrat of cars, such as a Jaguar or Porsche. The car you drive immediately says something about its owner, whether it be true or not. Jaguars and Rolls Royces state the fact that you have money. Porsches that you are successful and in a hurry; these are of course phantasms of the imagination because no one knows for sure what the person behind the wheel is really like. Not too long ago I owned a TR7. I was and still am not wealthy, many thought I was however, the police especially, who took a rather unwelcome fondness towards my car; I eventually sold it. The cost of running and maintaining it was too much and it attracted attention.

To me one of the most neglected issues surrounding the car is its environmental cost. The fumes generated as the waste products of the combustion process pollute our countryside, reducing the wildlife and plant kingdoms. Motorways are built often without due attention to the environment, bringing noise as well as other invisible pollutants.

Despite all the car's disadvantages there are its many advantages. It gives people a freedom which they did not have before and perhaps, most important of all, it provides a great service to industry; something we all benefit from. I do feel though, that a balance has to be set between the environment and the car so we do not lose what many of us have come to take for granted: our countryside.

Examiner's comments

This is a balanced discussion of the pros and cons of the car, written with good sense and humour. As well as offering a range of points on both sides, the writer introduces some of his own experiences as a car owner, to provide detail. The essay begins well, with a brief historical sketch of early motoring. The temptation to write a lengthy work on the history of the motor car, and by doing so risk a tedious opening, is avoided. The argument moves on from the historical sketch through a discussion of types of cars and problems of ownership to wider issues, e.g. environmental factors. The concluding paragraph is positive and realistic. There are some awkward expressions and a few errors, but this is a very competent discussion.

▷ Question 4   *Tutor's answer*

Notice that this question begins with the phrase 'How far …'. You will be expected to gauge the extent to which individuality should be expressed through appearance. Here is a topic which almost demands detailed examples. It is difficult to imagine a way of writing successfully and interestingly on it in wholly general terms. On the other hand, there is a danger that you might get too involved in the detailed examples and lose the thread of the argument. Once again, a simple outline plan will avoid this. Spend a few minutes writing one for yourself, taking care to support the main points of argument with good illustrations. The following would be a typical approach.

How far do you think individuality should be expressed through appearance?

1   **People judge by appearances**
   (a) Appearance makes an impact.
   (b) Some people like to go to extremes in this respect, e.g. Punks.
   (c) It is important to make your appearance appropriate for the occasion, though, e.g. weddings, interviews.
2   **Appearance is a way of expressing personality**
   (a) Most people experiment with different 'looks', especially when they are young.
   (b) On the other hand, young people tend to choose to look alike, e.g. wearing denim jeans.
   (c) Sometimes people have to wear a uniform because their role socially is more important than their individuality, e.g. the police.

(d) Sometimes whether a uniform should be worn is open to debate, e.g. school uniform.

3   **Conclusion**

(a) As far as possible let people have freedom of choice.

(b) Remember, though, there is a need for group identity expressed through appearance.

This is just one possible plan among many, but it does offer a structure and a degree of balance in discussing the issue.

▷ **Question 5**   *Outline answer*

The National Curriculum for both primary and secondary schools has been much discussed, so you would need to do a little research for this question. You could start with what you know, and list what you consider to be basic to the primary curriculum, using your own memories of that stage of education, and compare that with how the National Curriculum is working in primary schools these days. A well-informed essay would look at some of the arguments in favour of a more standardized approach to all learning in schools. The arguments against might mention the value of individual teachers passing on what they are enthusiastic about and enjoy teaching. There are also points to be made about equality of opportunity to learn, and the importance of a good grounding in subjects that pupils and society will need more of in the future, e.g. science or computing. This is a starting point. Try developing a plan along these lines for yourself.

▷ **Question 6**   *Outline answer*

In addition to deciding upon your main arguments, you have to think about impressing them on your audience – whether readers or listeners. I'm sure that you will be able to think immediately of a list of possible pupils' rights. Put them down, then check each one to see if it can be reconciled with working in a school community or with the different responsibilities that arise when young people are not at home. For example, you may think it should be a right for school children to leave the school premises at lunch-times. To deny them this may seem a limitation of their personal freedom. Yet what about the responsibility of the head and teachers for their students? How can they be sure that no accidents will occur to unsupervised young people? How would this fit in with their legal responsibilities?

When you have written your list, think about the likely audience – probably school students and/or teachers. To persuade, you have to sound as if you believe in the ideas you are putting forward and also show that you are ready to defend against opposing views. Look back at points made earlier in the chapter on how to keep and hold your audience's attention.

▷ **Question 7**   *Outline answer*

As this is a written speech, you should devote more attention to wording your arguments very carefully. Such an issue always has people strongly in favour and strongly against. In the first group might be those who wish to preserve the character of the town or village; who live in the main street and would like it to be quieter; who are concerned about the danger to people and buildings from increasingly heavy traffic. Against might be those who say that heavier traffic will bring more trade to the community and perhaps provide public transport too for the convenience of local people. If the traffic is diverted, the town or village may become a backwater – dead, rather than sleepy. Think of a town or village that you know well and relate these arguments, and any others you can think of, to particular circumstances.

▶ **Question 8**   *Outline answer*

The question gives you certain features to include. This must be a speech (you could use some of the advice on structure and on devices of style outlined earlier in this chapter). You have to argue *for* the proposition and in such a way that you persuade a specific audience – here teenagers. This could be quite challenging. Trouble with neighbours and the need to keep your distance is something everyone knows about, but it is parents who often have most contact with neighbours. Think about how neighbours can affect the lives of young people: complaining about noisy parties, motor bikes, being nosy; they can be friendly and supportive, too. You could take the idea of neighbours in a broader sense, such as the UK's European neighbours, but if you decide to do this make it quite clear at the outset of the speech that this is your interpretation.

A STEP FURTHER

Take opportunities to read effective discussions about important contemporary issues and to listen to the wide variety of public speaking styles in the media today. You will learn a good deal about ways of presenting argument: how best to order your points but also how best to have some impact on the receiver of your communication, whether reader or listener. In the latter case, non-verbal communication (NVC, for short) also makes a vital contribution: does the speaker look confident, sincere, honest? Do hand gestures seem vague or suggest the dictatorial? How does the speaker pace his or her utterances – slowly enough for the audience to take in and reflect on what is being argued. or too slowly, tending to drag, boring the audience and losing its interest? In writing, it is vital to keep the interest of your readers if you hope to convince them. Notice devices of style used by writers whose work you admire. Some of these might be experimented with in your own attempts at writing to persuade.

SUMMARY

▷   Essentials of effective argument are knowing your facts before you begin, planning argument, speaking with conviction, and interesting your listeners or readers.

▷   Some rhetorical devices of value to speakers and writers of argument were listed, including exaggeration, persuader words, repetition, and rhetorical questions.

▷   Balanced argument as well as arguing for and against a proposition were discussed.

▷   What is NVC? This question was answered, and you were advised about how it can enhance as well as detract from your verbal skills.

Descriptive writing

GETTING STARTED

In some English course books published earlier in the twentieth century there used to be advice on how to set about descriptive writing. The basic idea was what later came to be jokingly referred to as 'the two adjectives to every noun' kind of writing. Even so, the essence of good descriptive writing is to convey to your readers, as vividly as you can, the sensuous aspects of your subject – what they would see, smell, taste, touch and hear, and, rather more elusive to put down on paper, its spirit, so that it becomes like a living experience to the readers. All you have at your disposal to achieve this are words. Get into the habit of observing scenes around you closely and trying to capture them in words. The writer, James Joyce, and some others too, used to jot down on envelopes or scraps of paper ideas which occurred to them, rather as an artist uses a sketch book.

	LONDON	MEG	NEAB	NICCEA	SEG	WJEC	IGCSE	TOPIC		STUDY	REVISION I	REVISION 2
as coursework	✓	✓	✓	✓	✓	✓	✓	Using words with discrimination				
	✓	✓	✓	✓				Literal description				
	✓							Figurative description				
	✓	✓	✓	✓	✓	✓	✓	Comparison				
	✓	✓	✓	✓	✓	✓	✓	Contrast				
	✓	✓	✓	✓	✓	✓	✓	Sound effects in descriptive writing				

WHAT YOU NEED TO KNOW

Using words with discrimination

'Be observant!'

The words you choose when you write a description are very important, and should be thought about and selected carefully. It is a common mistake to suppose that you have to clutter your writing with lots of impressive words (worst of all load it down monotonously with 'two adjectives to every noun'). The essential principle is to use words with **discrimination**, so that they not only give a vivid and realistic impression of your subject but also help to create the spirit of the thing. You may use words **literally** or **figuratively** (see below for more details of this) but above all use them **aptly**. Figurative expressions can be very effective in bringing your subject to life, but use them sparingly and try not to 'overwrite', i.e. use a figure of speech in almost every line, so that readers find themselves tripping over them, instead of being carried along by them.

Literal and figurative expressions

Read and think about the following poem written by a fourteen-year-old girl.

The Pig

Smooth and plump and pink, the pig
With wriggly, curly tail,
Surveys complacently the yard
And the rim of the old tin pail.

'Now tell us, Pig, what are your thoughts?

What is it you can see?'
'I see my yard, my pail, my world –
The world belongs to me.'

'Why, foolish Pig, now don't you know,
Beyond this old stone wall,
There lies a world so very big
You cannot see at all.'

'Don't be absurd,' the pig replied,
'These things just cannot be.
The world is girdled by this wall,
The world belongs to me!'

Why is this simple poem so effective? Surely, because it presents the concentrated point of view of a limited-minded animal. The pig's world is defined by the boundaries of the wall: it has no words, and no ideas, for what is beyond it.

Now read and contrast this poem, written by the same pupil:

Birds

A robin, cheerful companion.
Snaps at caterpillars gaily,
Whistling in his throat so low
You have to strain your ears to hear.
And sparrows, underfed starvelings without fear
Flutter and run, and dart from tree to tree.
And there, so small she's difficult to see,
A tiny lady, a wren hiding shyly.
And in tuneful melody
A single blackbird mounts guard on the fence.
On the lawn, squabbling, a young thrush politician rants;
And a bluetit – tiny impudence –
Swings among the blackcurrants.

This is expressed much less literally: the language is more metaphorical. Both poems communicate very well, though, don't they?

A similar approach can be used in prose descriptions, too. Take a third example:

The pouncing fire leaps on its prey like an angry lion. It slowly slinks on its paws and then, with a gigantic leap, pours like a shower of sparks on its kill. Its jaws thrust open wide and with a sigh it is gone, sliding amongst the jungle and then, with a sudden spurt of anger, it quivers into lIfe again and rears and destroys.

This image of the fire is an excellent one by which the writer can explore the subject with an interest, complexity and emotional involvement beyond the potential of any amount of literal detail.

I referred earlier in this chapter to some English course books of a traditional style. These also often had lists of figurative expressions for the student to learn and, presumably, then imitate. There is a certain danger in this approach. Students can become self-conscious about using figurative language and can so easily overdo it. This is at least an enterprising and adventurous use of vocabulary, but it can have an adverse effect on the reader. It is as if the writer has not fully fused sense and expression: how do you feel about this next example?

'Avoid overdoing imagery.'

Dead! The news stuck like toffee in her mind. It felt heavy and indigestible. Whichever way she spun it out she could not get rid of it. It just stayed stuck!

I think this makes the point by itself! Remember, though, that those assessing your work are likely to be sympathetic to your experiments with words, and prefer to see you making some mistakes along the way, rather than not venturing into new kinds of expression at all.

Here, then, remembering the warning above, are some examples of **figures of speech** that you could try to use sometimes in your own writing.

▷ Figures of comparison

Simile

A simile is an explicit comparison between two or more things alike in only one respect. The comparison is introduced by 'like' or 'as':

> She glided cat-like.
> He climbed as sure-footed as a cat.

Well-worn or overworked similes in everyday usage are known as **clichés**, e.g. 'as white as a sheet', 'as red as a beetroot'.

Metaphor

A metaphor is a comparison between two or more things that are alike in some respects. The comparison is usually implied:

> The fog came on little cat feet.

The comparison is sometimes extended over several lines of expression, as in the following example, written by D. H. Lawrence:

> Naxos thousands of feet below the olive roots,
> And now the olive leaves thousands of feet below the lava fire
> Peace congealed in black lava on the doorstep.
> Within, white-hot lava, never at peace
> Till it burst forth blinding, withering the earth;
> To set again into rock,
> Grey-black rock.
> Call it Peace?

In this case it is called an **extended metaphor**.

There are well-worn cliché metaphors too. When several of them are combined in one utterance they become almost meaningless and sometimes amusing:

> We are the captains of our fate and must pull ourselves up by our boot-laces, to avoid the sea of troubles ahead.

Personification

This is a metaphor in which human characteristics are attributed to something inanimate:

> Winter whipped the trees bare.

On a larger scale, the **fable** and **allegory** are both forms of metaphor.

Fable

A fable is a short narrative, where animals usually represent some trait of human beings for a moral purpose. Often the moral is written separately at the end, e.g. Aesop's *Fables* from the sixth century BC. A more recent fable is George Orwell's *Animal Farm*.

Allegory

An allegory is a story with two levels of meaning: one literal and another more generally understood, e.g. Bunyan's *The Pilgrim's Progress*.

▷ Figures of contrast

Antithesis

This is a comparison in which one idea is set against another:

> Better to live happy and die poor, than live rich and die wretched.

Paradox

A paradox is a statement which seems to be self-contradictory, but which actually asserts something true:

The freezing ice burnt her hand.

▷ **Figures of sound effect**

Alliteration

This is the figure of speech in which the sounds of consonants occurring in words close together are the same, or similar:

The cold, cruel, keen northern wind.

Assonance

In assonance the sounds of vowels or syllables in words close together are the same, or similar:

She heard a crisp sound, as if of ice splitting and hissing.

Onomatopoeia

This is the figure of speech in which the sound of a word imitates a well-known sound, often in nature:

Miaow.

▶ **EXAMINATION QUESTIONS**

All the Boards are likely to give candidates an opportunity to write a 'set piece' description (either in a written paper, or as coursework), and you will probably include stretches of description in your other creative writing. For descriptive writing in response to a stimulus, see Chapter 17.

Here is a list of typical questions. (Some of them relate to passages, set by the Boards on GCSE papers, which have been discussed in earlier chapters. Page references have been given where appropriate, so that you can turn back.)

▷ **Question 1**   Write descriptively about an old and perhaps ruined castle or church.

▷ **Question 2**   Think of something you would really like to own (it might be a piece of equipment or clothing or even a toy) and write a description of it, explaining in detail what it is, where it can be bought and why you want it.   (London)

▷ **Question 3**   Imagine that you are the vet in the passage written by Jacqui Durrell. Describe your experiences of a typical visit to her home based on what you have read in the passage from *Intimate Relations* (see pages 110–11).   (SEG)

▷ **Question 4**   Write a description of a place you know and love well.   (NEAB)

▷ **Question 5**   'A Wet Day by the Sea.'   (MEG)

▷ **Question 6**   'A Walk in Autumn.'

▷ **Question 7**   'Clouds.'

▷ **Question 8**   Describe a crowded beach. As you watch, a thunderstorm breaks and the holidaymakers run for shelter. Describe the events as they happen and conclude by describing the deserted beach.   (WJEC)

▷ **Question 9**   The joys and miseries of a winter's afternoon on the school field.   (WJEC)

▷ **Question 10**   What is it like where you live? You may like to write about the kind of people who live near you, perhaps describing some of the well-known characters and/or some of the places that you think make your neighbourhood lively and interesting or dismal and boring.   (NEAB)

▷ **EXAMINATION ANSWERS**

There are two kinds of descriptive writing required by these questions: free writing, and writing related to a passage you are given. Remember that in the second case (Questions 1, 2, 3 and 4 above) you must write within the limitations of the details in the passage, unless you are specifically told that you may expand on them.

▷ **Question 6**   *Student's answer*

Here is a pupil's outline for an essay 'A Walk in Autumn':

> *It is Autumn*
> *Rough winds*
> *Cold weather becoming wintry*
> *Trees are bare*
> *Old houses are dominant and rickety*
> *Autumn fireplaces burn wood, creating smoke*
> *Three people walk down the lane*
> *A solitary gentleman and two women*
> *The surrounding lands are dying*
> *The lane is well worn, probably by horse and cart*
> *The twist in the road encloses the village*
> *The gentleman is going home for his tea*
> *The two ladies are out for an Autumn walk in the fresh, cool air*
> *The sky is filling with clouds as the blue clear skies of Summer fade away*

(continued)

> *The clouds ride the skies*
> *There are no animals to be seen as they are probably hibernating*
> *The valley to the left looks cold and secluded*
> *Snow is soon to fall.*

As you see, it is a list of quick impressions, moving from general ideas which characterize the weather and the appearance of the countryside at this season, to setting the scene in a particular village, where three people are out walking. The mood changes, towards the end, with hints that winter is coming: 'the blue clear skies of Summer fade away'; 'There are no animals to be seen as they are probably hibernating' and 'Snow is soon to fall'.

Now read the essay right through.

A Walk in Autumn

The figure of a gentleman briskly walks home from his day of work at his workplace. He is on his way home to his wife who will have prepared tea and biscuits to warm him from the cooling air of Autumn.

The rough winds blow the leaves from the trees and bushes as he passes them by. The trees are now looking bare and sodden as the Autumn gusts create a wintry feel to the air. The surrounding land appears to be dying as leaves turn to brown and die, falling gently to the ground.

The sky now begins to fill with Autumn clouds as the blue, clear, quiet skies of Summer fade away. The clouds are dark and glide briskly through the skies as they bring new weather to the scene.

The village lane appears well worn over the years by horse and cart as they would have crashed through the village. The meander in the road encloses the village houses as the lane disappears up the hill into the distance.

Two ladies are taking a walk up the lane in this cold evening scene. They are well wrapped up in cloaks and they are talking with one another. The cool air fills their lungs as they breathe in. They too are walking home like the gentleman.

The village houses appear old and well used. They have high chimney stacks releasing the smoke created by the burning warmth of the fire below. Smoke rolls from the stacks into the overcast evening sky. The dormant rickety old house at the front of the lane stands like a loner, away from the crowd of the other village houses. It appears empty and still, as if it has not been used for many years and shall soon crumble to a small waste.

There are no animals to be seen. They are probably now hibernating as the months of Winter rapidly build their wake of freezing chills.

The winds now blow and snow is imminent as the barren signs of Winter approach. The trees rustle and crack their branches together in the wind.

The valley behind the village to the left of the scene looks cold and secluded from the rest of the land. Fog is building up, soon to cover the village in a blanket of cool air.

Examiner's comments

In his final version, the writer changed his initial plan slightly. The opening has more impact, with the human interest of the gentleman hurrying home to his tea. The ominous mood has been kept and is built up through a series of details – the 'dying' land, the darkening clouds bringing new weather then the threat of 'freezing chills'. The ending, though, is a little flat and seems incomplete. Notice how well the writer has used contrasts, both to intensify the mood of the piece and to structure it, to some extent. One contrast is drawn between the bleak weather and the warmth of home: the gentleman hurries to tea and biscuits which will 'warm' him from the cooling air of Autumn. The ladies hurry home to village houses where chimneys smoke from 'the burning warmth of the fire below'. One empty house stands apart. That no longer has a human connection and seems likely to return to waste ground soon. Even the animals are sheltering, well away from 'freezing chills'.

The range of vocabulary is not very extensive but describes the scene quite well. There is appeal to four of the senses: sight, in the pictorial aspects of the scene; smell, in the smoke and warm tea; taste is involved there, too, perhaps, and touch in the suggestion of the 'rickety' and 'crumbling' house. The weather is effectively evoked: Autumn 'cooling', 'rough', 'gusts create a wintry feel'. Clouds are 'dark and glide briskly' unlike the 'blue, clear, quiet skies of Summer' – three simple words which make a good picture.

There is even an attempt at figurative language: a 'meander' is really a bend in a river, crossing a plain. Here, it is applied to the road. The house is 'dormant', i.e. wrapped in a long sleep, and has another human characteristic: it is isolated 'like a loner away from the crowds'. The trees have animation – they themselves, rather than the wind, 'rustle and crack their branches'. Finally the fog is said to be about 'to cover the village in a blanket of cool air'. All these images are well integrated into the writing: you probably didn't notice them all on your first reading. Altogether this is rather a successful short description of an Autumn scene.

▷ **Question 7**   *Student's answer*

Here is a pupil's essay with the title 'The Cloud'. It is chiefly descriptive writing but it is also a story, as you'll see.

The Cloud

Over the countryside a thundercloud formed. Heavy and grey, with an unholy line of light at its rim, it drifted across the setting sun, casting a sudden shadow. As the sun disappeared it grew, and passing over towns in the night gained a murky, yellowish-grey hue that only showed clearly the next morning. It was a cloud like smog; but it wasn't smog.

In the morning the sky was grey and overcast. The cloud drifted over towns to the countryside once more. As the rain began to fall, drops fell from the yellow cloud – large and impure, leaving a brown mark on whatever they touched. Most of the rain from the cloud fell into or drained into a moorland stream, that trickled its way and poured its poisoned waters into a river. The rain stopped falling. The river ran on its way. Imperceptibly at first, its waters became gradually slower and instead of being crystal clear it was now a poisonous brown. Sluggishly it slid through the countryside, past ploughed, brown fields, past grassy, muddy fields where cows came down to drink. The cows who drank from the brown river did not live long, but died the next morning, gasping for air and kicking feebly. No weeds grew in the ploughed fields, and when the planting season came the birds that pecked at the seeds died, quickly.

The river flowed on, carrying its poison with it. The sun, that had once brought sparkles to the clear surface, now only glinted dully in the water making it seem more miserable than before. During a day the leaves in the willow trees turned from green to brown. The rushes in the water turned brown as well and seemed to decay gradually.

A child was paddling in the river's edge and stumbled, falling into the water. The river was shallow at that point and he should have been able to regain his balance. But, strangely, once the brown water had covered him he did not come to the surface again. His body was washed up some miles further down the river. The same happened to a boy, who, climbing in a willow tree, felt the branch crumble beneath him where previously it had been steady as a rock, and he fell downwards into the river.

The river flowed on. Soon it left the countryside and came to a town. On one side it still had a grassy look but for some reason the grass withered and died, leaving only bare earth. Children fishing from the bank were disappointed when hour after hour yielded no fish, not even a tadpole. Anglers had no more success.

A child playing near the river bank scratched himself; a bit of mud from the river entered the scratch, and though the child washed it again and again he fell ill – some sort of tetanus, the doctor said – and the child died.

Where the river widened at one point it was usual for boats to be taken out. This had been done for several years – but only now did the paint flake off and a kind of wood rot come into the bottoms of the boats so that they became unusable.

The river flowed on, bringing death wherever it came. It left the town and crawled through the country again till it slid into the sea and scattered there.

Above the coastline a ragged wisp of yellow cloud appeared, that grew, towards sunset, and drifted away with the wind.

Examiner's comments

Although this reads at first as if it is simply descriptive the writer introduces ominous hints about the Cloud, with such words and phrases as 'unholy', 'murky' 'sudden shadow', and the first paragraph ends with the worrying sentence 'It was a cloud like smog; but it wasn't smog.' This suggests a double threat: something dangerous – and unknown.

By the second and third paragraphs the Cloud is openly stated to be poisonous, affecting the river and the vegetation that comes into contact with it. Soon afterwards, a child is affected too. While these events are unwinding, attention is being paid to the appearance of the river: 'The sun, that had once brought sparkles to the clear surface, now only glinted dully in the water' and 'The rushes in the water turned brown as well and seemed to decay'.

Progress of the story is maintained by the river's course; it flows next through the town, with similar results. Perhaps a chance was missed here to give details which would differ more from those given earlier – the child playing is almost a repetition of the earlier incident. A chilling detail is slipped in, though, with the description of the boats and the corrosive effect of the polluted waters upon them 'only now did the paint flake off and a kind of wood rot come into the bottoms of the boats so that they became unusable.' Moving towards the end of the essay, the writer increases the scale of the threat: 'The river flowed on, bringing death wherever it came.' The quiet 'ragged wisp' of cloud drifting away, suggests that the menace will be diffused even more widely.

This very restrained piece of descriptive writing is extremely effective.

▷ Question 8   *Outline answer*

A piece of work for this question should be built around the contrasts indicated. You could begin with the crowded beach and end with it deserted. It would be worth while thinking about that first: what details would you observe on the beach on a Summer's day? The sudden storm should be a dramatic happening causing panic and a total change in the behaviour of the sunbathers. You could conclude by observing the beach, swept by the rain and left to the gulls, soaring overhead. The wording of the question helps you to give a shape to your work, doesn't it?

▷ Question 9   *Outline answer*

Here you have a choice: the joys *or* the miseries. ... This title gives an opportunity for strong involvement, perhaps of enthusiasm for your favourite game, or wry humour, as you recall those foggy afternoons when you couldn't see the other players, let alone the ball! Giving a satisfying shape to your work could be a problem here. It would be easy to wander from detail to detail and not really know how to end. Some planning *before* you start is recommended, then. You could, for instance, follow a pattern of contrasts, similar to that in Question 8. Imagine the warmth of the changing rooms and the grim (or enticing) look of the misty field through the window; the numb fingers and toes gradually becoming warm through exercise and, finally, the welcoming sight of the open school door and the gust of warmth blowing out from the central heating!

▷ Question 10   *Outline answer*

This question, too, invites the use of contrast: you may choose to pick out the lively and interesting or dismal and boring aspects of the place where you live. This is only a suggestion, though, put in to help you get started, as are ideas about the local people or places. A short, honest consideration of the place where you live is the best way to start. Having jotted down a list of things you definitely must write about, think next about how to prevent your essay becoming list-like. Here is a chance to give some attractive anecdotes about local characters, or memories you associate with a particular place. A personal view is asked for, so this should be a very individual account.

▷ A STEP FURTHER

In a radio talk called 'Capturing Animals', the poet laureate, Ted Hughes, gave some excellent advice on writing descriptively. He recommended close observation and perception of what you want to describe: 'Just look at it, touch it, smell it, listen to it, turn yourself into it', and then choose words which will bring it to life, until, in short, you will have 'captured a spirit'. This advice could hardly be bettered.

SUMMARY

▷   The importance of the vivid and precise use of words was discussed, and how to avoid cliché.

▷   The difference between literal and figurative writing was explained.

▷   Some figures of comparison were mentioned: simile, metaphor, personification, fable and allegory.

▷   Some figures of contrast were mentioned: antithesis and paradox.

▷   Some figures of sound-effect were mentioned: alliteration, assonance and onomatopoeia.

Responding to a stimulus

▷ **GETTING STARTED**

Earlier, in Chapter 11, the way you might respond to the stimulus of something you had read and enjoyed or felt strongly about was discussed. Other kinds of stimuli, however, are also likely to be part of your work; for instance, looking at pictures and illustrations, watching television programmes, and listening to music. All these are recognized as being good starting points for talking or writing, e.g. the **London** syllabus for coursework includes 'personal response to such stimuli as pictures, music, poetry and prose'.

The stimulus may be suggested to you by your teacher or tutor, in which case you will probably be guided in writing a response.

If you are taking a written paper, you may be set a task based on a photograph or picture, e.g. a composition based on a photograph (**MEG**); a photograph to be written about in any way you wish (**NEAB**); or, write imaginatively in response to one of two pictures (**WJEC**).

Finally, it should be noted that responses to a stimulus also occur as *oral* coursework: **London, MEG, SEG, WJEC**.

LONDON	MEG	NEAB	NICCEA	SEG	WJEC	IGCSE	TOPIC	WRITTEN EXAM	ORAL EXAM	COURSE-WORK
✓	✓	✓	✓	✓	✓	✓	Responding to text	✓		
✓	✓			✓	✓		Responding to text		✓	
✓	✓	✓	✓	✓	✓	✓	Responding to text			✓
	✓	✓			✓		Responding to pictures	✓		
✓	✓			✓	✓		Responding to pictures		✓	
✓							Responding to pictures			✓
✓							Responding to music	✓		
✓	✓			✓	✓		Responding to music		✓	
✓							Responding to music			✓

▷ **WHAT YOU NEED TO KNOW**

▷ **Relevance**

'Find a good starting point'

The chief matter of importance in responding to a given stimulus is to be reasonably **relevant**. Unless specifically told otherwise (and it is unlikely that you will be), you must not talk or write about it for a few seconds and then move on to spend most of the time allocated on other things. The rule is to be certain that someone reading or starting listening to your response could see a clear connection between what you write or say and the original stimulus. Also, avoid being too original or unusual; when given a photograph of a tramp examining an old boot, one candidate wrote about a weekend job in a shoe shop!

▷ **EXAMINATION QUESTIONS**

The following is a selection of questions of the kind you might find on an examination paper, or that might be suggested to you by your teacher or tutor for coursework.

▷ **Question 1**   Look at the photograph (Figure 17.1). Write about it in any way you wish.   (**NEAB**)

Figure 17.1 (BBC Hulton Picture Library)

▷ **Question 2**   Write imaginatively in response to *one* of the pictures (Figure 17.2 or Figure 17.3). (**WJEC**)

Figure 17.2 (BBC Hulton Picture Library)

Figure 17.3 (BBC Hulton Picture Library)

▷ **Question 3**   Write a story, a description, or other composition suggested by *either* Figure 17.4 *or* Figure 17.5. (Your writing should be about the subject of the picture, or take some central suggestion from it.)

Figure 17.4

Figure 17.5

▷ **Question 4** Use the picture (Figure 17.6) supplied with this paper as a basis for your writing.

Figure 17.6

▷ **Question 5** Listen to a recording of the opening of Wagner's *The Flying Dutchman* or Handel's *Water Music*, and write a story or a description based on your response.

▷ **Question 6** Compare reading a play with seeing it on television or in the theatre.

▷ **EXAMINATION ANSWERS**

▷ **Question 1** *Outline answer*

A photograph of children playing is an attractive stimulus. It could lead to memories of the games you played as a child, a description of the children in the picture or perhaps a story, featuring them as characters. Children and games should be a central concern of the writing.

▷ **Question 2** *Outline answer*

A tower block suggests quite a range of kinds of writing. You may decide to write about the disadvantages of living in such accommodation, compared with living in a house with a garden. Town architecture may suggest itself as a topic, or you could write a story about the loneliness of a young mother and her children in a tower block, or even something dramatic like a fire or explosion. There are many possibilities.

A group of police officers awaiting some event obviously leads to wondering why they are waiting, and what will happen next. One problem here could be that you get so involved in writing about the event, e.g. a royal visit, that you forget all about the police officers. That would matter only if you were asked to make a clear link between your writing and the details of the picture, though.

▷ **Question 3** *Outline answer*

Suppose you wanted to write about the beach photograph. I think it suggests a story of some kind. The small boy seems to be setting off alone along the breakwater, on an apparently deserted beach. The shadow may suggest that it is late afternoon. What might happen next? To write so that the photograph is central to your concerns, you should keep his adventures of a kind likely to happen. For example, he goes too far along the beach; later, his worried parents search for him; some people say they have seen him – every clue as to his whereabouts is eagerly seized upon; meanwhile, the small boy is sitting by a rock pool in a cave, perfectly content. This is just one possible approach.

The photograph of an old inn with a mountain towering behind it has no suggestion of period. You could write a story of smuggling in the nineteenth century, or set your scene in the present day: the inn looks isolated, and would be a good hide-out for someone. Perhaps it has a more innocent story: you spent a very enjoyable holiday there. Whatever you choose to write on, the inn and its lonely situation should be highlighted.

▷ **Question 4** *Outline answer*

A picture of a natural scene seems to invite descriptive writing, though not necessarily. You might imagine a group of characters who were just about to enter the scene, or who had just left. Try thinking about the location of the place shown and the season of the year it depicts: are the trees bare? Look for clues in the picture to help to make your writing more realistic.

▷ **Question 5** *Outline answer*

Responding to a piece of music poses problems because it is subjective. Although many may agree as to the effect of certain musical instruments – e.g. heavy base drumming sounds ominous, slow violins sound peaceful – probably no two people would write similarly in response to listening to music. The pieces suggested in the question are what is termed **programme music**, i.e. they have titles which tell you something of what the music was meant to represent. That is a helpful clue, though you would not be tied to such an approach. The first piece is lively, dynamic music, perhaps suggesting a storm at sea or some other violent action. The second seems more stately and calm, though equally dramatic, suggesting perhaps a march, or something progressing steadily until a climax is reached. Those are my responses; yours could be very different. Whatever you write about, remember that your reader may not know the piece of music, and that your story or description should be able to stand by itself as a piece of satisfying communication.

▷ **Question 6** *Student's answer*

Here is a piece by a sixteen-year-old girl, after watching G.B. Shaw's *Pygmalion* on television, and comparing that with her own reading of the play.

Eliza Doolittle from the play 'Pygmalion'

Before Eliza became a duchess she was a poor flower girl. When we first met her she was sitting on a plinth of the column, sorting her flowers. She was about eighteen–twenty but not any older. She wore a little sailor hat made of black straw which was very dirty and had hardly been brushed. Her hair needed washing badly, the colour was hardly natural, she wore a black coat which went down to her knee. She had a brown skirt with a coarse apron and her boots were not fit to wear. By the time Professor Higgins finished with her she was just as good as a duchess, maybe even better. She wore fine and expensive clothes and jewellery, she looked much cleaner and the main thing was she could speak proper English, just like a duchess.

An important incident at a tea party was although she could speak better English, she didn't know what to say like she said 'somebody pinched it', and 'what I say is, them as pinched it done her in'. Another

(continued)

---

one is when she went to the garden party she passed as a duchess but, when they came back Pickering and Higgins didn't thank her or even congratulate her for her appearance at the garden party

Eliza Doolittle reminds me of a film on television which was called 'My Fair Lady'. The girl was exactly like Eliza and she even talked like her and the story was the same, because both the teachers were teaching the pupils to speak English properly.

Eliza doesn't get on with Professor Higgins very well, she always gets into arguments with him. Eliza gets on quite well with Pickering because I think Pickering understands Eliza better than Higgins. Higgins treats Eliza as a common flower girl and as if she is worth nothing. Mr Doolittle doesn't like Eliza very much and she doesn't like him; they don't get on very well.

I think Eliza is a clever girl because she learnt her lessons quick and well. Eliza is a kind girl because she goes to her father's wedding although he was wicked to her she said 'Oh well, just to show there's no ill feelings'.

I think that the play was very good because it was all about Eliza learning to speak English properly. The story was also very good. Twiggy and the rest played their parts very well. I enjoyed the play very much.

Examiner's comments

The writer achieves quite a good balance here. She tells us quite a lot about the plot, but does give some of her own responses as well, e.g. 'Eliza gets on quite well with Pickering because I think Pickering understands Eliza better than Higgins. Higgins treats Eliza as a common flower girl and as if she is worth nothing.'

She conveys a keen sense of enjoyment of both reading and watching the play. It might have been better, perhaps, if she had discussed some of the ways that a television version is different from the text of the play, because a different medium is used, e.g. close-ups can emphasize details that we would not necessarily notice much when we read: cuts may be made to the text, or, as in the case of the film version of *Pygmalion*, a happy ending substituted because that has more box-office appeal. One version ends with Eliza Doolittle approaching Professor Higgins and saying dreamily, 'I washed my hands and face before I came.' The camera produces a close-up shot with soft focus, to create a mood of romance. We are left to conclude that the next development will be marriage and a happy-ever-after relationship, which was hardly what G.B. Shaw had in mind! There are errors of expression, though not enough to impede communication seriously.

▷ A STEP FURTHER

Look out for pictures in the newspapers, especially any that are striking and seem to tell a story. Imagine how you could write about them in different ways. Another interesting thing to do with pictures is to get a set and try sequencing them in a different order: how does the story differ, for example, if the picture of the isolated inn comes last, instead of first? A set of pictures can help you to plan your piece of writing, because it offers you several stages along which to progress.

SUMMARY

▷   This chapter discussed using pictures, music and multi-media approaches in speech and writing.

▷   It was pointed out that there needs to be a clear connection between your work and the original stimulus.

▷   Differences of approach between text and film were mentioned.

Chapter 18

Personal writing

▷ **GETTING STARTED**

Personal writing, or writing based on your own experience, is probably the easiest to get started with as it has been said that 'there is one book in each of us'. Even so, given a free choice, it can be hard to choose one thing from many possibilities. It is a good idea, then, to keep a list of things you would like to write about, when they occur to you; ideas can come along when least expected. All sorts of things experienced can make successful pieces of writing – a conversation overheard in the supermarket, a family argument, an occasion when you were suddenly filled with strong emotion and felt that this was a very significant moment in your life, and so on.

Perhaps because describing it comes naturally, extra care is needed in communicating what happens in real life to a reader: some shaping will usually be needed. The advantage of writing from experience is that the piece often has a great deal of impact and interest because of your involvement in what you are saying.

LONDON	MEG	NEAB	NICCEA	SEG	WJEC	IGCSE	TOPIC	WRITTEN PAPER	COURSE-WORK
✓	✓	✓	✓	✓	✓	✓	Personal writing	✓	
✓	✓	✓	✓	✓	✓	✓	Personal writing		✓

WHAT YOU NEED TO KNOW

▷ **Select what is important**

The first important thing to do is to think about the experience you have chosen and **select what is important to you.** That will give it immediate shape. Sometimes, if it has been in your mind for a long time, it will already have taken on the shape from your recalling the experience again and again.

▷ **Be realistic and vivid**

Second, do not drift into far-fetched or imaginative extensions of what happened. **Be as realistic and as vivid as possible.** Ways of doing this include describing how you acted and what you said and felt, as honestly as you can, and reporting exactly how other people who were involved reacted. Remember, we are very close to our own experiences and must make them extra clear to readers who have not shared them – extra explanations may be necessary.

▷ **Write about an everyday experience**

You can begin straight away by writing about something that happens as part of your **everyday experience.** At first thought, something personal like this may seem unlikely to be very interesting to other people; but this is not necessarily so. Your personal experiences could well be very interesting to someone not familiar with the way that you lead your life, especially if you can describe them with skill and detachment.

As an experiment, try writing a short account of your family at meal-times. When you have written it, put it aside for a few days, then critically re-read what you have written and ask yourself the following questions:

'Four rules for writing from experience'

▶ How have I presented myself?

▶ How have I presented members of my family as characters?

▶ What have I left out?

▶ Have I started and ended in a satisfactory way?

Such an exercise can be very instructive: you should learn something about the differences between life and written accounts of it, and also of your own ability to select and describe incidents, and portray character in personal writing.

Here is a pupil's attempt at this exercise. She chose to write about Saturday lunchtime when she came home from her weekend job for a meal with her family, and tended to see them in a new light because she had been away from them for a while.

The Family at Dinner – Saturday

I stalk into the house via the open front door, throw down my coat and proceed to climb, with unladylike eagerness, up the stairs to enquire as to what is for dinner. I have one hour in which to cram enough fuel into my stomach to last me for another two hours' work in the shop, and I make sure that I make the most of the time allotted for this enjoyable necessity.

Mum is usually bent over the steaming cooker preparing some delicious meal and Dad, at this time, is usually pottering about in the garden. When the cry 'Grub!' goes up, we all instantaneously leave whatever we have been attending to and gallop for all we are worth to the kitchen, where the meal is on the table. My sister is the fondest of her food and naturally is always the first there. The conversation following is typical.

DAD	*Been busy?*
ME	*Yes.*
MUM	*We saw you in there …*
ME	*Oh. [Various assorted sounds of eating and clanking.]*
SISTER	*We went up to get some wood.*

[Silence. Two minutes' pause.]

ME	*What for?*
DAD	*Cupboards.*

[Four minutes' pause.]

ME	*This is lovely. I'm starving.*
MUM	*There's no more.*
SISTER	*Ooooh! [disappointment]*

[Two minutes' silence.]

ME	*I've got piles to do.*
DAD	*You can help wash up.*
ME	*I've got too much to do.*
DAD	*Never mind about that. You could have done it last night. You help your Mother.*
ME	*But …*
MUM	*You haven't helped me for a long time.*
ME	*But …*
DAD	*She can help as well [referring to my sister, who offers no excuse but a disturbing scowl].*

[We finish eating and we sit for a couple of seconds and, as usual, my sly sister sidles out of her chair and makes a dash for the toilet.]

ME	*I knew she'd do that, Mum. It isn't fair!*
MUM	*She'll be out in a minute.*
DAD	*Can't you help on your own for a change?*
ME	*I did it on my own last time. [Whimpering protest.]*
DAD	*Look, Sally, are you going to help your Mother or not?*
ME	*[Muffled protest].*

Mum gets up and puts the dishes in the bowl and starts running the hot water. My sister suddenly appears, and with a horrified look because the dish-washing has not yet started, disappears into the hall once more. This time, she is caught in the act of escaping by her father, who whisks her off to the kitchen and presents her with a tea cloth.

By this time there is nothing left of my lunch-hour in which to do any chores, so I am 'let-off' with a warning that I'll be doing it next time!

You can see that the writer is very self-aware at the start: she 'stalks' into the house and shows 'unladylike eagerness' for her food. Next, she sketches a typical Saturday lunch-hour scene with Mum bent over the cooker and Dad pottering about in the garden. Her sister is first introduced as 'fondest of her food' and 'naturally ... first there', when food is on the table. This may strike you as slightly critical, and it soon emerges that there is indeed rivalry between the sisters.

The move into dialogue in the central stretch is strikingly realistic; the reader seems to be allowed to overhear the family's conversation. The piece ends with a little drama: a sly sister not managing to get out of helping with the washing up but the writer's good excuse accepted – with a warning. This concludes the piece in a satisfying way.

When these comments were made to the writer, she was very surprised. She thought she had just written it as it had happened, not thought about the impression the piece would make, or tried to shape it at all.

▷ SUGGESTIONS FOR COURSEWORK

Here is a selection of titles you might like to write about for coursework. Try making your own list, too.

- ▷ My life from two to fifteen years.
- ▷ A frightening experience.
- ▷ The world around me.
- ▷ How I would like to change my life.
- ▷ My first day at school.
- ▷ Harassment.
- ▷ My first journey abroad.
- ▷ Sisters! or Brothers!

▷ EXAMINATION QUESTIONS

You will probably wish to include one or more pieces of personal writing in your coursework, and most written papers, except those concerned with factual material, will give some opportunity for this. Here are some examples from specimen papers.

▷ **Question 1**   Tell a story about the time when you were embarrassed when you discovered something about yourself or your relationships with someone. (Here are some suggestions which you may use, if you wish. You may write about your own private thoughts and feelings, or about how other people did not understand you or made you feel worse because they mocked you.)   (**NEAB**)

▷ **Question 2**   You have been called unexpectedly to a person in authority over you, at school or work. You do not know why you have been sent for. Write about your feelings before and during the interview.   (**London**)

▷ **Question 3**   Write a story beginning with the following words: 'Looking back, I now realize it was a stupid thing to do.'   (**London**)

▷ **Question 4**

My Mum and/or My Dad.   (**WJEC**)

Question 5   'I have never felt so ashamed in my life!' Write about a personal experience – perhaps a joke that misfired or a time when you unthinkingly hurt a loved one – which ended with your feeling very guilty and ashamed.   (**WJEC**)

 Question 6   Write about an occasion when, for the first time, you succeeded in doing something which many other people find quite easy.   (**MEG**)

 Question 7   A question of loyalty.   (**MEG**)

 Question 8   Write an account of a visit you made with your parents to the seaside. You may write in any way you like but you might like to try writing about a time when you were younger and particularly enjoyed new challenges such as swimming, climbing on the rocks, or going out in a boat; *or* you might like to write round the idea of being lost, or cut off by the tide. The account can be real or imaginary.   (**MEG**)

EXAMINATION ANSWERS

 Question 1   *Student's answer*

Here is an account of a misunderstanding based on something that happened to two friends at school. It would make an appropriate piece of writing for this question. Read it through and think about how the writer has given her work shape. Then consider what we learn about her feelings, and Angie's feelings. How do we learn this: through action, speech, or in some other way? Which details make the account seem real and vivid?

Misunderstanding

It was three fifty-five in the afternoon. I was waiting for Angie outside in the playground. I was getting impatient and restless as I had already waited twenty-five minutes. Me and the rest of my class thought Angie was slow witted and dumb. We thought she didn't know anything about her schoolwork, but I didn't know why I was the closest to Angie, although I didn't like her very much.

Angie was very innocent and she looked it too. She would never answer anyone back or ever argue, she even hesitated to answer questions in class. Most of the time she kept quiet and hardly gave her opinion towards anything or anyone, except once, when we were having our Biology lesson. It was about the way the muscles in the body worked. Angie told Miss James, the teacher, that in her previous school she had done this project. Miss James suggested that Angie should tell the rest of the class about her experience.

At first she was very nervous and wished that she hadn't told Miss James and because she did, she had to face about twenty-four people and explain about the way the muscles in the body worked. Miss James quietened the class down. Angie stood up in front of the class and started explaining, I could hear giggles at the back of the class. Some girls were laughing at Angie because of the way she talked. All her words were getting jumbled up as she was very nervous. I felt embarrassed because she was my friend. After about six minutes of explaining Miss James asked Angie to sit down. She came and sat next to me. Eventually the pips went. I was glad it was our last lesson and we could go home.

Angie and I were going down stairs to the exit when Angie remembered that she didn't get her Mock exam grade to say whether she was doing basic or Higher Maths. She told me to go down and wait for her while she went to see Mr Smith the teacher to ask about her grade. I could have easily told her that she failed because she wasn't in the school long enough to do all the coursework required for the exam. I thought that I would let her get the shock for herself. I went down and was waiting. It wasn't long until me and the other people in our class were proved wrong.

(continued)

> *Angie came down with a surprised look on her face, but she also was very happy. She came running down the ground floor corridor and when she saw me she burst out with the news that she came second in the class with eighty-seven per cent. I asked her who came first thinking she would say my name, but to my disappointment it was Louise, brain box of our class. I asked Angie how many marks I got. She replied sixty-two per cent. At that moment I felt so jealous that I could have killed Angie. I felt so ashamed that Angie had only been in the year for the last five months and she managed to pass the exam with a better grade than mine. Angie, seeing the look on my face, wanted to comfort me because to her I was her only friend. She said 'Never mind, Chris, at least you passed and beat some people in our class. Sixty-two per cent is quite good. If you work hard I'm sure Mr Smith would enter you in for the 'Higher' exam.' I felt good when Angie said that to me. I thought to myself that although I didn't like Angie in the past, she saw me as her very close friend. At the end it seemed that I was the stupid one for misunderstanding Angie.*

Examiner's comments

The opening paragraph of *Misunderstanding* tells us a great deal quickly. The first sentence, 'It was three fifty-five in the afternoon' sets the scene, and by the end of the paragraph we know what is essential to know about Angie and her relationship with the writer. After that the writer lets the natural course of events – e.g. during the Biology lesson – take over. Angie's ordeal is dealt with in one paragraph; the second part of the incident turns the tables. Chris feels inferior and inadequate, and Angie takes the role of comforter. The final three sentences conclude the episode neatly, and sum up what Chris feels she has learnt from it: 'I felt good when Angie said that to me. I thought to myself that although I didn't like Angie in the past she saw me as her very close friend. At the end it seemed that I was the stupid one for misunderstanding Angie.'

Most of the account is circumstantial – what happens in school on that afternoon – but there is variety, with some dialogue and quite a lot about the feelings of each girl: 'Some girls were laughing at Angie because of the way she talked. All her words were getting jumbled up as she was very nervous. I felt embarrassed because she was my friend.' But later, in contrast 'Angie came down with a surprised look on her face, but also she was very happy. She came running down the ground floor corridor and when she saw me she burst out with the news that she came second in the class'. There are very vivid touches, in addition to what has already been mentioned – the way Angie's words were getting 'jumbled up as she was very nervous' (how like life!) or how she came 'running down the ground floor corridor' and 'burst out' with her happy news. There are some faults of expression, but altogether this is a well-shaped, honest and attractive piece of personal writing.

▶ **Question 2**   *Outline answer*

A piece of writing based on this idea seems likely to fall into two parts: the feelings, possibly of apprehension, that you have before the interview and the encounter itself. Events will be presented from your point of view and so may be very one-sided. Unlike the balance often required in argumentative writing, one side of the truth in personal writing can be a good thing, as it can offer a definite point of view. Suppose, for instance, that you were to be told that you had been chosen to represent the school on a visit to a pupils' conference abroad. Imagine how surprised and excited you would be and, legitimately, how these feelings would swamp the piece. The pleased and proud attitude of the head teacher would have its place, but would be of lesser importance.

▶ **Question 3**   *Outline answer*

You are invited to write a story. This may not be direct personal experience, but you will almost certainly be able to think of occasions in your life when you have said this, or something like it, to yourself. Spend a short time thinking of incidents that would be an exploration and analysis of your own behaviour, looking back afterwards. There is likely to be a contrast between how you felt when you entered into the experience and how you felt later, and, possibly, some realization that you had matured as a result of it all.

▶ **Question 4**   *Outline answer*

A portrait in words is asked for here. As you have to concentrate on one member of your family, you will need to sustain your comments for some time. It may seem that you could write almost for ever about your Mum or Dad, because you know them so well, but a few moments spent thinking about what details you want to include, perhaps their appearance, early life, likes and dislikes, relationship with you, hobbies and interests, jobs, friendships and so on, will be time well spent. As with other topics where a lot of detail is included, you may find that you have a tendency to write in a list-like way, so reserve a little time in your planning for thinking about how best to arrange your ideas, and how to begin and end effectively, or be selective like the writer of 'Two Drivers – Two Personalities' in the Student's answer to this question.

Two Drivers – Two Personalities

Both my father and mother drive. My father is a big man, and with his powerful arms he seems to be playing with a toy when he is driving. My mother is a small woman and it is almost difficult to detect her behind the wheel. As the car she drives does not have power steering, it looks as if she is physically moving the car when she has to steer. But these are not the aspects I want to discuss. I want to talk about my firm belief that people's personalities come into evidence when they are driving.

My father is Italian and my mother English. I can almost detect their cultures in the way they drive. My father is a good driver. Technically, his driving is perfect but when we go travelling together, I don't feel tranquil or at ease. When he is driving in town, especially, I can hardly recognize him. He becomes mad at the world. He is in a mood of constant anger, and curses everyone to his right and left. His aggressiveness makes me so nervous that we are either going to have an accident at any moment or he is going to get into a fight, so that at the end of the trip I am exhausted.

I went to a local school for eight years. In all those years my father may have driven my brother and I, all in all, not more than ten times, none of them that I can remember without an incident of some kind. In fact, we never wanted him to drive us; it was always my mother who took and brought us back. My father can never accept the disorderly and impulsive driving of others. He cannot help be frustrated, even though he has driven for most of his life.

My mother learned to drive in London, although I cannot say that she drives in a city style. Being English, she has a feel for what the other drivers are thinking. My father will not change his speed until he is right behind a car and has to put the brakes on. My mother starts slowing down, even at a distance. She evades possible close situations, and tolerates those drivers who seem to be determined to do what they are not supposed to do.

Technically, my father's driving is perfect. He has a mastery of the car. I cannot say he drives too fast or too slow. There are times when he drives at speed; he is always relaxed and calm when he is driving fast. My mother, on the other hand, is a fast driver in the city. Although calm, she is also cautious and always alert. She takes all these to the extreme while on a highway. She is the only person I know who actually slows down when she is passing another vehicle on the highway. When I ask her why, she says 'There are all kinds of crazy people on the road; I want to make sure that this driver is not going to do anything crazy just when I am passing him.' Because she is so cautious, she is never relaxed while driving. It is very strange, but she can be the calmest person in the world and yet so tense behind a wheel.

My father's aggressive personality and intolerance as to what he thinks is not right comes out when he is driving. In the same way, my mother's tolerant and mild personality comes out when she is driving. She is not a weak person, she is not afraid to drive forcefully, but she tolerates others. My mother's English background is evidenced by her capability to adapt to driving situations. My father's intolerance to situations which he considers wrong also is evidence of the Italian impatience culture.

Examiner's comments

By concentrating on one aspect of his parents' behaviour – driving – this candidate has been able to explore the chief contrast in their personalities and the cultural differences between them. The 'my father/my mother' contrast may seem to be repetitive at first (notice how these phrases open several paragraphs) and to some extent it is, but it does offer a balanced account. In fact, we learn by inference something about the writer and his amused observation of his parents' vagaries. By working on a limited scale (think of the enormity of trying to write about both parents in detail in a short essay) he succeeds quite well.

▷ **Question 5**   *Outline answer*

This question, like Question 3, asks you to look back at a past experience – this time one of embarrassment or shame but involving someone close to you. Similar procedures should be followed to those outlined in the notes to Question 3. Notice, though, that you are told how to end this time: with feelings of guilt and regret.

▷ **Question 6**   *Outline answer*

This is an interesting question. I suppose there may be some people who have never had this experience, but they must be few and far between! Most of you will have had the uncomfortable experience of being slow to learn something, whether it was tying your shoe-laces, coping with a subject at school, or, later, learning to drive. The feelings of inadequacy, loss of self-respect and even, in some extreme cases, of desperation and of hopelessness which such an experience can cause may be painful to recall but are likely to make a powerful piece of writing if you can communicate them honestly and clearly. Try to avoid generalizing too much about the experience. Go through the stages of learning, as far as you can remember them, and your reactions each time you failed. Perhaps the experience turned out well in the end, in which case you can conclude with the disproportionate joy you felt when you eventually succeeded.

▷ **Question 7**   *Outline answer*

This could be a story without any particular personal slant. It would be a good title for personal writing, however. Loyalty to friends, family, beliefs, or a cause that matters to us is a basic human response and, again, one often very strongly held. If you can think of something you had to defend because you really believed in it and can write about it, then by communicating the same strength of feeling you may be surprised at how good a piece of writing you produce. As usual, though, to achieve a successful piece of work it is essential to have good planning, careful selection of incident, honest recall of how you felt and what happened, and an overall satisfying shape to the work.

▷ **Question 8**   *Outline answer*

This piece of writing may be real or imaginary. In either case, it should be based on your own experience. The first option suggests that you might like to recall a seaside experience from the past, when you were younger and faced some challenge. Likely challenges are offered but you do not have to write about those. This is the sort of topic where vivid recall of the detail of the experience will help to bring it to life for the reader. If you were to choose to write about rock-climbing you could try to remember what the rocks looked like; the physical experience of trying to get a foot-hold on slippery, jagged or narrow surfaces; the emotional experience you might have had – fear as you suddenly found that there was nowhere safe ahead to move to, or pleasure at reaching the top. These are only a few possibilities: your own experiences will be much richer.

The second option suggests something definitely dramatic: lost, or cut off by the tide. Something like this may actually have happened to you. If so, your task will be easier because you can draw on your memory of what it was like. If not, try to think yourself into the likely events, and your corresponding feelings, remembering to plan and shape your work, and trying, above all, to write realistically once again.

▷ A STEP FURTHER

Fluency and skill in writing about personal experiences come, as do most things, partly through practice. You should try to acquire gradually a good sense of what is both interesting and important to you and likely to be of wider interest and significance, as well as increasing your ability to communicate effectively. One way of doing this is to write regularly, e.g. keep a diary, even try writing poems, or short descriptive sketches of episodes in your life that you want to explore and remember. One writer who did this spoke of producing verbal 'snapshots'! It is something you could try for yourself.

SUMMARY

▷   How to be vivid and convincing when sharing your personal experience in writing was discussed.

▷   The value of observing with sympathetic detachment the lives of other people and maybe storing some detail as mental 'snapshots' was also mentioned.

Chapter 19

A sample coursework folder

▷ **GETTING STARTED**

This sample coursework folder has *five* pieces of work, involving personal, narrative and dramatic writing, letter writing and imaginative writing. Seeing such a folder will give you some idea of what a range of assignment work might look like. You could try to make your *own* estimate of the material presented before looking at the Examiner's Comments which follow. There is also the teacher's or assessor's record of the pupil's oral work.

Here is the front cover of the coursework folder, which will help you to see what is covered in this chapter.

	Written Expression	
Units 1 2 3 4 5		
Title/Question		*Nature of Task*
Unit 1 *Personal Writing* THE CHALLENGE		Writing from personal experience
Unit 2 *Narrative Writing* DOG		Writing a short story
Unit 3 *Dramatic Writing* THE GOVERNORS' MEETING		Writing a short play, based on a school situation
Unit 4 *Letter Writing* LETTER TO MR AND MRS KEATING LETTER TO MR SAMUELS		Writing formal and semi-formal letters
Unit 5 *Imaginative Writing* A FRIGHTENING EXPERIENCE		Writing in response to a picture

▷ **Personal writing**

The Challenge

I got up stretching and yawning. I felt terribly sick and worried. I had to do it. I couldn't back out now, I thought to myself. I slowly got dressed and went downstairs to have a wash and brush my teeth. When I had finished washing, I went into the kitchen and sat down at the table. My cornflakes were already set out on the table. I saw something white out of the corner of my eye. I got up and walked over to the draining board. There was a note. I picked it up and read it:

'Michael,
I've had to rush out early today and I'll be back a bit later than usual, so don't stay in on my account. Go out and play with your friends and I will see you when I get back.
Lots of love,
Mum.'

Why couldn't she have forced me to stay in for once? I thought. Well, I could tell my friends that I had to stay in, and then they would want to see the proof, or they would call me 'chicken' . So that idea went down the drain. I was so scared and frIghtened about going ahead with my challenge. Why did I say 'yes' in the first place? I asked myself over and over again in my mind. I put down the note and sat down again. I poured lashings of milk over my cornflakes with a sprinkling of sugar. I ate as slowly as possible, and when I finally did finish I washed up my bowl and spoon and put them on the draining board to dry. I sat down once again with my head in my hands. I had to think of something. I just couldn't bear to hear them all calling me a chicken.

As the day wore on I managed to convince myself that I was going to do it, that I was going to win, even if it killed me. My thoughts were interrupted by a knock at the door. My heart seemed to beat faster like the beating of a drum. Thoughts of who it could be were going through my mind as Gary, Peter and John had come rather early, if it was them. I thought maybe it could be the milkman, but no – Mum had paid him yesterday. As I walked towards the front door I was nearly convinced that it must be one of Mum's friends. But as I opened it I knew that my fears were realized, for there, standing at the door, were Gary, Peter and John. My heartbeat was faster than ever and the same old sickly feeling came flooding back into my body.

'You ready, then?' asked Peter, with a big grin across his face.

'Not chickening out, are you?' said Gary, grasping hold of his sports bag.

'No, I'm just coming. But you're early, aren't you?' I asked, scratching the itch in the back of my neck.

'Well, we're just making sure we don't have to get a replacement, you know!' snapped Peter, as if he was almost implying that I was going to cry off.

'Well, you don't!' I snapped back. 'I'll just get my stuff together now.'

I shut the door and went upstairs. I got together all my swimming gear and bunged it in a plastic carrier bag. As I reached the street door I felt very apprehensive but I couldn't back out, I kept telling myself.

'Come on, Michael!' I heard them shouting outside. I opened the door and stepped out onto the street. We caught the bus and made our way down to the beach. When we reached the beach there were crowds of people sitting and lying all over the sand. I looked beyond the crowds and noticed a sign 'ALL BOYS TAKING PART IN THE COMPETITION LINE UP HERE'. Standing by the sign there was a man dressed in a dark blue tracksuit, and a blue cap with a whistle around his neck. That must be the coach, I thought. We made our way down to the spot where the race was taking place.

'Changing rooms over there,' he said, pointing to a few huts. We went inside them and changed from our clothes to our swimming trunks. I walked across the sand and made my way down to the water's edge, where everyone was ready and waiting for the big competition to start.

'Right! Listen, boys,' shouted the coach. 'The first one to reach the black rock is the winner.' Everybody was lined up against the edge of the water.

'Are you ready? On your marks, get set (there was a pause), GO!' He blew his whistle and everyone jumped in. I swam as fast as I could. I was in the lead, but for how long? Within ten minutes I was very tired. As I started to struggle, I could feel my legs and arms getting weaker and weaker. But I had to go on now that I had got this far. Just a few more yards, I kept saying to myself. Just a few more yards. By now I was slowing down and tiring out but all the other boys were way behind me. I could see that they too were tiring. A few of them had dropped out altogether. I was now doing a doggy paddle and breast stroke, whereas before I was doing front crawl. I was getting weaker and weaker. Only a few more strokes. I had to do it. I could faintly hear the crowds on the beach shouting: 'Come on, Michael!' By now I was coughing and choking. One more stroke – I had done it! I could just about hear the crowds on the beach cheering and shouting. I had won!

▷ **Narrative writing**   **Dog**

'Get out of here, you disgusting dog!' The rubbish bin was all over the floor and there were tins and the remains of last night's dinner scattered everywhere.

'Marian!' a voice called out from the living room. 'What's happened?'

'The dog has had the rubbish out all over the floor!' she shouted back, picking up all the rubbish.

'Where is the little runt?' John, her husband, got up out of the chair and picked up a belt from the sideboard.

'Come here, dog. You're going to get it now!'

The dog was cowering under the table, and John dragged him out by the scruff of his neck and whipped him right across the muzzle with the belt. The dog yelped in pain, but John persisted in beating him.

'You've had it now, boy.' He beat him again and again. He dragged him out of the room and straight out of the front door.

'Now keep away from this house and take your bloody rotten fleas with you.'

He went inside and slammed the door behind him. The dog stood yelping on the pavement, throbbing with pain, and blood oozed out of his wounds. As he limped off down the street he was whining and crying in pain. He limped on about a mile before he came to a lake. He drank as much water as he could and cleaned his wounds with his paw.

He travelled for days until one late afternoon he woke up to find himself surrounded by two children pitying him. He could hear them speaking and his first instinct was to crawl away from them, but he could feel a warmth and a kind of feeling between them. He stood up and walked over to them, wagging his tail with great effort.

'Look at him; he looks as though he hasn't been fed for a week,' one of the children said, stroking his sore back. The dog felt pain as she touched him gently, but he was able to bear it, as he could feel she meant well.

'Let's take him home to Mum,' the other one said. They reached the huge gates of the house where the two young girls lived and they both rushed off inside the house.

'Mum! Mum! Look what we have found. We've found a dog.' They jumped up and down with excitement. The dog walked into the kitchen and cowered down under the table as the children's mother came closer to him.

'Hello, boy. You look as if you need a good feed.'

'Where did you find him, Jennifer?' she asked. The younger of the two replied, 'We found him sleeping in the Park.'

'Well, he certainly looks ill. Was he with anyone?' she asked.

'No, Mum. He was on his own.'

The mother of the children bathed his wounds and put some food down on the tiled floor. Within seconds the dog had wolfed down every scrap of meat.

'Oh, look at him. He must have been very badly beaten. If only he could talk. If only he could tell us who did this to him. He's such a beautiful dog. People who ill-treat their dogs should be horse-whipped.' She bent over to stroke the dog.

'He's an alsation, you know.'

'Oh. Mum can we keep him, please?' pleaded the elder of the two.

'Oh yes, of course, but if the owners contact us we will have to give him back.'

A few days passed, then a few weeks. As the dog got stronger he filled out and became fit and healthy again, just like an alsation should be. His beautiful brown and black coat shone again and looked a whole lot better than the day they first found him. They treated him well and the dog loved them very much. But he still had the memory of his former owners who beat him and starved him deep in his brain. His immediate instinct was to get his revenge.

One night, the family had all gone to bed and everything was quiet in the house. The dog stood up, shook himself and trotted off out of the back yard and onto the pavement. He trotted on down the street, and turned the corner.

The next morning the family came down into the kitchen where the dog was curled up in his basket, sound asleep.

'Hello, boy. How are you this morning?' they said. The dog got up quickly and ran to greet them at the kitchen door. He was wagging his tail frantically. He looked very pleased to see them and also a look of satisfaction was all over his face. The morning papers had just been delivered and Jennifer came rushing back with them in her hands. She gave them to her mother who was sitting on a chair drinking a cup of coffee. There was a sudden look of horror on her face as she read the front page.

'Oh my god!' she said. 'Look at the state of her!' She was reading the headlines: 'COUPLE SAVAGED BY MYSTERY ANIMAL.'

'Mrs Marian Jones and her husband, John Jones. They were mauled to death, attacked by some animal in the night, probably by a wolf. Lucky that we have a dog to protect us all.'

The dog curled up in his basket. He knew exactly what had happened.

▷ **Dramatic writing**

The Govenors' Meeting

This play is set in the office of the head mistress, Mrs Catherine Williams. Five people are attending this meeting: Mrs Margaret Keating (the mother of the pupil being discussed), John Andrews (best friend of Ken Samuels, the teacher who was attacked), Walter Richmond (friend of Margaret Keating's husband) and Elizabeth Walker (Chairperson of School Governors).

WALKER Would you like to come in, ladies and gentlemen? [*They all go into the room.*]

WILLIAMS Take a seat, please.

[*They all sit around a large table.*]

WALKER First I must say thank you for attending this meeting. Now, we are all here to discuss the incident involving Jennifer Keating and Mr Ken Samuels, the Humanities teacher. I have made out five copies of the report. Would you all please take one.

[*They all take one and read it.*]

KEATING This isn't fair at all! This is not what happened! He's lying! This report is all lies!

WILLIAMS Calm down, Mrs Keating. Perhaps you would like to give your account of the incident.

KEATING Well, Jennifer was talking quietly to a class mate when she was told to shut up in the most rude way. Anyway she refused because of the way he spoke to her. She was then asked to leave the room and she refused still. So he took her by the arm and pulled her out of the chair to lead her out of the classroom and she pulled away and he fell over and hit the floor. That's what happened. No big deal! You see, Mr Samuels should be sacked for dragging my daughter about, not my daughter expelled for just defending herself.

WILLIAMS Well, Mrs Keating, if that's the case, then it makes no difference. You see, she still refused to do as she was asked, so she still would be punished.

KEATING Yes, but why should she do anything anyone tells her to do? I'm her mother, I tell her what to do, no-one else!

WALKER Mrs Keating, you are not being very co-operative at all! While Jennifer is in school she is under our authority and we have every right to tell her when she is in the wrong.

ANDREWS Mrs Keating, imagine if you can, that you are looking after a friend's daughter. Now this little girl happens to be helping herself to your dinner for the night. Tell me, Mrs Keating, would you think that you have no right to tell this little girl what is wrong to do and what is right to do or would you tell her that it is wrong to take something not belonging to her, and take it away?

KEATING I'd kill the little cow if she pinched my dinner!

ANDREWS Well, there you are, so what makes you think that only you can tell people what to do and nobody else is permitted to, especially with your daughter?

KEATING Yes, all right. I was being a bit stupid, wasn't I? But that's stIll no reason to expel my daughter.

WILLIAMS Well, Mrs Keating, we will decide that at the end of this meeting.

WALKER Let's get on with the meeting shall we? Now, going by Mr Samuels' report, Jennifer was talking and chewing gum when the rules clearly say that chewing gum is strictly forbidden. So that's one rule broken. Another is, one way or another, Jennifer Keating did actually assault Mr Ken Samuels.

RICHMOND Yes, but only because he assaulted her!

WILLIAMS Ah, but Jennifer gave him reason to.

RICHMOND I see. If it was the other way round then Jennifer would probably still get the blame.

WALKER Mr Richmond. It doesn't matter what you would like to think, the truth is she did assault Mr Samuels so there are no ifs and buts about it.

RICHMOND Yes, O.K. I'm sorry.

WALKER Now, another broken rule was swearing, and swearing is also strictly forbidden and we will not have our pupils abusing the teachers no matter what!

WILLIAMS Well I'm sorry but the only possible thing we can do is to suspend Jennifer for a little longer, in order to be fair to both sides. It is not a serious enough case for Jennifer to be expelled. Mr Samuels was hurt but it wasn't intended that way. So I have decided that she should be given a clear warning and told not to do it again. If she can abide by these rules then I am willing to have her carry on at this school. Is everyone agreed?

KEATING Yes, that sounds fair to me. I'm sure she won't do it again.

WALKER Well, we shall have Jennifer back in two weeks from today. [*Everyone mumbles, some with relief and some with disagreement. They all get up and leave the room.*]

▷ **Letter writing** *Letter to Mr and Mrs Keating*

Dear Mr and Mrs Keating,

Following the governors' meeting on Tuesday, I am writing to convey to you the decision taken about Jennifer after discussion of the incident that took place last week in school.

It was agreed that Jennifer should send a written apology to the teacher concerned and be suspended from school for two weeks, starting on Monday. We expect to see her back on Monday, 19 March.

Yours sincerely,

Elizabeth Walker
Chairperson of Governors

Letter to Mr Samuels

Dear Mr Samuels,

I am writing to inform you that Jennifer Keating is to carry on at school after a two-week break. We have come to this decision because, although she was being very tiresome, it is clear that she did not intend to hurt you.

I understand that she is very sorry, and she will be asked to offer an apology which we hope you will accept.

She will be returning to school on 19 March, in two weeks' time.

Yours truly,

Elizabeth Walker
Chairperson of Governors

▷ **Imaginative writing**

A Frightening Experience

A young boy, by the name of Max Maddison, was walking along the street all alone, frightened and worried, after running away from his foster parents. He was a young boy of ten, with dark skin and black hair, wearing jeans and a jacket made of denim. As he walked along the gloomy street he passed many different people. Some were black, some white; some not quite black and not quite white. It was very strange to him, as he had not been allowed out of his foster-home alone after his real parents had neglected him when he was only five months old.

'Hello, son,' a voice called out from behind him. 'Who are you, then?'

Max looked at the man, very frightened. He peered up at his brown complexion. He was carrying a jacket across his shoulder and Max noticed a gold watch on his wrist, and he wished he had something like that.

'What's the matter, son? I only asked who you are? I mean, it's not every day I see a young boy like you walking around the streets all alone.'

Max became even more frightened. He leaned against a lamp-post and stared up into the strange man's face.

'Would you like to come home with me, then? I have a very cosy house. You can stay tonight if you want to.'

Max was so young, so naive that he didn't know that this man that had picked him up could mean serious trouble. He did not know whether to turn to the nearest police station and be taken home again, to be locked up behind four walls, or he could go with this complete stranger and be safe out of this street full of other people. He did not know. But this man was a stranger to Max.

'Well, then. Do you want to come with me, or not?' the man said again.

Max just managed to force a few words out: 'No, I don't want to, thank you.'

He slid along the lamp-post, and took off down the street, around the corner and down an empty alley-way. He walked slowly and got his breath back. He felt very lonely and sad. At least at home he had a nice warm room with plenty of central heating to keep him warm. For the first time since he had run away he wished he was back in his welcoming room. He walked down the High Street and looked into the show window. He thought of his foster-parents being worried sick that he had run away. Max knew that he had to return home. There was no way he could survive out in the dirty, gloomy and smelly streets. He made his way home. The flat door was half open and half shut when he arrived. Perhaps they hadn't even noticed that Max had run away. He pushed the door to behind him. He was very scared.

He walked into the living room and saw his foster-parents sitting on the sofa, watching television. They noticed him standing there and Max's heart beat faster than ever.

'Hello, Max. There's a good programme on television. Come and watch it, if you want.'

Max looked very surprised, but he didn't mind that they didn't know. He sat down to watch television.

'Mum, can I have a watch?'

▷ **Speaking and listening**   The candidate's record of assessment for the Speaking and Listening component is shown in Figure 19.1.

Figure 19.1

UNIVERSITY OF LONDON EXAMINATIONS AND ASSESSMENT COUNCIL: GCSE NATIONAL CURRICULUM/KEY STAGE 4

ENGLISH 1202: ENI COURSEWORK FRONTSHEET FOR PAPER 1A: THE SPEAKING AND LISTENING COMPONENT JUNE/199

Centre Number	Candidate Number	
Surname & Initials		Candidate's Mark for Enl /50
Subject Number *1202* Paper Number *1A* Subject title **ENGLISH**		37

Date Work Completed	Title of Assignment	Conditions in which work was produced	Teacher's Comments
14/11/9	Debate on hypothetical closure of British section.	Individual speech.	A calm and confident speaker. A fluently presented speech. (38/50)
13/3/9	"The Drover's Wife": H. Lawson.	Pair discussion, followed by presentation	Thoughtful ideas, showing a sensitive response to the text. Ideas clearly expressed, though the presentation could have been more dynamic (36/50)
26/3 and 2/4/9	Comparison of two poems: "Sometimes It Happens" and "Absence"	Group discussion and presentation	Perceptive exploration of meaning, mood and structure. Engages effectively with partners and present analysis fluently and confidently (38/50)
10/4/9 (video)	An interview with Edith Wharton about "Ethan Frome"	Role-play interview – video. (pair)	Takes the role of interviewer – thoughtful and interesting questions. Is able to ask questions/comment to develop partner's ideas. A confident and competent performance (39/50)
10/4/9 (video)	Relationships between parents and teenagers	Group discussion, in response to newspaper articles	Fluent and thoughtful speaker. Responds to text effectively. Makes interesting comments throughout. (35/50)

SIGNATURE OF EXAMINING TEACHER _____   DATE *16th May 199*

MODERATED: _____   *Instructions for the Conduct of the Examination 1202*

Examiner's comments

Considered as a whole, this folder would certainly be assessed at a good C grade. There might be some concern about the balance between creative and transactional pieces (the two letters are the only sample of the latter). In other respects, though, the student has presented a good range of imaginative writing. The piece of personal writing is convincing, well-shaped and accurately expressed. The short story 'Dog' handles the emotions of all concerned effectively and with restraint. The ending is particularly successful in this way. The short play not only develops the situation clearly, it is well-planned, with clashes of feeling and resolutions of disagreement among the speakers, and the dialogue is good. The letters are written in an appropriate tone, are quite well expressed and sensibly paragraphed. The layout is correct, apart from the missing addresses. The final story is delicate in its understatement of the implications of the situation. The child's confusion is sensitively handled, and the ending does not try to do too much: mixed with the childlike wish for an impressive possession, which might have led him to make a wrong decision, is a drawing nearer to his foster-parents. It offers hope for a better life for Max.

The candidate has presented a variety of items for the Speaking and Listening component and all have been capably carried out.

Overall, this folder of work shows a standard of achievement that any candidate for GCSE/Key Stage 4 English could be pleased with.

Figures 19.2, 19.3 and 19.4 are some sample assessment sheets for three of the activities listed on page 202.

Figure 19.2

NATIONAL CURRICULUM/GCSE ORAL ASSESSMENT
NAME   DATE *14/11/9*
TASK: *British Section debate: speech*   INDIVIDUAL/PAIR/GROUP
A)   CONTENT   *(Mayor of Colomiers)*
   Good points, thoughtfully developed.
B)   INTERPERSONAL SKILLS
i)   Listening/responding to others
   N/A
ii)   Ability to initiate/sustain discussion
   N/A
iii)   Non-verbal communication
   Good – looks calm & confident
C)   USE OF LANGUAGE
i) Range of language/style/vocabulary
   Ideas expressed articulately. Wide range of vocabulary
D)   CLARITY OF EXPRESSION
   A calm and confident speaker. Fluently presented speech
OVERALL MARK *38*   NC LEVEL *8*

Figure 19.3

NATIONAL CURRICULUM/GCSE ORAL ASSESSMENT
NAME   DATE *13/3/9*
TASK: *'The Drover's Wife': presentation*   INDIVIDUAL/PAIR/GROUP
A)   CONTENT
   Lots of thoughtful ideas – sensitive response to text.
B)   INTERPERSONAL SKILLS
i)   Listening/responding to others
   Generally OK.
ii)   Ability to initiate/sustain discussion
   Begins presentation (avoid "OK, well . . . ") Good.
iii)   Non-verbal communication *Fine – look at audience*

C)   USE OF LANGUAGE
i) Range of language/style/vocabulary *Fluent, effectively phrased.*

D)   CLARITY OF EXPRESSION
   V. good at times. Lots of 'ums' at others. Could generally be more dynamic
OVERALL MARK *36/50*   NC LEVEL *7/8*

Figure 19.4

NATIONAL CURRICULUM/GCSE ORAL ASSESSMENT

NAME   DATE   *22/1/9 and 24/1/9*

TASK: *'Tackling Racial Tension in School': problem –*
           solving role-play. (CRE representative)   INDIVIDUAL/PAIR/⟨GROUP⟩

A)   CONTENT

     Makes interesting points about gangs' tendency to be racist. Could have been
     developed further. Generally, contributions thoughtful but undeveloped

B)   INTERPERSONAL SKILLS

i)   Listening/responding to others

     Listens carefully – could have responded more readily.

ii)   Ability to initiate/sustain discussion

     This is an area which he needs to work on, but he is not entirely at ease with role.

iii)   Non-verbal communication

     Seems relaxed.

C)   USE OF LANGUAGE

i) Range of language/style/vocabulary

     Sound, and appropriate to role

D)   CLARITY OF EXPRESSION

     Points which he does make are clearly expressed, Has potential to be very fluent,
     forceful speaker.

OVERALL MARK *32*   NC LEVEL *7*

Chapter 20

Checking and correcting

▷ **GETTING STARTED**

This chapter aims to give you advice about going over your work when it is finished, looking at it critically and correcting any errors you may have made. As it comes last it will remind you of matters considered earlier in the book and serve as a form of revision of some of them for you.

Your techniques for checking work will vary considerably, depending on the kind of task you are involved in, and whether you are taking a written paper or doing coursework. Certainly, you will be able to spend much less time correcting an answer in a written paper than revising a piece of coursework.

Remember that all published work that you read has not just been written down and printed. It has probably gone through several drafts and revisions before reaching its final form. This is likely to be true, too, of radio talks or other pre-recorded performances: they are usually edited before transmission. Much of the work you do for the examination should be seen as 'work in progress', your progress along the road to becoming a more accomplished writer or talker. Even so, you are presenting some of what you produce for assessment, and will want it to be the best you can do at that stage. What follows should help you to achieve this.

▷ **WHAT YOU NEED TO KNOW**

The amount of time you have available largely determines the checking you are able to do. Let us consider basic aspects in three sets of circumstances:

1 Checking answers in the examination room
2 Checking coursework
3 Checking oral work component.

Always leave yourself five to ten minutes for checking over your exam paper. There are several basic points to look for here. Check that you have

▶ followed the instructions
▶ written relevantly
▶ written accurately.

▷ **Checking answers in the examination room**

'You can't make too many checks.'

Have I followed the instructions?

It is obviously very important to read all the general instructions (or **rubrics**), as well as the wording of questions in an examination very carefully.

Many people understandably do not feel very calm in an examination room, and nervous haste can lead to errors and, in the long run, loss of time. It is far better to read, then re-read, the whole question (or even paper) carefully before you begin. Remember that a major mistake, such as misunderstanding the general instructions or how to tackle a particular question, often cannot be corrected.

Make sure that you read all the pages of a paper: you would be surprised how many pupils in examinations forget to turn over the page, if it happens to finish with the end of a paragraph.

The most common ways of *not* following the instructions are:

'Five don'ts for the
examination room.'

▶ answering too many questions
▶ leaving out important aspects of a question
▶ using an inappropriate tone or style
▶ ignoring word limits
▶ ignoring the marks awarded for a question.

Answering too many questions

Think how frustrating it must be to discover, when you are checking, that you have written three essays, when only one was asked for! If you do find yourself in this position, do not despair. Most probably your longest or best essay will be assessed. One candidate tore her paper into quarters when she realized that she had written more answers than she was asked for, and left the examination hall in tears. The invigilator taped her script together again, sent it in with the rest, and she passed the examination. Take care not to make the same mistake yourself: you might not be so fortunate! If, however, you do something of this sort, and realize it at the end, it is probably best simply to leave it to the examiner to consider the situation. The examiner will mark the paper, within the requirements of the mark scheme, in the way most favourable to you.

Leaving out important aspects of a question

This mistake usually comes about because examinees skim-read, or read carelessly in nervous haste. For example, you might be asked to write a speech at a public inquiry discussing a certain proposal, and read 'opposing' instead of 'discussing': or, for another question, not notice that a report supporting *or* opposing is required and not one offering a balanced discussion of the issue. Again, you might be asked to write a newspaper article with a headline and subheadings, and forget the subheadings. Hasty attempts to put right this sort of mistake in your final five or ten minutes usually make matters worse, although in the case of subheadings, you could insert them in the margin at the appropriate point.

Using an inappropriate tone or style

Sometimes the audience to which you direct your writing is specified and this immediately should indicate to you something about style. A report on fellow pupils' views about curriculum problems will be rather different if written up for a meeting of the school governors or for the school notice-board; a letter to the manager of a travel firm will be more formal and restrained than one to a personal friend, and so on. If you fail to take in the kind of audience you are meant to be addressing, you lose marks for writing in an unsuitable tone or style.

Ignoring word limits

The most common error here, of course, is writing too much on one question and running short of time for the rest, or even failing to answer part of the paper, because of poor timing.

The best advice is *not* to exceed a word limit. In a short piece, where conciseness is an important factor, you may well have work disregarded after the word limit has been reached. In a larger piece, such as a five hundred word essay, the more you write the more errors you make, so you will be losing marks for yourself. Every examiner knows that an extremely long essay, written in examination conditions, is very often a weak essay. Not only will there be problems of accuracy but also it will almost certainly be rambling, expansive and dull. Avoid these problems by respecting the word limit: it is there to help you. But if, when you are checking, you find that you have exceeded it, you could quickly re-read your piece of work to see if you can make any cuts, *without damaging the overall style and shape of the work*.

Ignoring the marks awarded for a question

The number of marks awarded for a question is another indication of how much time you should spend on it. To take the example of a comprehension exercise where you have five marks for the first two questions, ten marks for the next two, and twenty marks for the final one, you should spend about four times as long on the last question as on the first. And if you are pressed for time, it will probably be best to begin with the last question. Again, when you are checking at the end of the exam, you should clearly devote most time to improving your answer to the last question.

Have I written relevantly?

Stress has been put on the importance of relevance more than once in this book. In written papers, where candidates are all being assessed on the same range of tasks, it is a serious weakness to stand out as not fulfilling the necessary requirements, but instead, doing something either quite different, or only roughly related to the task in hand. It is good advice not to try to be wildly original or experimental in an examination. By all means, if you have what seems like a very good idea for an answer and are keen to try it out, do so, but not before asking yourself firmly: 'Am I really answering the question or am I indulging a personal enthusiasm which is taking me away from the question?' As has already been stated (see Chapter 17) ingenious interpretations of topics, or writing on something you have prepared beforehand and so must attach to a topic, are all best avoided. This advice has been given before, but it is worth repeating. An experienced teacher and examiner always said the following to her pupils in the final lesson before a written examination: 'I have three pieces of advice to give if you hope to succeed in the examination – be relevant, BE RELEVANT and BE RELEVANT!'

If you find, when checking your paper, that you haven't been strictly relevant you may sometimes be able to do something about it. Suppose, for example, that you had written an essay with the title 'Junk Food'. You had started quite relevantly in the first paragraph, explaining that you enjoyed eating junk food, but that it was never provided at home. You then wrote three or four paragraphs describing the wonderful traditional meals cooked for you by your mother, which you also loved eating, and had finished with an account of a recent particularly splendid meal. A moment's reflection then told you that you had wandered from the point and, in a way, reasonably, because you rarely had the chance to get any junk food. You could, in such a case, quickly make a few insertions. In the central stretch of the essay, you could slip in occasional remarks, such as '*far from spending Saturdays eating hamburgers … we always have grilled fish …*', or add something along the lines of 'When Sunday lunch comes I find on my plate roast beef, baked potatoes, Yorkshire pudding and cauliflower, *not Kentucky Fried Chicken*'. In conclusion, you could add '*I do really enjoy eating junk food, on the rare occasions that I have the opportunity to get some …*'. This would not be ideal, but it would signal to the marker your intentions to bear the title in mind in the writing.

Have I written accurately?

Obviously, in written papers, whatever the audience you appear to be addressing in your work, the actual reader will be the examiner and he or she will be comparing your work with that of others. Part of the examiner's concern will be with how well you are acquainted, not only with the grammatical structures and vocabulary of the English language, but also with what may be called 'the conventions of written English': correct spelling and punctuation. The examiner will also much prefer you to write legibly. It is doubtful if you will have time at the end of an examination to work on the grammar of your answers, but you may be able to improve the punctuation and spelling, especially if you are allowed to use a dictionary.

Before leaving the examination you should make some final checks.

First, look at the cover of your answer book. Are your name, examination number and Centre number clear and correct? Have you listed the numbers of questions and parts of questions you have chosen, in the order you have answered them?

'Finally …'

Next, check that you have numbered each question, or part of a question, clearly within the answer book. Also, cross through all rough work or false starts – anything you do not want to be assessed.

Finally, make sure that any supplementary sheets are firmly attached to your answer book!

▷ **Checking coursework**

A piece of coursework will often exist in draft for some time before it is submitted for assessment, and so there may be opportunities for your teacher, and perhaps some of your friends, to look at it critically and give you the benefit of their advice. There are three main forms of evaluation:

▶ Teacher evaluation
▶ Pupil evaluation
▶ Self-evaluation.

If you take advantage of all three, you should get a good deal of advice about how best to present your work.

Teacher evaluation

Sometimes your teacher or tutor may find time to discuss a piece of coursework in school or college with you. Ideally your teacher's personal comments should help you a good deal. Also, try to go back over several of your pieces of work and build up a picture of your strengths and weaknesses, as they emerge from these comments. Teachers and tutors often complain that pupils seem to make no real use of the comments they spend so much time making on their work. As explained in Chapter 1, GCSE assessment is based on criteria, so remarks and marks on your work for the examination will be telling you how you measure up to the set criteria, as well as offering you personal encouragement and response.

Pupil evaluation

Have you tried working with a friend, or in a small group, exchanging ideas about each others' work? You can discuss errors you have made (especially of spelling or punctuation), any parts of the work where you have not been quite clear, ways of developing good ideas that you have had, and possibly different ways of setting out or presenting the work.

Self-evaluation

'Do you evaluate your work?'

Your own checking is best done some time after finishing the piece of work, if possible, since you will then be able to look at it as editor, rather than creator. If the work is of some length, or incorporates different pieces of material, make sure that it is properly arranged and easy to read. Now is the time to do any necessary pruning.

If your piece of coursework has been done under supervised or controlled conditions – and usually each folder should have at least one piece of this kind included in it – then you will have to depend upon yourself for the accuracy and presentation of the work. Most of your work, though, will probably be produced as part of normal classwork or homework.

When the work has reached the final draft stage, it is time to do some 'proofreading' or sometimes have an editorial conference with teacher, tutor or friends, as part of normal classwork. It is a good idea to get used to a set of symbols which will show exactly what needs to be done to correct the work. Below you will find detailed advice on how to do this. Remember that you should include the draft work, with the corrections made, and a note about the help given, along with your final piece for assessment in the examination folder.

▶ **Checking oral work component**

Your teacher or tutor will put in the Speaking and Listening component records. Check the items through with him or her, and make sure that your best pieces of work are included.

 USEFUL PRACTICAL APPROACHES

Punctuation and spelling are probably the things that are most easy to improve in a piece of written work, so here are some final remarks on these matters.

▷ **Punctuation**

It is helpful to think of punctuation as marks to help the reader to follow more easily the sense of what is written. In the eighteenth and early nineteenth centuries punctuation marks were much more frequent in a piece of writing than they are today. The growth of modern

'Don't forget the full
stops!'

business practice, among other developments, has led to much lighter punctuation. Even so, candidates in examinations sometimes write several pages without a single comma or full stop! That can mean that a reader has to go over stretches of the text again, to be sure of what is intended.

Punctuation can be used differently, according to what you are writing. It can pace your work most effectively. Consider the following three examples:

> As he entered the dark wood he suddenly felt tense: he could almost hear the silence. Then, suddenly, there was a sharp crack. Crash! The bough of a tree smashed through the thick canopy of leaves, somewhere to his right. He turned quickly. There was only a slight patter, as leaves settled on leaves.

> 'But you did see the thief, didn't you!' she shouted, accusingly.
> 'Well … I can't be sure. It was so gloomy in the room. There was someone there, in the far corner, I believe.'

> The grass was springy and fresh and Jack threw himself down on it and lay absent-mindedly, pulling at a blade of rye grass, gazing up at the clear, blue distant sky.

I think you will agree that each depends on punctuation to achieve very different effects. The first is dramatic and needs careful pacing to build up suspense gradually. The second is also dramatic, but more urgent: punctuation here suggests how the voice would emphasize particular words in speech, or in reading this aloud. The third is slow-paced. Only a comma or two is needed to indicate slight pauses.

Occasionally you may like to try working in a pair or as part of a group at an editorial discussion of draft work.

As you read through the piece you should indicate any mistakes you find by a mark in the text. Some of the marks used for this purpose are in the *central* column of Table 20.1. At the same time, you also make an explanatory mark in the margin, level with the mark in the text – for these, see the *right-hand* column in the table. For example, if you think the writer should have started a new paragraph, you make the appropriate mark in the text and write 'n.p.' in the margin.

Table 20.1 gives a version of some of the symbols used by publishing houses for proofreading authors' work.

As you discuss the piece with others you may find sometimes that there is disagreement about, for instance, whether a comma is really needed, or a capital letter, in a particular case. Talking over these points will help you to learn more about the need for certain punctuation marks, as well as increase your own level of accuracy.

Here is an example of a piece of a student's work corrected, using the marks given in Table 20.1.

'Try a little proofreading.'

Meaning of mark	Mark in text	Mark in margin
Word or letter left out	$\wedge$	$\wedge$ plus word or letter
Full stop left out	$\wedge$	$\odot$
Comma left out	$\wedge$	$\wedge$
Question mark left out	$\wedge$	?
Quotation marks left out	$\wedge$	$^{\prime\prime}$
Apostrophe left out	$\wedge$	$^{\prime}$
Change to capitals	$\equiv$	cap
Begin a new paragraph	$\sqsubset$	n.p.
Run two paragraphs together	$\supset$	run on
Figures or abbreviations to be spelt out	encircle words or figures to be altered	spell out
Take out	/	$\mathcal{O}$

Table 20.1

Moving House

It was dreadful weather when we moved house of course but as mum said that was only to be expected. The removal men came early they kept tramping through the house, bringing in mud from the garden. They went to and fro, lugging huge packing cases as if they were nothing at all. One labelled Glass – with care was half thrown into the back of the van. Mum said she felt relieved when the van finally drive off. The men seemed very cheerful because half of their work was over but we felt miserable to leave our old house. As the van turned the corner I took a last look at our big apple tree the one where I use to swing on a tyre when I was little. I felt sadder and sadder all the way to the new house. It was only about ⑤ miles away, but it was in a totally different area. When we got to the new house, it looked horrible through the rain the garden was terribly overgown and the convolvulus was even creeping in at the window. Why did we have to come here, mum? I asked, but she just stared glumly through the car window. It really was an awful first impression.

(margin annotations: ✓ ✓ / ⊙/ cap/ / ✓ /handle/ ✓ / o/ / ✓ / r/ ✓ d/ / spell out / ⊙/ cap/ / ✓/ ✓)

▷ **Spelling**

'Good spelling habits.'

If you follow the advice given in Chapter 5 about improving spelling for yourself you should not be too worried about it. Some students, though, have chronic spelling problems that are not easily overcome. If you feel that this a weak area for you, get a friend, or your teacher or tutor, to indicate which words are wrong in your work, but *not to write in the correct spellings*. It is more valuable for you to find out the correct version for yourself using, as appropriate, a dictionary, writing it down to see if your visual memory tells you that it 'looks right', applying an appropriate rule (if there is one), and (though this is least rewarding, since English is not a regularly phonetic language) 'sounding out' the word. The last is at least usually a check that you have the right consonants and number of syllables.

Don't let weak spelling loom too large in your thoughts. It should not be so very worrying, for example, if you try a word you do not often use, e.g. 'charismatic' or 'environmental', and get it wrong. The spellings to concentrate on first are those of commonly recurring words, and of words that you use frequently in a particular piece of work. If you can get those right, what you are trying to communicate will be clear to the reader, for the most part.

Although the advice given in this book is intended mainly to help you to prepare for the GCSE/Key Stage 4 examination in English, it may also extend your range of speaking, listening, reading and writing experiences. When the examination is over you should continue to enjoy doing some of these. If you do, you will also continue to improve your skills.

SUMMARY

▷   How to check your work in the examination featured in this chapter.
- Have you answered too many questions?
- Have you left out parts of a question?
- Have you written in an unsuitable style?
- Have you overshot or ignored word limits?
- Have you noticed the number of marks for each question?
- Have you timed your paper wisely?
- Have you written relevantly?
- Have you checked your paper for errors?

▷ How to check your coursework also featured.
- Is teacher evaluation included?
- Is pupil evaluation included?
- Have you fulfilled syllabus requirements?

▷   There were some last thoughts on punctuation to bring out meaning, on proofreading your work and on checking spelling.

Index

Longman - for all your study guide needs

Addison Wesley Longman publishes a wide range of curriculum-related books to help you with your studies. If you have enjoyed using this book and have found it useful, you can now order others directly from us - simply follow the ordering instructions below.

Don't forget to tell your fellow students about *Longman Study Guides* -
they might find them useful too!

HOW TO ORDER

A full list of titles is given overleaf. Decide which title(s) you require and
then order in one of the following ways:

by post
Fill in the quantity alongside the title(s) you require, select your method of payment, complete your name and address details and return your completed order form and payment to:
Addison Wesley Longman Ltd
PO BOX 88
Harlow
Essex CM19 5SR

by phone
Call our Customer Information Centre on 01279 623923 to place your order, quoting mail number: HESG1

by fax
complete the order form overleaf and fill in your name and address details and method of payment, and fax it to us on 01279 414130.

by e-mail
E-mail your order to us on awlhe.orders@awl.co.uk listing title(s) and quantity required and providing full name and address details as requested here. Please quote mail number: HESG1. Please do not send credit card details by e-mail.

Mail no: HESG1

Your Name _____

Your Address _____

_____

Postcode _____ Telephone _____

Method of payment

☐ I enclose a cheque or a P/O for £ _____ made payable to Addison Wesley Longman Ltd
☐ Please charge my Visa/Access/AMEX/Diners Club card

Number _____ Expiry Date _____

Signature _____ Date _____

(please ensure that the address given above is the same as for your credit card)

Prices and other details are correct at time of going to press but may change
without notice. All orders are subject to status.

☐ *Please tick this box if you would like a complete listing of York Notes*
Literature Guides (suitable for GCSE and A-level English students)

LONGMAN   Addison Wesley Longman

LONGMAN HOMEWORK HANDBOOKS (KEY STAGE 3)
£7.99 each unless otherwise stated

QTY *(0582)*

1	_____	29330 8	English (KS3)
2	_____	29331 6	French (KS3)
3	_____	30423 7	French pack*(KS3) (£12.99)
4	_____	30425 3	French cassette (KS3) (£6.00)
5	_____	29329 4	German (KS3)
6	_____	30427 X	German pack*(KS3) (£12.99)
7	_____	30428 8	German cassette (KS3) (£6.00)
8	_____	29328 6	Mathematics (KS3)
9	_____	29327 8	Science (KS3)

LONGMAN GCSE STUDY GUIDES
£9.99 each unless otherwise stated

10	_____	30481 4	Biology
11	_____	31538 7	Business Studies
12	_____	30482 2	Chemistry
13	_____	31539 5	Economics
14	_____	30484 9	English
15	_____	30483 0	English Literature
16	_____	30485 7	French
17	_____	03839 1	French pack* (£14.99)
18	_____	03836 7	French cassette (£6.00)
19	_____	30486 5	Geography
20	_____	30487 3	German
21	_____	03837 5	German pack* (£14.99)
22	_____	03838 3	German cassette (£6.00)
23	_____	30495 4	Higher Level Mathematics
24	_____	30494 6	Information Technology (£10.99)
25	_____	30496 2	Mathematics
26	_____	30497 0	Music
27	_____	31540 9	Physics
28	_____	28700 6	Psychology
29	_____	31542 5	Religious Studies
30	_____	30498 9	Science (£10.99)
31	_____	22651 1	Sociology
32	_____	22652 X	Spanish
33	_____	24509 5	Spanish pack* (£14.99)
34	_____	24511 7	Spanish cassette (£6.00)
35	_____	23771 8	Technology
36	_____	30545 4	World History

LONGMAN GCSE EXAM PRACTICE KITS

37	_____	30381 8	Biology £4.99)
38	_____	30383 4	Business Studies (£4.99)
39	_____	31191 8	English (£4.99)
40	_____	30384 2	Geography (£4.99)
41	_____	30385 0	Mathematics (£4.99)
42	_____	30379 6	Physics (£4.99)
43	_____	30380 X	Science (£5.99)

LONGMAN GCSE REFERENCE GUIDES *£6.99 each*

44	_____	05788 4	Biology
45	_____	05790 6	Chemistry
46	_____	05072 3	English
47	_____	05077 4	French
48	_____	05074 X	Mathematics
49	_____	05794 9	Physics
50	_____	05076 6	Science

GCSE SURVIVAL GUIDE *£2.95*

51	_____	05078 2	

_____**YORK NOTES LITERATURE GUIDES** *(see overleaf)*

LONGMAN A-LEVEL STUDY GUIDES
£9.99 each unless otherwise stated

52	_____	22569 8	Accounting (£10.99)
53	_____	31545 X	Biology
54	_____	31652 9	Business Studies
55	_____	31546 8	Chemistry
56	_____	05782 5	Computer Science
57	_____	27688 8	Economics (£10.99)
58	_____	31656 1	English
59	_____	05784 1	French
60	_____	24495 1	French pack* (£14.99)
61	_____	24497 8	French cassette (£6.00)
62	_____	05173 8	Geography
63	_____	31654 5	German
64	_____	24498 6	German pack* (£14.99)
65	_____	24508 7	German cassette (£6.00)
66	_____	28702 2	Government and Politics (£10.99)
67	_____	31549 2	Law (£10.99)
68	_____	31550 6	Mathematics (£10.99)
69	_____	31551 4	Modern History
70	_____	27690 X	Physics
71	_____	31655 3	Psychology
72	_____	27691 8	Sociology

LONGMAN A-LEVEL EXAM PRACTICE KITS *£6.99 each*

73	_____	30386 9	Biology
74	_____	30387 7	Business Studies
75	_____	30388 5	Chemistry
76	_____	30389 3	Mathematics
77	_____	30390 7	Psychology
78	_____	30382 6	Sociology

LONGMAN A-LEVEL REFERENCE GUIDES *£6.99 each*

79	_____	06394 9	Biology
80	_____	06390 6	Chemistry
81	_____	06396 5	English
82	_____	06398 1	Mathematics
83	_____	06392 2	Physics (£7.99)

LONGMAN HANDBOOKS *£7.99 each*

84	_____	09965 X	Botany
85	_____	08810 0	Chemistry

LONGMAN PARENT'S AND STUDENTS' GUIDES
£2.99 each

86	_____	29971 3	Longman Parent's Guide to Pre-school Choices and Nursery Education
87	_____	29975 6	Longman Parent's Guide to Key Stage 1 of the National Curriculum
88	_____	29974 8	Longman Parent's Guide to Key Stage 2 of the National Curriculum
89	_____	29973 X	Longman Parent's Guide to Key Stage 3 of the National Curriculum
90	_____	29972 1	Longman Parent's Guide to GCSE and Key Stage 4 of the National Curriculum
91	_____	29978 0	Longman A-level Survival Guide
92	_____	29969 1	Longman Students' Guide to Vocational Education
93 to	_____	29970 5	Longman Students' Guide to Returning Learning
94	_____	29976 4	Longman Students' Guide to Higher Education

* pack = book and cassette